T0163400

It is often said, correctly, that Paganism is an umbrella term covering a rich profusion of traditions, attitudes, experiences and beliefs. What better way to reflect that reality within one book than to get so many good writers to represent it?
Professor Ronald Hutton

This is a much-needed book that gives voice to the diversity of ideas and opinions being voiced by contemporary Pagans. As I read it, I felt as if I was sitting in a circle, in a community of like-minded souls,hearing new points of view, challenging ideas, old ideas expressed in different ways. Warmth, humanity, creativity all flow from these pages.
Philip Carr Gomm, author and Leader of The Order of Bards Ovates & Driuids.

This book is far from your average Paganism 101 book. In this book will be found a fantastic range of people commenting on a wonderfully diverse selection of topics. Just looking at the list of topics explored in the book should give an indication of how wide ranging the book is in terms of exploring Paganism. But the decision to include 101 different Pagans discussing those topics gives a sense not only of the richness of diversity within modern Paganism, but also hints at an underlying commonality of worldview. Something that is hard to capture with the words of just one author. I thoroughly recommend this book as an introduction for people who are exploring Paganism for the first time, and also to Pagans who have been walking their paths for some time for the insights it provides into how other Pagans view and experience their paths.
Mike Stygal, President of the Pagan Federation.

The very idea of a Paganism 101 reader co-authored by 101 pagans is a breakthrough in itself. This excellent sourcebook highlights significant recent writing by practitioners of Druidry, Wicca, Shamanism, Goddess worship, Herbalism - and a whole lot more. Highly recommended.

Dr Nevill Drury, author of *The Shaman's Quest* and *Pan's Daughter*

A fascinating diversity of genuine experiences offered from a wide range of key earth-centred practitioners today. Sharing their personal stories with courage, wit and honesty about their paths, clarifying The Big Questions many around the world of 'all faiths or none' have today about the rapidly growing Pagan traditions. Organized in three parts: 'Who We Are', 'What we Believe', and 'What we Do', each story provides a river of wisdom all its own, a cornucopia to feast on for all readers...Highly recommended. **Dr Karen Ralls**, historian, religious studies scholar, member of OBOD, and Oxford-based author of Medieval Mysteries & Music and the Celtic Otherworld

Paganism is undoubtedly a faith in need of definition – and here it is, *Paganism 101* makes essential reading for anyone seeking building blocks for the modern movement & for all those followers a little unsure of what they have found.

Mark Olly, author, TV presenter and archaeologist

In this wonderfully multi-voiced collection, 101 Pagans demonstrate that contemporary Paganism, rather than being a single religion, is instead a diverse religious *movement* -- a gathering of related spiritual traditions. In sections dealing with Pagan identities, beliefs, and practices, Paganism 101 offers a balance of well-informed descriptive essays and reflective, personal pieces. The collection captures the evolving quality of Paganism as a new religious movement where important issues are actively being negotiated: some of the essayists explicitly respond to each other, reflecting the lively debates that characterize Pagan community. This intelligent anthology is sure to spark the interest of readers new to Paganism and offers excellent discussion prompts for Pagan and interfaith study groups.

Christine Hoff Kraemer, Managing Editor, Patheos.com Pagan channel

Paganism
101

An Introduction to Paganism
by 101 Pagans

Paganism
101

An Introduction to Paganism
by 101 Pagans

Trevor Greenfield

MOON

BOOKS

Winchester, UK
Washington, USA

First published by Moon Books, 2014
Moon Books is an imprint of John Hunt Publishing Ltd., Laurel House, Station Approach,
Alresford, Hants, SO24 9JH, UK
office1@jhpbooks.net
www.johnhuntpublishing.com
www.moon-books.net

For distributor details and how to order please visit the 'Ordering' section on our website.

A CIP catalogue record for this book is available from the British Library.

Design: Stuart Davies
www.stuartdaviesart.com

Printed and bound by CPI Group (UK) Ltd, Croydon, CR0 4YY

We operate a distinctive and ethical publishing philosophy in all
areas of our business, from our global network of authors to
production and worldwide distribution.

CONTENTS

Preface

Moon Books came to life in January 2012, as a new imprint from John Hunt Publishing, specialising in Pagan / Shaman titles. From the start we were determined that we wanted to be more than just a traditional publishing outlet. Sure, we wanted to sell books but side by side with that we wanted Moon Books to become an online community of authors, writers, bloggers, poets and readers. We also wanted Moon Books to become a valuable resource for the wider Pagan / Shaman community. So it followed that we set up a blog, something we continuously develop, and which currently hosts bloggers, poets, photographers and people writing books online as works in progress.

The idea of a bigger project, of a Moon Books Community book, came to me one day when I was browsing some Amazon titles. One of them was called *Wicca 101*... I had an idea... wouldn't it be cool if the *101* referred not only to the book's introductory nature, but also to the number of contributors! How much more knowledge and wisdom you could disseminate if that many people could be given a voice.

Paganism 101 is the product of my light bulb moment. It's been an honour and a pleasure to work with everyone involved in the book, to engage with their ideas, stories and beliefs. But it doesn't stop there, because now, you, the reader, become an equally important part in our collective endeavour. I hope you enjoy the book.

Trevor Greenfield

Introduction

In a time of unprecedented freedoms to choose what to believe and invest our faith in we have actually lost access to the largest proportion of our belief systems, collectively known as 'paganism'...until now. In looking for the answers to the 'big questions' in life, more people than ever before appear disillusioned or dissatisfied with the handful of principally Judaic schools of thought, and struggle to find a credible alternative that has not been demonised or made a mockery of.

As a keeper of earth-centred traditions myself, I am often asked what 'wiccans', 'shamans' or 'witches' are, for example, and what they stand for. And in the mere five to ten minutes I have to answer I try to convey first and foremost that before we all had 'names' we simply just worked with Nature in the ways and by the means most appropriate to where we lived. 'Titles' were secondary to thoughts, words and actions. When titles did become necessary they were more as a way to recognise those most proficient in a particular art, say healing or teaching or herbalism, than to ridicule or segregate.

As a child I was labelled many things; stupid, lazy, crazy and a witch... Unsurprisingly the last label was not meant as a badge of honour (as is redefined in this book), but as most people today would think of – manipulative, evil, bringer of harm... inhuman. What I later discovered to be wonderful gifts to respect and share, (when I finally meet my first 'pagan', Swein McDonald, The Highland Seer), caused me nothing but harm and confusion in front of others. But at least I had Swein and then another pagan, Lakota Elder, Ed McGaa, Eagle Man to teach, guide, and show me who I am and who I am not.

Paganism 101 demystifies the labels given to all people who follow earth-centred traditions so that you can easily understand their core principles through their own candid words and their individual practices explained here in detail and without pretence. Based on the 'wisdoms' (defined as knowledge plus experience) of this collection of well-respected teachers, you get the rather rare opportunity of tuning in to 101 voices, all willing and eager to speak to you directly of what resonated with them and why, in order that you can find the same.

Where in the world today could we gather such a diverse group of living practitioners who, though not necessarily likeminded, do share a likeminded purpose to help others walk their path; discover a life with greater meaning, that is respectful, sustainable, creative and limits suffering while being true to your being... pagan or otherwise.

The tapestry of life is made richer, not poorer, by the vibrancy and diversity of its threads, and *Paganism 101* allows the reader to experience the weaving of this tapestry and find in it the images most pleasing to them that may also point to a spiritual path or authentic expression that finally aligns them with their most natural way of being.

Barbara Meiklejohn-Free, author of the best-sellers *The Heart of All Knowing* (Moon Books) and *The Shaman Within* (Moon Books), shaman and advocate of our earth-centred traditions.

PART 1

WHO WE ARE

DRUID

HEATHEN

WITCH

WICCAN

SHAMAN

CHRISTO-PAGAN

GODDESS FOLLOWER

ECLECTIC PAGAN

Druid

Graeme K. Talboys

Being Druid. Is it about donning robes and standing in the rain at Stonehenge, planting trees, chanting obscure bits of ritual, sharing tea and cake? Possibly. Ask ten Druids what it means to be Druid and you will get eleven answers. This is because it is personal. That does not mean it is made up by the individual to include anything they want. It is about having a relationship with the world, one that is based in certain principles but which, because it is a relationship, is shaped into a unique form by both partners.

Some people find this difficult. They believe following a spiritual path means blind obedience to a very precise set of rules. It doesn't work like that. It can't work like that. Develop rules for a desert culture, for example, and they will make no sense to people who live in dense woodland; or people who live in a desert a millennia or two later. Things change. If that fundamental fact of existence is ignored the rules are worthless.

Others will ask what makes being Druid distinct from being on any other path. Being Druid is about being guided on and viewing the path via the medium of Celtic history, myth, folklore, images, and symbols. The path probably leads to something beyond this particular forest; perhaps the same place to which all other paths lead. We don't know. For a Druid, that possible destination is nowhere near as important as how you behave on the journey.

Our actions along the way depend on a way of looking at the world which recognizes we are part of the whole and have an intimate relationship with the rest of the world. Reaching this understanding is when the fire in the head first flickers into life. For some it is a sudden explosion, a great burst of light like sunrise. For others it is a candle flame in the dark.

The metaphysic in question is derived from sources held in common with ancestral Celts as well as from writings that were made from the beginnings of the historical period. Nor is it solely that because it is as modern as it is ancient, drawing in contemporary culture and thinking. It is from this fertile ground that the maxims of modern Druids are gleaned.

When people become Druid, it is usually out of a realization that they have already developed a view of the world that is akin to the Celtic metaphysic and are living their lives in accord with it. All they lack is a formal framework through which this can be expressed. Not everyone in this situation is attracted by the pagan Celtic view of the world; not all those who do follow a Celtic path call themselves Druid. The important point is that they have already chosen to live by certain codes of behaviour.

For many, it never goes beyond an overall expression of an idea, being as much an emotional response as it is intellectual. However, if we look to what we know of ancestral Celtic thinking, it is possible to tease out some of the tenets by which Druids live their lives today. Central to them all is truth.

These days, truth is usually considered to be the preserve of language. Yet it has a much broader scope. Indeed, it applies to the rightness or fitness of *all* things, in whatever form they exist or are made manifest – spoken and written statements, certainly, but also actions, constructs, thoughts, emotions, places, and ideas. Notions of falsehood take their shape from this.

Underlying the universe are patterns and relationships that constitute what some call the natural order and others call the laws of nature. Understanding and working in concord with those principles to achieve some particular right end is what Druids do. This is also sometimes known as magic.

If we were to make a distinction, it would be that magic is the right working with those principles whilst truth is the right measure of those principles. That is, magic is understanding the rightness or fitness of a word, of an action, of behaviour, of the way we live, and using that understanding to achieve some right desired end. Truth is the degree to which the word, the action, the behaviour, the way we live is in accord with those principles.

Ancestral Druids understood this. Being aware of and understanding this is what they do today as well, but in a world more complicated than our ancestors could have imagined. Which means that those who follow the Druid Way work to understand the universe and the patterns and relationships on which it is based as well as the way in which it evolves in the here and now. This is the truth we seek.

Truth provides the raw material with which we work because knowledge and understanding are quite meaningless unless they *are* applied. The work we do is known as service. For ancestral Druids, service was ultimately concerned with maintaining material, social, and spiritual balance. Today, it is about restoring the balance that once existed – showing that there are boundaries, that the universe has a voice that must be heard, that there are better paths to tread.

Seeking out truth, be it reaching for the distant absolute or working with particular instances, enables right action. Right action has two essential elements. The first is that it should be in accord with natural law; the means to an end should be in harmony with the end, otherwise the enterprise fails before it begins. The other is that the end should not be personal. Right action does benefit those who undertake it, but that should not be the goal – otherwise it is not right action. If you grow vegetables organically, it is done because it is in accord with the universe and beneficial to wildlife. You still get tasty and wholesome vegetables. The difference is that the means by which the end is achieved is in harmony with natural law and increases the degree to which unity is achieved.

As mentioned, an important aspect of service is the way in which work is done. Although Druids have no single definitive moral code handed to them by a deity or a prophet, we do have a highly developed sense of ethics. Because the rules are not available in a handy little book, however, we have to work all the time to ensure the things we think, say, and do are ethical and relevant. Adherence to the central importance of truth, combined with a belief in freedom of will, leads to the practice of a form of Situation Ethics. That is, an ethical stance based on certain precepts, but dependent upon the circumstances of a given situation.

Social structures, ethical considerations, and the judicial system were very different two thousand and more years ago in the Celtic world. Yet the basis on which Druids approached ethical questions is still workable and relevant today, even in a world dominated by strict and complicated legal and ethical systems that are backed up with the threat of retributive punishment for those who transgress.

The trouble with a system like that is that it exists outwith the person. There is no sense of inherency, no sense of engagement. In particular, responsibility is perceived as lying elsewhere. Society is so complicated and disjointed, so highly competitive and adversarial, that it is easy to feel that laws and ethical systems are lacking in relevance to everyday life. Law-makers, enforcers (a term that says a great deal in itself), judges, and moralists are rarely part of the community they are meant to serve and increasingly behave in ways that put them at odds with that community.

Honour and responsibility, if they are to flourish, require an intelligent and free response to life in general and to all specific situations. Freedom of will is crucial. If someone has no genuine choice, then no matter how well that person may seem to behave, it has not been done honourably. It is the same with responsibility. Where one acts from freedom of will, one has to be prepared to accept responsibility for what one has done. No one and nothing else can be blamed. The two – honour and responsibility – are inextricably linked, part of a cycle. To take responsibility (in any sense of the word) is to behave honourably. To behave honourably is to take responsibility for one's place in the world.

That place is not always a comfortable one. Many Druids live unconventionally and their metaphysical stance often places them at the edge of or completely 'outside' of the society in which they live. This can make life difficult, but we do not consider ourselves beyond or superior to society. We are respectful of the ways of others, even if we do not always like them. This does not mean that Druids are acquiescent. Where there are points of conflict, our instinct is to work to resolve these issues. If there are aspects of society we feel to be wrong, we work to change them. However, that is always done in a way that is in accord with our principles.

Respect is not confined to the human realm. The world and everything in it is endowed with spirit. This does not mean the world should not be touched. What it does mean is that we recognize an essential unity of life. Believing that all things are connected, we identify with the rest of the world. That means we take care to live here as lightly as we can.

For some this means embracing vegetarianism or becoming vegan; and those that do not, take care about the sources of their food, eschewing anything produced by factory farming and artificial genetic modification. We are generally well informed on these and other issues and are often actively involved in work to protect animals from cruelty, forests from destruction, the land and the sea from wholesale devastation, the displacement of indigenous peoples by large corporations, and so on.

This is part and parcel of our sense of identity. Most people might consider or express their connection with the natural world by analogy; Druids believe they are identical. This stems from the distinction that we learn to make between what is our self and what is not our self.

Whilst genetics create some of the parameters within which

we are and can be influenced, who we are is the result of all the environments in which we circulate. Within those environments, the single largest influential factor is other people and we evolve as persons by interacting with them. We all do this in different ways and to different degrees but it is people who make people.

Whilst important to recognize, this is often to the neglect of other elements of the many environments in which we exist. Even with no people around, we constantly interact with our physical, social, psychological, and spiritual environments. And that, too, constitutes a series of relationships.

If this is so, where does each person stop and the rest of the world begin? This is not a spurious question. It is fundamental to the way in which we treat the planet. If we answer that, as persons, we stop at the epidermis and the rest of the world starts from there, we alienate ourselves from everything else that exists and cannot truly claim to know anything about the world with any certainty. The world becomes other, unknowable, and untouchable. Thus isolated, our vision of ourselves becomes synchronous and synonymous with our body. That becomes our central concern. We become truly selfish.

Pagans in general and Druids in particular have a different perspective: that we interact with the world and that what we are is due (if only in part) to that interaction. Therefore, as persons, we do not stop at the epidermis, but extend beyond that to include all that we experience at any given time. This will include other people, animals, plants, objects, machines, ideas, sensations, dreams, and so on.

If during normal, everyday life, our being enfolds all that we interact with and experience, then we are inseparable from the world. We go through life expanding and contracting in a vital dance in which the essential self lives its own life without ever being separated from creation. We are all part of one another, part of every creature, part of every stone and star, part of all that is.

If we harm any part of the world, we also harm ourselves. We cannot avoid changing the world as we pass through; that is a function of living. We can recognize, however, that we are a part of it and a part of other people as much as it and they are part of us. Our passage through the world should be a gentle one – if only to minimize harm to our self. Do this and we become, not selfish, but self-interested, and that is synonymous with becoming interested in others and, through the many overlapping fields of being, the whole of the universe.

There is, of course, a great deal more than this, although it is invariably derived in some way from the basic precepts mentioned above. By its very nature, the Druid Way is organic and those who follow it explore at great length, read widely, think deeply, and act with care. The sources from which they draw their teachings and from which they draw their ethical positions are often enigmatic. This means that nothing ever becomes rigid for each new contribution to the debate and each step in the relationship moves things forward in a way that keeps these ideas alive and relevant, firmly rooted in the real world.

This then constitutes the fire in the head and once that sacred flame is kindled, it helps light the way through what can be, at times, considerable darkness. Becoming Druid is to change one's whole attitude to the world and to society. It is not easy. But there is always help for not only is it the light of a visionary experience, but it also represents that other aspect of being Druid – community. No matter how much you may work alone (and there are probably more solitary Druids than there are Druids within the formal structure of Orders), being Druid has always been about community, so that flame is also the hearth around which we all sit, the place from which we venture out and the place to which we return.

Ask ten Druids what it means to be Druid and you will get eleven answers. This has been the twelfth.

Graeme K. Talboys is the author of a number of books

including *Way of the Druids – Rebirth of an Ancient Religion* and *The Druid Way Made Easy*. He lives in Scotland.

Judith O'Grady

By its very nature, the Druid Way is organic and those who follow it explore at great length, read widely, think deeply, and act with care. The sources from which they draw their teachings and from which they draw their ethical position are often enigmatic.

What is being said by Graeme Talboys? In this instance I am reminded of when I was in university as a biology major and for a little extra money tutored students who were having trouble with general biology. We were going over a failed test question by question and got to one about mitochondria (whom I love). First, I showed my student how to use the index in the text and we looked up the reference in the required reading, something like, "mitochondria are a part of every cell and have difficult and complex interactions with the other parts".

"So what was the answer to the question?"

"In every cell."

Then I digressed and drooled on for a bit about my love of mitochondria – coming mysteriously from elsewhere to be a part of us and everywhere – and thought to ask,

"What do you think that means, 'difficult and complex'?"

"Ummmm..."

"In Science-Speak, that means 'no one really knows and I do not really understand, myself'," and we had a spirited and rewarding discussion about biology (the study of Life Herself) and far more interesting and lovable than science professors.

I have already outed myself as science-oriented (so I think of 'organic' as 'carbon-based' unless I am specifically discussing my food) but I am an Irish descendant as well. I see having opinions, being argumentative (ideally in a fact-based and non-accusatory way), and engaging in story-telling as typical of the culture. Thus, "the sources" can also be described as "stories" and as such must, in order to be requested by listeners at the campfires and correctly passed down through the ages into the lore, be entertaining – full of battles, passion, heroic decisions, and cows. In many of the stories, the protagonists are not well-educated, icily dispassionate Mind-Lords but short-thinking wrong-acting bullies who set the trap of bad endings with their own poor self-serving actions.

Violent endings are more interesting, so much so that the lore is often commented on as placing positive value on sadness. It is not the sadness, but the Iron-Age equivalent of car chases and explosions tangled with the teaching that all actions bring down reactions. As well, the careful listener can extract the moral obliquely and with a satisfying sense of pride at perceiving the pitfall that the blustering protohero does not. It is not "right" or "wrong" answer but "least-harm" answer. This is not enigmatic, but rather subtle. Without an ethical deconstruction behind the car chase/cattle raid, the story will not last.

Lorna Smithers

The quest for inspiration takes a Bard to many places. Amongst my favourites are the river Ribble, Round Loaf on the West Pennine Moors and Glastonbury Tor. However, forming a relationship with places close to home can be just as rewarding as visiting recognised sacred sites.

Behind my street lies a thin strip of woodland on the banks of a diminished brook, sole remnant of farmland covered by houses during the late 1970s. On the lower side unmanaged trees have grown up close, slim frames of birch competing with beech, ash and lime. Shrubs of holly and young yews bring dark splashes to the hazel understorey. The steeper bank hosts alder and hawthorn draped with ivy tumbling from the crooked branches and dressing the ground with cordate leaf.

Magpies strut ostentatiously across the green when they are not defending their territory from rooks or flying between the branches tapping and cawing. A squirrel scrambles up a tree crossing to the next in a spectacular display of aerial acrobatics. Gathering midges hover close.

Relating to a place takes more than ritualised sitting. I'd removed over twenty bags of litter from the valley before I glimpsed a pair of nature spirits – leafy figures from the margins of my eyes and recognised I was on the right track.

Getting to know Fish House Brook taught me a valuable lesson about the way we treat our streams and rivers. There isn't an inch of her course from the concrete source to where it is culverted into the Ribble that has not been artificially changed. Two years ago it was awash with litter, obstructed with leaves and polluted by overflow. Following the clear-up it is possible to hear her song unmuted. By sunlight her water takes on the golden timbre of honey, providing a hint at her lost name.

Meditating on ivy and seeing her pulsing life force as key to the valley's survival, providing food and greenery for the birds in winter and binding the eroding bank in place, I met an ivy-clad fae who became one of my first teachers of the relationship between this world and Faery. Then there's the mighty dryad of the trysting oak who holds rule at the crossroads and will grant entry to the Otherworld if asked correctly. These encounters inspired me to begin a collection of poems and set up a Friends group to encourage others to treat the valley with respect.

Maintaining the relationship isn't easy, particularly for someone who prefers speaking with trees than to people who litter and let their dogs soil the path. Sometimes I wish I lived near Glastonbury Tor where there is rarely sight of rubbish, the local springs are revered and they chair a Bard every year. Yet there the struggle is won whilst here in this unrecognised place it has only just begun, there are spirits unknown and songs unsung.

John Awen

From about the age of seven until about the age of ten, I was forced to attend Church of England Sunday school. To say I was reluctant would have been an understatement. I remember distinctly, even at a young age, churches just seemed to be too oppressive, even though I didn't know fully what they stood for. Still, off I went each Sunday to learn about this book called the Bible and the teachings in it. I remember clearly to this day, sitting down with the other children and being read what I would now call parables, stories then. As if it was yesterday, I can clearly remember sticking my hand up constantly, several times each Sunday and each week thereafter, asking how and why these so-called miracles could happen. This probably didn't stand me in good stead with the Sunday school teacher as after several weeks even with my hand waving frantically in the air, I was readily being ignored. I had then and still have an enquiring mind and will not settle for just being told. I like to find out all of the answers so I am able to weigh it out for myself; basically I want to know the truth about it or my perspective of the truth, which can vary from person to person. I admit now, and told both my parents since, that I did abscond for about the last year of this and I could be found at these times, even at the age of nine and ten, walking through woods, touching trees and sitting under them, wildlife spotting and watching the seasons change and also enjoying being outside in all the elements.

Looking back now, I can see that I have always been of pagan belief, I just did not know that then, but even then this was going to stand me in good stead and eventually placed me on my journey to becoming a Druid. I have over the years looked into several different beliefs/faiths, and was always left asking more and more questions and not feeling satisfied with their portrayal of that belief/religion. It was only upon researching about Druid/Druidry, that I realised for me personally this is the one belief that totally ticked every single box. I decided about two years ago to label myself a Druid and walk this earthly path as, for me, it totally encapsulates all that has been, all that is now and all that will be. Be it in reach, up in the sky and out of reach, in other realms and many things we cannot even perceive to understand, it warms a deep rooted core and sparks a fire inside me. To not only breathe the air, but to taste it; to not only hear the bird sound, but truly listen to it; to watch the buds come on the trees and the seasons change; to stand freezing cold and soaked to the skin on a stormy day or night. To raise your hands in the air, to exhale and to feel the spirit that dwells within. To be comforted by the spirit when you're feeling lonely. To feel warm when you know you're cold. To look at the bigger picture and to just be aware of all that is. There is so much more to being a Druid and none of us should ever stop learning. This for me personally is the base and the glue of what being a Druid is about and I am so grateful to be walking this path and treading along this journey. So mote it be!

Scott Irvine

I blocked the Oak King's staff with mine, shifted my body weight round and took a swing back at my twin brother, the Light aspect of myself. The Oak King saw it coming and blocked my attack with ease. Another attack from the Oak King displaced my crown of holly. I stepped back to replace it, getting a crack on my knuckles in the process.

It was Midsummer at Stonehenge and I had been asked by the Archdruidess of the Cotswold Order of Druids if I would like to represent the Holly King at short notice as the person that was going to do it had to cancel. Of course I would fill in; it was an honour for me to do battle in the ancient temple of Stonehenge.

I had met up with Veronica, the Archdruidess, the year before at the Summer Solstice ceremony at Rollright Stone Circle where I was photographing the event and was invited to attend their ritual at Stonehenge the following week. It was then that I realised I was a Druid. I had followed the pagan path for a number of years but up to that moment I was unsure of which path to follow.

Having been asked to be the Holly King, fighting with a bow staff, I had two weeks to prepare. I had never held a bow staff, or any weapon for that matter and I discovered that my opponent was an experienced battle re-enactor. He was determined to floor me before allowing the Holly King to win. I was just as determined that he would not. The battle lines were drawn. I purchased a book on karate to practice footwork and balance and borrowed a curtain rod to practice the bow staff moves I had checked out on YouTube.

The Oak and Holly Kings are the Light and Dark aspects of the Stag Lord Cernunnos. Twice a year at the Solstices they battle it out for dominance over the Sun. The Holly King reigns from Midsummer to Midwinter and represents the inner knowledge of the Universe and brings about the beginning of the Sun's descent into darkness. It was a fight I had to win or else the balance of the universe would be upset.

The Druids were split into two groups, each to rally behind one of the Kings once they had been crowned. I asked the Goddess for strength, courage and protection before the battle commenced. My practicing served me well; the Oak King could not floor me. After five minutes of fierce battle my strength sapped but luckily it was the same for the Oak King. We agreed to hit the staffs three times then I would hit him on his back and he would go down. Although it was all predictable it still felt like scoring the winning goal in the F.A. Cup Final. The Druids cheered, the balance of the universe was ensured for another six months.

Heathen

Alaric Albertsson

I first met the Medoburg Kindred at a private residence that was known, then, as Aurvangar. The property, located in western Pennsylvania, possessed a natural beauty throughout its hills and ravines. A carpet of ivy cascaded over a sloping hill above the front patio, and a gentle brook passed under the house's side porch. The people gathered on that porch mirrored Aurvangar's simple and unpretentious splendor. There was nothing extraordinary in their appearance or behavior. I would never have guessed that the petite, quiet woman sitting in one corner of the porch was a college professor, or that her slender, lanky boyfriend had been one of the first Ásatrúar in the United States.

Our host, a man named Richard, had invited me to meet with his kindred at Aurvangar for a ritual they called a blót. Richard and I had corresponded through email, and I was curious about this group and their ways. By the 1990s I had started to feel estranged from the general Pagan community; more and more I had become a loner, with ideas that did not mesh well with the more eclectic, free-wheeling traditions of my peers. That afternoon, after talking extensively with the members of the Medoburg Kindred, I finally had a way to express those odd ideas that burned inside me. I was still very much a Pagan man, but now I knew of a more descriptive word.

Heathen.

Historically, the words *pagan* and *heathen* were synonyms; both denoted a rural person in a disparaging way, much as we would use the word "hick" today. The difference is in the cultural origin of the two words: *pagan* has a Latin origin, whereas *heathen* is a Germanic term.

In the 21st century, and indeed since the 1970s, the word Pagan (with a capital P) has been embraced by polytheists and earth-worshippers to describe a wide range of spiritual paths. Likewise, the word Heathen (with a capital H) has been claimed by people who follow a specific style of Pagan spirituality. Whereas Pagan is a vast umbrella term for almost any spiritual paradigm incorporating polytheism, earth-reverence and/or feminist spirituality, Heathen is a much smaller umbrella term. There is still an array of diversity within Heathenry, but two points of agreement are shared by all Heathens, and it is these two points that define us and distinguish us from other Pagan paths.

First, we are Germanic. While I have met some Celtic reconstructionists who identify themselves as Heathens, the majority of people who use this word as a descriptive draw their spiritual inspiration from the indigenous beliefs and customs of Norway, Sweden, Iceland, Denmark, England and, of course, Europe's continental Germanic tribes. Collectively we tend to be very focused on our spiritual identity. Very few Heathens describe themselves as eclectic.

Equally important if not more so, Heathens are true polytheists, believing in many deities. While our worship as Heathen people is focused on Germanic deities, most of us acknowledge the gods and goddesses of other cultures as being equally real. And when I say "real", I mean in the sense that you and I are real. For Heathens, the gods are distinct and independent individuals, not aspects or facets of an all-encompassing divinity.

Beyond this are other customs and ideas shared by most Heathens, but our essential defining characteristics can be summed up as Germanic polytheism. Within that designation can be found a great deal of diversity.

Ásatrú is the most widely known expression of Germanic polytheism, and is a word used by some people as a term for all Heathens. The word can be traced back to the 19th century and essentially means a belief or faith in the gods. Ásatrúar are reconstructionists, which means they seek to recreate Germanic (especially Scandinavian) religious traditions based on historical literature and archaeology. Much emphasis is given to two 13th century Icelandic manuscripts known as the Eddas, which are highly valued as source material. Because of this, Ásatrú might be thought of as Icelandic Heathenry or, in a broader sense, Scandinavian Heathenry. The people of Medoburg are true to this path, going so far as to use the Younger Futhark (a set of runic symbols specific to the Norse and Icelandic cultures) rather than the more popular set of 24 runes sold in bookstores and new age shops. One of the Medoburg Heathens, Ann Groa Sheffield, has even authored a book about the Younger Futhark called Long Branches. However, there are many other Ásatrúar who take a more general approach to their spirituality, borrowing freely from the Anglo-Saxon and continental Germanic cultures rather than focusing on Scandinavian practices. The beliefs, customs and attitudes of Ásatrú can vary greatly from one group to the next.

Solitary practice is not discouraged, but Ásatrúar often organize themselves in groups known as kindreds. Unlike the Wiccan coven, there is usually no initiatory hierarchy within a kindred, and the emphasis is on social ties and worshipping the gods rather than on working magic.

Less well known is another Scandinavian path known as Forn Sed or Forn Siðr, meaning "the old customs". In Europe, Forn Sed is an active religion in Norway, Denmark and Sweden. It differs from Ásatrú in that Forn Sed is inspired primarily by Scandinavian folklore rather than the Eddas and other writings. As far as possible, followers of Forn Sed eschew reconstructionism in favor of living traditions expressed in song, dance and festival customs. Of course they are still reconstructing the spirituality of their ancestors; the difference is in their method.

Followers of Anglo-Saxon Heathenry like myself represent what may be an even greater distinction within Heathenry.

When Germanic peoples settled in England their culture developed in unique ways. We revere many of the same gods and goddesses as our Norse and Icelandic friends do, although by slightly different names: Woden (Odin), Frige (Frigg), Tiw (Tyr), Thunor (Thor), Ing (Freyr) and Fréo (Freyja). Nevertheless, the pantheons are slightly different. Anglo-Saxons have deities like Eostre, Hrethe and Weland, who are not found in Scandinavian mythology. Conversely, if the Norse god Loki ever set foot on England's shores there is no record of it.

One trait shared by Anglo-Saxon Heathens is an emphasis on the tribal unit. While kindreds are optional for Ásatrúar, the Anglo-Saxon equivalent – which might be known as an inhíred, a mót or a théod – is almost a requirement for those of us who find our inspirations in the beliefs and customs of the pre-Christian English. No, there is no rule requiring anyone to be part of a group in order to worship the old gods, and of course there are many Anglo-Saxons who, simply because of their circumstances, must function as solitaries. But for us this is never a *desirable* lifestyle. Early English society was structured around a tribal model, and contemporary Anglo-Saxons are still today very "pack oriented".

An Anglo-Saxon movement known as Theodism was created in 1976 by a man by the name of Garman Lord. In contrast to most other expressions of Heathenry, Theodism is a reconstructionist movement that attempts to recreate pre-Christian Germanic social structures as well as Germanic spirituality. The social unit is the théod, a word meaning tribe, which always has a hierarchical structure.

But not all Anglo-Saxon Heathens are Theodsmen. There are others, including myself, who describe their path as Fyrn Sidu, which means exactly the same as Forn Sed ("old customs"), but in Old English. As in the practice of Forn Sed, followers of Fyrn Sidu are less concerned with reconstruction and more with preserving the qualities of pre-Christian spirituality that live on in folklore and custom. The tribe is just as important, but in Fyrn Sidu this social unit is more often known as an inhíred (household) and has a less formal structure. These social units may be conventional nuclear families, but more often than not they are families of choice.

I am going out on a limb here, but I think it may even be appropriate to add Seax Wica to the list of Anglo-Saxon Heathen traditions. Ten years ago I would have dismissed the idea. Seax Wica sprang into existence in the mid-1970s when Raymond Buckland published his book *The Tree: The Complete Book of Saxon Witchcraft*. The new tradition introduced new ideas, such as self-dedication and democratically elected coven officers, but it nevertheless adhered to the Wiccan cosmology of only two deities; a Horned God and a Mother Goddess. These deities are called upon by the names Woden and Freya, and much of the other symbolism within the Seax tradition was inspired by pre-Christian Anglo-Saxon spirituality. In recent years I have encountered Seax practitioners who say that they have broken away from the duotheistic God-and-Goddess cosmology to embrace a true polytheism. In their magical work they continue to primarily acknowledge Woden and Freya (Fréo), which is entirely appropriate as these are the two Anglo-Saxon deities associated with magic. However, they recognize that these are not the *only* Anglo-Saxon gods.

To further illustrate the diversity within modern Heathenry, I would like to mention Urglaawe. This is an expression of Germanic spirituality that focuses on the cultural traditions of the Pennsylvania Deitsch. In the Deitsch language, Urglaawe means "the original faith". Followers of Urglaawe draw their inspiration from time-honored customs such as Braucherei (healing practices) and Hexerei (magical practices).

With the exception of Seax Wica – which of course uses Wiccan rituals – most Heathens perform a basic rite usually known as a blót. Ásatrúar always use this term for the rite; it means a sacrifice. In Old English (and probably in Old Norse as well) the word is closely related to blood, and among Anglo-Saxon Heathens there is some disagreement as to whether the word is appropriate for a non-blood offering. For those of us who believe the word is misleading, the term húsel is often used instead. In my inhíred we say húsel, but since this is a discussion of general Heathenry we shall use the word blót.

Blood offering? Well, yes, in pre-industrial societies people routinely butchered their own meat. It was a fact of life. Today very few people are directly involved in slaughtering animals, and, as you might expect, the typical blót is a non-blood offering.

The details of the rite vary from one group to another, but they almost always share several key elements. Above all else, a blót is not an act of magic, it is an act of devotion. A gift or gifts are given to one or more spirits intentionally honored during the rite. In a kindred or an inhíred there will first be a group offering before any individual offerings are given. The honored spirit may be a deity like Odin or Thor, or it may be a collective group of entities such as ancestral spirits or land wights (nature spirits). Mead, an alcoholic drink brewed from honey and water, is the usual choice for this group offering.

The ritual area may or may not be consecrated at the beginning of the blót. In my inhíred we consecrate the ritual space by carrying fire (most often a lantern or candle) around the perimeter. Other Heathens, both solitary and groups, use a hammer rite which involves making hammer symbols (and thus evoking the power of Thor's hammer) at the four cardinal points as well as above and below the ritualist.

A drinking horn is filled with mead for the group offering. After a brief prayer to the honored deity or spirits, the horn is passed among all of the participants. Each person gives thanks to the honored deity and takes a drink. When everyone has partaken, the horn is then emptied either onto the ground or (if the ritual is held inside) into an offering bowl. In a large group this may be the extent of the group offering, but smaller groups usually extend this to three rounds of drinking. The first round is always devoted to the honored deity, but the second and third rounds can be directed to other gods or spirits who the participant would like to thank.

Following the group offering, participants may be invited to come forward with individual gifts, and these can be almost anything. Most gifts are tangible – drinks, baked goods, small trinkets – but I have also watched people recite poems or sing as their offerings to the gods.

Another rite common to many Heathens is the sumbel or symbel. This is essentially a group ritual of drinking and speaking. Oaths are often given during a sumbel, as it is believed that anything a person says carries more weight when spoken during one of these rituals. As with a blót, a horn is filled with mead and passed among the participants. Some groups, particularly in Ásatrú, pass the mead horn three or more times. During the first round the horn is raised in a toast to the gods and goddesses, with each participant choosing which deity he wishes to honor. The second round is devoted to ancestors and to personal heroes who have passed on. During the following rounds participants may give oaths, share poetry, brag about their accomplishments or sing songs.

Some groups follow a different format than this. Theodish Heathens practice an especially structured symbel which is believed to affect the luck – hopefully in a good way – of all those participating. In the Theodish symbel are two specific boasts; the first a boast of one's past deeds or ancestors, and the second a boast of something the speaker intends to accomplish. There is a metaphysical principle underlying these boasts, which are intended to expand and strengthen the luck of the théod.

From my description of the blót and the sumbel it may seem like there is a lot of drinking going on, but in practice Heathens are no more disposed to consuming alcohol than other people are. Drunkenness in Heathen rituals is strongly frowned upon, and in fact it is entirely possible to be a practicing Heathen without ever taking a drink at all. Those who cannot or choose not to drink simply touch the mead horn respectfully to their lips and pass it on to the next person. If the ritual is outdoors, the person may pour his or her portion onto the earth before passing the horn.

Heathens do not conveniently fit into any one stereotype. We are of many paths, with different political views, different approaches to our spirituality and different sources of cultural inspiration. Other than being Germanic and being polytheists, there are few common qualities or practices that we all share. And yet we know who we are. A Heathen, above all else, is a man or woman of honor, striving to be a credit to the northern gods and to his or her ancestors.

Alaric Albertsson is a native of Missouri, but currently lives in western Pennsylvania. He is the author of *Travels Through Middle Earth: The Path of a Saxon Pagan*, *Wyrdworking: The Path of a Saxon Sorcerer* and *To Walk a Pagan Path: Practical Spirituality for Every Day*.

Silvia Rahmani

Alaric Albertsson gives us a very vivid and detailed description of his personal experience as a Heathen in the United States. However, being a German, I would like to focus on the more spiritual and folkloristic background of many Heathens nowadays in Germany.

I grew up in a little village north of Frankfurt and remember very well that Christian holidays were often celebrated with the folkloristic continuation of the old Heathen beliefs and practices.

Mayday, for instance, was celebrated by us youngsters with much noise the night before, with "hexing", which meant flowerpots and doormats would disappear and wooden shutters were being unhinged and carried away. It was the joy over spring and welcoming the light of the sun. The dark spirits of winter were chased out of the village by banging old pot lids together, whistling and whips clashing. There was dancing and flirting. Houses were decorated with young tree shoots and daisies were thrown into the river while making a wish for a future husband or wife. Even the cows were decorated with chains of flowers on their way to the meadows, it all was about fertility and growth.

The Christian Church, of course, ruled the holidays and everyday life, but in the houses and neighbourhoods of the village, it was the old mothers and grandmothers, with their tales and stories which were written down by the Gebrüder Grimm long after they were first told and the customs were Heathen.

Many of us German Heathens have our roots in these early days of childhood. Heathenry never was rooted out in the remote villages. We were living in unity with nature and the seasons because we depended on them. Our beliefs were carried to us since the first mass migration of Iron Age. Our Heathen Gods never died, because they lived on in the tales of our grand-mothers, in the rocks, rivers and trees. We still live by the Nine Noble Virtues. The art of civilisation was taught to us by the crafts God Loki.

Modern Heathenry, wherever in the world it is practised, can only be fruitful if the old Germanic paths are remembered, a way of life with the gods and spirits around us, in unison with nature and honouring those who were before us.

Christopher Courtley

Despite my strict Christian upbringing, as a teenager two of my favourite subjects were Norse mythology, and witchcraft. I was also fascinated by the runes and by hex signs, the latter of which I was introduced to in a "Wendy the Good Little Witch" comic of all things.

At thirteen I had read Anton LaVey's *The Satanic Bible*, which left me with the false impression that all modern witches were Satanic, but I had also recognised a survival of paganism in some of the lore concerning witches. So I decided to "invent" pagan witchcraft, which is pretty funny in retrospect. Of course, I had no idea at the time that it already existed. I didn't find that out until a year or so later. But I decided early on that Wicca was not for me. I was more inclined toward sorcery and Traditional Witchcraft, and it was through the latter that I eventually discovered Heathenry.

In Heathenry I found a kinship not only in the worship of the northern gods, but also the intense study engaged in by Heathens and, above all, their insistence on keeping a clear distinction between the actual lore and what they call one's "Unverified Personal Gnosis", or UPG.

By now I also found myself being drawn toward Theodish and other Anglo-Saxon Heathen groups because I felt a strong identification with the Anglo-Saxon lore and language. I suppose this may have been the result of an early influence on my childhood imagination by the writings of J.R.R. Tolkien, but I also believe it is due to half my ancestry having sprung from the British Isles.

My evolution into an Anglo-Saxon Heathen was more or less complete after I read Alaric Albertsson's *Travels Through Middle Earth: The Path of a Saxon Pagan*. Just prior to that I had read Brian Bates' novel *The Way of Wyrd*, which also spoke to my Trad Witchcraft leanings, and so of course from there I went on to read Albertsson's *Wyrdworking: The Path of a Saxon Sorcerer* and Edred Thorsson's *Witchdom of the True: A Study of the Vana-Troth and the Practice of Seiðr*.

For me the practice of Heathenry has included two different approaches of modern Heathens: reconstructing the ancient ways of our ancestors, as with the blót or húsel, and carrying on (or rediscovering) the legacy of our folkish customs and traditions. For example, like many, I consider as part of my practice of Heathenry keeping the Yuletide traditions of decorating an evergreen tree, burning a Yule log, wassailing the apple trees, hanging holly, ivy, and mistletoe in the home, and so on. I don't think anyone really knows for certain how far back most of these traditions go, but they are valid living traditions today, so I make them a part of my religious observance.

There's nothing wrong with choosing one approach to Heathenry over another of course; I just feel more complete with the inclusion of both in my daily life and worship.

Gerrit Orgers

We live as Heathens, but what happens when we die? Not all Heathens go to Valhalla, in fact, very few of us will likely make it there. In order to qualify, you will need to be an exceptional warrior. And let's face it, unlike our forebears, we are no longer a warrior people. The majority of us live civilian lives. And although many Heathens also practice some form of martial art, civilian life mostly comes before that part-time warrior thing.

So... where do Heathens go when they die? Well, most of us will end up in Hel. But our Hel is not to be confused with the Christian version, for whereas that one is filled with fire and brimstone, ours is actually a cold place, located in Niflheim (Mist-Home). In Hel, the Goddess of the same name presides over the souls of those who did not die in battle. It is a place filled with artists, farmers, craftsmen, etc. Good, hardworking people, who also sit out the long wait till Ragnarok, our version of the end of this World. The Goddess Hel has survived in modern times, in many ways. It is said that she is the same as Frau Holle, in the tales of Grimm. And in Holland, her part is played by the local Goddess Nehalenia. There are other examples to be found all over Germanic parts of the world.

In Heathen belief, our forefathers and mothers play a vital role. We are an extension of them and thus, what we do is in part thanks to them, but also reflects on them. In order not to shame them, it is very important for a Heathen to live an honourable and productive life. How we define that is mostly up to ourselves, but the main consensus is to live by the Nine Noble Values (Honour, Discipline, Courage, Perseverance, Hospitality, Truth, Fidelity, Self-reliance and Industriousness). It is also important to honour and remember our forebears, for they are the ones that made us, and they have formed who we are.

When we face certain problems, it is not uncommon to ask our forebears for guidance and advice. In Heathen belief, we acknowledge that the Dead look upon our lives and when properly asked, they may indeed provide useful feedback. One of the ways to do this is to visit a grave of an ancestor and meditate beside or even on top of it for some time. It is also considered good practice to set aside a place at the table, for the Dead, at family or tribal gatherings. The Dead also receive a part of the meal which we share and so continue to form a 'living' segment of our society.

So it's not a bad thing to go to Hel. We can play a part in this world after we die, aiding our offspring in a similar manner as our ancestors have aided us. And in doing so, we will remain a part of life, of family, of our Sibbe or Tribe. And hopefully, we will have given our children enough of our values, love and knowledge, to ensure they too will live an honourable life and continue to remember us kindly.

Joe LeVasseur

A long time ago when I was a solitary Heathen, I found it rather hard to establish a direction. All I really understood were the basics of the gods and the lore. "What do I do now," I constantly asked myself, "and where do I go from here?" Many spend years in that same place never knowing anything else about Heathenry. One thing that helped me get a leg up was when I attended a class on Asatru (Icelandic Heathenry) at a Pagan bookshop. After that class, I spoke with the presenter and he invited me to a ritual that his kindred was hosting in honor of the ancestors. People from at least four or five different Heathen groups were there. That was the beginning of my introduction to the Heathen community. Eventually, I was able to meet enough people so that myself and three others could start our own group, Saxnot's Hearth. Although the knowledge from the initial class I went to was valuable, I found the social connections that I made as a result of attending that class to be a hundred times more valuable.

Over the years I have realized being part of a community is an essential part of Heathen spirituality. In the epic poem Beowulf they describe the sumbles – great gatherings in the mead hall that involved the whole community, to toast the heroes and the slain, and to make oaths before those present. In the Icelandic Sagas, people gathered yearly at the All-Thing to discuss business, politics, and religious matters. Community has been key to the Heathen religion all the way down to daily life on a feudal manor. Heathenry developed in the time of tribalism and feudalism, when large groups of people worked the land together, and when our networks and bonds with one another were crucial for survival. Community celebrations, feasting, and games were such a big part of Heathen tradition that laws were even passed during the conversion to ban people from taking part in Heathen gatherings.

Today, the Heathen community serves more as a social network. Ties within the Heathen community allow us to grow our networks, to learn from the experiences of others, and to share new experiences with others. Solitary Heathens are able to take steps towards building kindreds, and established kindreds can meet with other kindreds to collaborate on Heathen projects. Human beings are social creatures and not only crave, but also thrive within community.

My advice to anyone interested in Heathenry is to go out and get to know other local Heathens. You may initially meet some people you don't get on with, but eventually you will meet people that you do. Attend social events, meet other Heathens, and you will solidify your spiritual direction and growth.

Witch

Dorothy Abrams

There are as many different kinds of witches practicing the craft as there are other kinds of pagan paths. There are green witches, white witches, red witches, black witches, good witches, ditch witches, hedge witches, family trad witches, feminist witches, Dianic witches, web witches, solitary witches and oodles more. There are male witches and female witches, teen witches and old witches.

One of the major differences I perceive is between US witches who tend to include more ceremonial white light workings and UK witches who boldly tend to straddle the line between the light and the dark. Both are earthy and practical but the temperament seems different. Suffice it to say then, no matter what I write in the introduction, there is plenty room for disagreement and discussion. I enjoy an exchange of views, so I invite diverse opinions and experiences. Since witches name themselves, witchcraft is what we make it.

Witchcraft is a secretive practice, one played close to the chest with a knowing smile between those who recognize its telltales and those who look askance with awe or fear. The rest of the population counts our experiences as odd coincidences. Magic experiences are not odd nor chance. Witchcraft is intentional, wise and learned in the ways of nature. I first learned the craft from a US hereditary witch named Lydia. Her mother, grand-mother and great-grandmother before her combined Irish, French, Romani and Cherokee magic into a family tradition generally resembling what Starhawk wrote about in her fairy tradition. In fact the first book Lydia gave me to read was *Spiral Dance*, an introductory text I still use. With Lydia, we cast circles, called the Elementals, invoked the God and Goddess, raised a cone of power, recited chants, entered trances and cast spells and charms. We used incense and herbs in the east, candles in the south, water and shells in the west and a pot of earth and pentacles in the north. We learned to ground, speak with Spirits, and release them. We approached all creation as inter-related if not as part of the great All Being. We cultivated a personal relationship with the Goddess and created miraculous manifestations. My favorite spontaneous appearance is the spirit gift of an old athame stuck randomly in Lydia's new apartment window sill, appearing literally from nowhere.

However, Lydia led a celebratory circle. Her highest magic was performed as a solitary. Quite honestly none of us were up to it in those days. She preferred not to teach, so she hived my partner Merlin off with me to establish a teaching circle now known as The Web PATH Center. Twenty years later we are still here. Having learned a lot, we do all we did with Lydia plus drawing down the moon, past life regression, healing, cord and candle magic, and a good many conversations with the dead. Our witchcraft has a strong dose of core shamanism in it including dismemberment journeys, journeys to the Summerland, and psychopomp intervention for those spirits needing help crossing over. Witch workings rely on animal allies usually referenced as familiars in witchcraft and power animals in shamanism. These beings guide the power of magic and help to actually create the vehicle by which magic is accomplished.

The other practices common to witchcraft involve plants and plant spirits. In the Web we work most with the plant spirits, not in preparing concoctions or spells. They are our familiars or fetch friends, working healing in the humans' spirit bodies that then sink into the physical bodies. A few of our number excel in charms and spells, potions, elixirs, poppets, talisman and soul dolls, all of which incorporate plant magic. We teach these skills so that individually people can move on and learn their craft according to the direction of their guides and their own talents. We have experts to consult if those skills are needed in the community, since as we frequently say to the beginner, "Everybody cannot do everything."

On the other hand, I strong believe every witch ought to have one divination practice such as tarot or runes, in which the witch excels. Excellence in understanding the tools and the process of psychic reading and prophecy as well as learning to read apart from the ego takes a concentrated investment of time. Reading also takes a depth of wisdom in the Craft that helps us understand what time is and is not; what cross-dimensional information is and how it can confuse an earth-dimensional mind; when to give information offered from the spirit realm and when to withhold it. As I said, witchcraft is a secretive practice. We have no business telling everything we know to people who are not prepared to hear it.

I also believe every witch should have an alternative healing modality in which they excel. Being a healer requires certain ethical decisions. The first is to do no harm. This is as true for the witch as it is the licensed physician. The second is to be well prepared. In our healer-mode, we need a reasonable education in anatomy and physiology so we can best understand what the spirits show us. Merlin and I took adult noncredit courses from a nearby medical school in its outreach program. We bought anatomy texts with good pictures. We have charts and a doll with the acupuncture meridians clearly defined. The old hedge witches did not have those opportunities, but those of us who do should take advantage of them. We read alternative healing texts, take workshops and work with our familiar spirits in creating a healing environment. When indicated, we create healing rituals with charms and small ordeals for the ailing to achieve. Becoming whole and healing the body is facilitated by a witch or physician or other practitioner. The real healing is completed by the ailing soul.

Having said that, across our community of pagans and witches, we have many Reiki masters, body workers, three good sound vibrational healers, two acupressure researchers, a licensed massage therapist who also knows cranial-sacral response, two licensed herbalists and several others with skill, a couple of nutritionists who work with healing foods, aura cleansers, pranic healers, and several chakra balancers. There are a couple of people working with aromatherapy and several shamanic healers able to do extractions and soul retrievals. When we work for each other within the community, we make no charge. Some of us offer our services free as a matter of spirit instruction. Others have been called to make healing their life's work so it is how they earn their living. All of this healing can be part of anyone's spiritual practice. It is also the practice of witches because witches heal.

Witches create magic. What does that mean? We change ordinary reality. Sometimes we interrupt an accident about to happen. Sometimes we create surprising outcomes from crisis situations. We find things that are lost. We protect the vulnerable and shield ourselves. We bring blessings and prosperity to our families. Sometimes, like the Reclaiming Tradition founded by Starhawk *et. al.*, we intervene in politics. These acts of magical intervention may be done quickly with the mind and a gesture. They may be carefully prepared according to the stars and the moon phases. They may be a group working when we draw down the moon or at some other auspicious time. They may be a collective of solitary workings sent out through an internet request. Nearly every morning Merlin and I do a white light meditation for individuals with health problems that are either very serious or chronic without successful treatment from western medicine. We work on half a dozen people at a time. When one is healed, we include another.

The important thing for a witch to remember in setting up a magical working is to be very specific in one's wording. The spirits are quixotic; they love a good joke. One woman doing a spell to spend more time in meditation asked to watch less television. The picture on her screen immediately began to shrink.

They key to effective magic for a witch is not elaborate recipes as in ceremonial magic, but an intimate relationship with the spirit world. We know Elementals by their names. We have patrons among the Gods and Goddesses who agree to work with us, correct us and make a spell come out right. That is not the same thing as always getting what we want. In the Web, we partner with these spirits to make magic. We share our lives. They ride with us on our journeys. Sometimes they are also spirit lovers, though not always. Sometimes they are the missing parent who agrees to cuddle us in their laps as we grieve. Sometimes they are a tough taskmaster who will give no quarter in their demands on what to do next. Sometimes we negotiate. Being in a human body means I accept some limits that they do not.

A witch is psychic. We can read a metal object and learn something of its history and the people who held it. We can speak to each other silently and finish each other's sentences. We can astral project from one room to another, from one town to another, or around the world. When you know how, you can. We can dream and change our dreams. We recall past and future lives, and know that they are all concurrent. We can enter a photo and learn something of the people's history. We can act as mediums for the dead and channels for the spirits and other worldly beings. We can manifest events and objects. We can be invisible and we can shapeshift. Again, everybody cannot do everything, but all of us can do some things. The more we practice, the more we can do. Our guides, familiars and mentors take us as far as we dare go and then a little farther. Once I asked for a specific sum of money. Within the week a lawyer wrote and offered me the exact amount for a piece of property I held but was not for sale.

There are some magical witchy powers we may not choose to

include, but which are possible. The deciding factor there is whether or not the working is for the good of all or if it is of the ego. For example, a hex or a binding spell is a reasonably simple matter to accomplish. Should we do it? My best advice is no, because who you love and who you hate, who you bind and who you hex all become linked to you by karma. Do you really want to continue to work this out across your many life stories? I have yet to see a witch's life prosper when she or he is involved in hexes or binding spells. I have seen them struggle and wonder why their lives are fraught with crises and disappointments. At least that is how I see it from the outside of their situations. There is such a thing as the rule of three, though that is an arbitrary number. My grandmother used to say "cast your bread upon the waters and it will return nine-fold." What goes around comes around. If you start a fight it will finish with you. Witches are brave and take chances, but it is never smart to overestimate your strength.

Conjuring spirits is another practice available to witches. We can call them up and expect an appearance. Some will see them and others will sense them, but they will be there. If we are calling them for a service or mission against another, then we are inviting chaos. We can create guardians/egregores for our property. If we do, we should be very clear about their duty and limitations. Someone trying to steal my computer need not be electrocuted. It isn't a capital offense. Better that they be scared away from the property in the first place. When you evoke an egregore, know why and what you expect and for how long. Beyond that, spirits of history, spirits of my family members, spirits of the disincarnate all can come alongside to help or communicate. They answer us and work best in partnership. This is the 21st century. We need not command though we must stand in our own power and take no nonsense – not from spirits and not from humans.

In ritual practices in the US most witches celebrate the wheel of the year with eight sabbats. We also observe the phases of the moon by holding ritual on or around the full moon. In these rituals we tell each other the stories of the seasons, of the spirits and ourselves in relation to the season. We may perform magic associated with that season. We may seek insight and information. We may also observe other holy days sacred to our patrons. Ancient feast days or national celebrations in other cultures are clues to the timing of these events. Saturnalia, the Green Corn Festival, and the Tet New Year come to mind. Some of us celebrate the days of the week for the Gods and Goddess they name: Moon, Mars, Mercury, Thor, Freya, Saturn and the Sun. That works well in one's personal practice. It is something to do every day at home.

In addition, witches venerate the Earth as Goddess Mother and Gaia. She is sentient. She is conscious. She supports us. She grounds us and heals us. We return excess energy raised in our workings to her through the rocks so she can use it as she will. We work to protect her from the crazy schemes of industry and exploitation. We work for the seventh generation forward, that they will have cleaner water, purer air and fertile soil. We recycle. We plant gardens and seek out organic food when we can. We spend time outdoors to feel the earth beneath bare feet and between our fingers. We meditate on her mountains and lakes. We hear her voice and sing back to her. We know the drum beat is the heart of the Earth.

This is what witches do. We all do some of it. We all can do more. We are men and women, girls and boys, dedicated to the Lady and Lord in all their guises. Some of us follow a long-established tradition. Some of us make up our own. Some of us are solitary. Some of us are in covens of 13. Some of us work with two or three friends. Some of us are in communities that number scores or hundreds. Some of us are open about who and what we are. Some of us are safely in the broom closet. Some of us keep it very simple. Some of us push the boundaries out as far as we can and then cross them. All of us are taught by the spirits. All of us will do this again.

Dorothy Abrams is a Central New York feminist Witch, co-founder of the Web PATH Center and author of *Identity and the Quartered Circle*

Sherrie Almes

I'm a witch. I don't make any bones about it. I'm completely out of the broom closet. This means I have had many occasions to share my spiritual path with others who don't understand what being a witch means. I welcome these opportunities to de-mystify the Craft by using more familiar terms to help others' understanding of what witchcraft is and isn't, without imposing my beliefs on others or demeaning theirs.

As part of my path, I incorporate herbalism using plants for healing in the form of teas, elixirs, potions, lotions, incense and oils, as well as for rituals; divination primarily using intuition, clairvoyance, clairaudience and other forms of mediumship, as well as the use of pendulums, runes, Tarot cards, and reading signs in nature. For many years I facilitated healings using personal energy and stones. Several years ago I also became a Reiki Master/Teacher. This isn't witchy since one can be a Reiki practitioner and not a witch or vice versa. The same can be said for psychic tools.

When explaining that many Christian beliefs and practices are adaptations of pagan ones, I have met with disbelief and resistance. I feel it's vital when talking with a non-pagan that I don't come across as ridiculing their beliefs. For example, I point out the similarities in our belief systems, such as how in celebrating Yule, I'm recognizing the birth of a new king and the promise of growth and prosperity, and that Ostara is celebrating rebirth, renewal, and new beginnings; that what I call a 'spell' is what others call 'prayer'; and what I call 'cakes and ale' is commensurate with Holy Communion. However, as a witch I take a more active role by creating the ritual and tailoring it to a specific intent enhanced with the use of herbs, stones, energy work, and the cycles of the sun and moon, and the seasons.

When it comes to working magick I have pointed out that burning candles and incense, the use of color and plants, and the raising of energy by singing, prayer and meditation are all things that are used by the Episcopal Church I was raised in and many other Christian denominations' church services. As a witch, these spiritual tools help me call the elements and the deities to my aid as well as to better prepare me to receive their energies, guidance and wisdom.

When the opportunity presents itself I feel an obligation to raise the consciousness of folks who are ignorant of the true nature of witchcraft. I live in the United States where witches (and non-witches) were persecuted and murdered during the late 17th century. Sadly, even in the 21st century this still occurs in many other countries. I feel it is imperative that we try to educate those whose notions about us are rooted in fear and misunderstanding.

We have fought for centuries to be accepted in the community at large, to be recognized as healers and instruments of the Divine, as people who have a conscious relationship with Nature in all her manifestations. As a witch, I must be aware that what I do, what I say, and how I comport myself will reflect on the entire pagan community. Whether I am aggressive or gentle, rude or kind, dismissive or accepting, or deliberately creepy-weird versus affable and earnest to those of a different faith path, may well determine that they will walk away thinking all who walk a pagan path are of the same ilk.

Bridgete Isabela

Witchcraft, being a Witch, is a way of life more than a religion. It is a way of being and a Path one accepts and chooses as the Way also chooses him/her. Following the Path of Witchcraft takes one on an interior journey, an initiation, to learn the ways of old and to learn about oneself completely and totally. The magic of Witchcraft is this knowledge of self combined with knowledge of the old ways to influence reality.

My own personal tradition is that of the Crone, and its foundation is Purification, Initiation and Transformation of the self in the world. Meditation plays a huge role in this tradition because spending time within is one of the best ways to get to know oneself and to be open to learning the old ways from ancient teachers who are with us at all times to teach and assist.

The first step in becoming a Witch is to accept the title and the way of being that it represents. That means to commit to spending several years seeking and learning everything you can about cycles, energies, meditation, herbs, divination, correspondences, gods and goddesses, symbolism, spells and learning to know yourself completely and how to get into a frame of mind that sees the world as magical and connected.

Books will literally fall into your hands, you will become aware of groups and classes, and the cycles of nature will teach you lessons as you open up and begin to see what has always been around you waiting for you to be ready. Some of the lessons will be difficult because nothing worthwhile is given away without work.

As you progress along this path of seeking and learning the time will come when you will know if it is the Path for you, or not, and if it is a part of who you are you can then claim the title Witch by saying three times, I am a Witch, preferably on the night of a full moon or dark moon. Then you will continue to seek and learn because there is always more knowledge to be gained on the path of Witchcraft.

Benediza Shortt

I am in a circular forest clearing on a metal folding chair. The trees are green with mid-spring growth. I have been sitting here waiting for something. The sky is bright and cloudless. I watch birds: robins, blue jays and cardinals, hop from tree to tree or pop into nests inside tree holes. There is a big screen TV in the middle of the clearing. That does not belong here. I am dreaming.

Scenes are played out there of depths of ocean, stretches of blue darkness. The channels begin to change of their own accord. There is a remote control on the ground near my feet. The TV is loud, frightening the birds away. A predator bird swoops down from the center of the sky. Is She a hawk? An eagle? As She comes down, the sky dims and droplets fall. There is a flash of distant lightning and rumble of thunder. It is going to rain. The TV crackles with static.

I know the remote has little battery life. Some buttons are missing. I do not expect it to be useful. I fall on my knees searching around the TV for some other way to shut it off. The birds have flown away, except for that predator sitting in a tree staring down at me. There is no way to shut off the TV from the screen.

"What am I supposed to do? I can't shut it off. I can't do it."

"Take the control. You need to take the control and shut it down."

The voice is resonant feminine. I am not sure if it comes from the bird or sky. I protest. I just cannot do it. She insists that I can, and I must. "Take the control in your hands," She tells me. Finally, with effort I press into the hole where a missing power button should be and turn off that TV.

That dream stays with me because I asked for it. One of my first rituals was to ask for guidance through dream. I will not say that witchcraft is not helping others, healing imbalances in communities or connecting to the web of life outside our microcosms. It is for all those purposes. It is also for the immediate concerns of life.

Asking guidance of the Great Mother/Father while honoring

the consequence and responsibility of individuals to participate in life, co-creating solutions and celebrating manifestations within the individual's life are as meaningful as engaging the greater community of the living universe. Witchcraft is working with the forces of nature, archetypes, elements, elementals, ancestors, or gods to create or bring forth balance to fractured situations.

The ways we do this are many and varied, but we are all doing it. We are all taking control and participating in life instead of watching it go by as on a screen, helpless to effect change for ourselves and others.

Robert Scott

What I do, in my witchcraft, is what many people pretend, imagine, or play at doing. I first realized this when I was having the typical Monday morning conversation with fellow male co-workers in the field of information technology, of what we did the past weekend. When it was my turn, I mentioned I was working on herbalism, and my co-worker responded with, "Oh were you playing a video game?" No, I really did work with herbs. On another occasion, the same Monday morning conversation, I told how I spent the weekend training first aid, and also went fishing. Yes, I really did forge a blade. It was at this point, when their first reaction was to suspect these fairly reasonable trades and crafts they first expected to be "within a game", I knew it would be out of the question to mention other things I do, such as other crafts, and my witchcraft.

I perform rituals individually, and within groups. I raise power and energy. I perform divination, and seek omens in a variety of ways. I see, hear, and sense things at times that are beyond the normal senses. I connect with land and ancestor spirits. I speak, and listen to animals. I honor, and communicate with, old gods and goddesses. I strive to learn a variety of skills, and wisdom. I have experienced things that cannot be shared. I recognize that there are more levels to this present reality than most can, or choose to, deal with. I perform spell work, but prefer to live in an intentional and magical way. My witchcraft is a blend of religion, spirituality, art, craft, and science. I have learned through books, teachers, and spirit. In contrast to information technology, my witchcraft is more of a wisdom technology. I am a male modern witch, and a walker between the worlds. I take this very seriously, and this is no game.

Wiccan

David Salisbury

Of all the traditions and paths within Paganism, Wicca has to be the largest and most popular. It's constantly in the news, in movies and television, and represented in large droves at all of the world's big Pagan festivals. Wicca has had a lot of time to grow and mature within the Pagan movement. Our ministers have become known for international interfaith work. Our physical worship and gathering sites are growing at a rate that's much faster than many other traditions. And now we're seeing infrastructure like temples and community centers popping up faster than ever before. Why is this the case? What makes Wicca so special?

To really understand Wicca, you have to know about its strange and unique origins. Although the religion has a lot of ancient influences, the way we practice it today comes from humble and somewhat recent beginnings. In the early 1950s, a British civil servant by the name of Gerald Brosseau Gardner put together the movement and religion that today we call Wicca. Gardner didn't use the world Wicca to describe his religion though. Instead, he simply called it witchcraft, insisting that it was a unique system taught to him by traditional witches in the New Forest area of England. The fact that Gardner called the religion "witchcraft" and that it later became known as "Wicca" has caused a lot of confusion for newcomers to Paganism. But once you know a little more about Wicca, it becomes pretty clear why the word is used to differentiate between the religion Gerald Gardner started and the broader practice of witchcraft.

Gerald Gardner was quite the cunning man, well-traveled and charming. He was also a bit eccentric for his time, being a nudist in addition to a witch. While being a witch and nudist would even today cause a lot of people to recoil in suspicion, it was absolutely outrageous for ultra-conservative England in the '50s. That didn't stop Gardner from quickly gaining a following though. As his coven grew, he came into contact with other witches and magick practitioners who would later become known as foundational icons within Paganism. One of those icons, the infamous Aleister Crowley, contributed a lot of information to Gardner's religion that he would incorporate as part of Wicca's fundamentals. He even had some adversaries too. Robert Cochrane, who was influential in what would later become known as "traditional witchcraft" despised Gardner, contributing to a tension between Wicca and more traditional forms of witchcraft that is still felt today. Regardless, Gardner pressed on, determined to revive the ancient Pagan ways in the modern form of Wicca.

So what exactly do Wiccans believe? Wicca, although very traditional in some ways, is a syncretic religion. That means our belief system and practices are a collage of many different influences from all over. On one hand, Wicca is very much based in the ancient Pagan beliefs of animism (the idea that spirits are present within nature). On the other hand, it's also heavily influenced by what we call "Ceremonial Magick", which is the material that Gardner incorporated from his relationship with Aleister Crowley. Both of these influences place a heavy focus on nature as sacred and the idea that humans are forever connected to nature's cycles of birth, life, sex, death, and rebirth. It is this reverence for the natural world that makes up the core and focus of the Wiccan religion.

Wiccans acknowledge and commune with the cycles of nature primarily by looking at the stories of our gods. Wicca is mostly a duotheistic religion, which means the divine is organized in the form of two beings. These two gods of Wicca are simply called the Goddess and the God. You might also hear them referred to as Lady and Lord, Mother and Father, or together as "The Great Ones." The Goddess and God are usually considered to be perfectly equal in their roles, although some Wiccans may place a special emphasis on either the Goddess or God in particular.

Wiccans are encouraged to grow their individual relationships with the gods, which explains why there are so many different thoughts on who they are and where they come from. Most Wiccan creation stories say that the Goddess came first, being born out of the black void of space during the Big Bang. As the Goddess expanded outwards, she created the limitless expanse that we know as the universe and all things within it. Eventually, she longed for a companion, someone to share the joys of creation with. So out of her desire she bore the God, her lover, other half, and co-creator. In their love, they gave birth to the stars, planets, sun, moon, and Earth.

Gazing upon the Earth and celebrating their creation, the gods created animals and then eventually humans, beings who could populate the Earth and share in the love of one another just as they do. The Goddess and God are born out of the whole universe, but they are very much of the Earth as well. Just like the stars themselves, the gods are always in the process of birth and death. Matter gathers together to form stars, they have their life, and then they die, creating new life in the midst of their destruction. We see this on a smaller scale when we look at our own Earth. Each spring the Earth "wakes up" and new life is born. That life grows to a height then begins to wither and die. While everyone is aware of that process in the form of the seasons, Wiccans believe that we humans and our gods are also a part of that cycle throughout the year.

The lifecycle of the Earth and our gods is celebrated in Wicca throughout the year in the form of sacred holidays called sabbats. There are eight sabbats in one year and each one mirrors the life stages of the Earth and the gods. The ancient people were heavily reliant on the planting and harvest cycles and so they created special days to keep track of the growing seasons. Many cultures believed that participating in the cycles of nature would bless the crops and ensure a prosperous and happy life. Although most of us don't need to do any farming ourselves, we still recognize the importance of observing and communing with these cycles. As we move through the year in communion with these forces, we better align our bodies and souls to the wisdom of the Earth. In doing so, we gain wisdom of our own.

The first sabbat on the great wheel of the year is Yule and falls on the Winter Solstice, just before Christmas. At Yule, we celebrate the birth of the god in the form of the rising sun. Fir trees are brought indoors and decorated with special charms, children are given gifts, and families feast. It sounds a lot like another popular winter holiday, doesn't it? You'll notice that since many Wiccan holidays are based on ancient feast days, they look very similar to some modern civil holidays. Yule is an example of a holiday that looks just like Christmas, since many Christmas practices actually come from Winter Solstice customs.

After Yule we arrive at Imbolc, which falls on February 2nd. Imbolc honors the spirit of hope and the idea that although the land is still covered in an icy chill, the first shoots of spring are starting to push up through the hard soil. Wiccans specifically look at the maiden Goddess in the form of Brigid, the great smith of the forge who transforms the metal of our lives into a pure "gold". For this reason, Imbolc is a day of quiet transformation and a time that's used to look within.

The next sabbat is Ostara, the Spring Equinox. At Ostara, we see the Goddess as maiden beginning to transform into the mother, looking upon the God with attraction and love in her heart. In the joy of her love, she dances around the Earth and wakes everything up, causing the land to become green and new again. Ostara is a happy time in Wicca and focuses on the great potential of things we have begun. Seeds are blessed and planted at Ostara to symbolize the start of the growing season.

Beltane comes on May 1st and is one of two highly important sabbats on the wheel. Beltane is the celebration of life and is the time when the Goddess and God come together in marriage. Big feasts are held, the maypole is danced to bring fertility to the land, and the union of couples is blessed by the priestess or priest.

Litha is the Summer Solstice and marks the height of the adult life of the Goddess and God. Here, the God is at his full power and unleashes his blessings upon the land. It is believed that Litha is a wonderful time to perform magick and commune with the spirits of nature because of the high amount of power adrift in the air on this day.

The next two sabbats are Lughnassadh (August 1st) and Mabon (the autumnal equinox). Both days look similar since they are the first of three "harvest days" in the year. Lughnassadh is when the God acknowledges that his power is waning and that he must prepare to descend to the land of death. The Goddess mourns, knowing that with his departure will go the fertility of the land. At Mabon, the second harvest comes in and the air becomes chill. But still the mood is light since it's not winter just yet. Families will gather to feast and we give thanks for all of our blessings throughout the year. We can think of Mabon as a sort of Wiccan Thanksgiving.

Finally, we reach the eighth sabbat which is called Samhain. Samhain falls on either October 31st or November 1st, depending on the tradition. It is really both since it begins at sunset on the 31st and lasts until sunrise on the 1st. Opposite Beltane, Samhain is the other highly important sabbat. At this time, the God dies and makes his way to the Underworld for rest. The Goddess, in her mourning crone form, casts the Earth into darkness so we might all rest along with him. Wiccans spend Samhain honoring our beloved dead, the ancestors of both our blood and spirit, known and unknown.

Besides the eight sabbats, Wiccans also observe the cycle of the moon each month. When the moon goes from new to full, we focus on things we wish to bring into our lives. When it decreases in size from full to new, we work to banish unhelpful influences. The phases of the moon reflect the monthly journey of the Goddess in her transformation from maiden to mother to crone, and back to maiden again. The moon reminds Wiccans that change is an essential value that must be cherished if we're to grow deeper in our path spiritually.

The biggest way that Wiccans celebrate the cycles of the seasons and the moon and the presence of nature is through ritual. Ritual is very important in all Wiccan traditions. Ritual aligns us with energy, marks a special time, and helps shift our awareness into different spiritual states. Most Wiccan rituals have a standard layout that consists of casting a circle to bless the space, calling on the guardians of the directions and elements, and invoking the presence of the Goddess and God. After that, the middle part of the ritual will depend on whatever the particular working is for. Usually, most workings involve the raising of energy through song and dance or the recitation of sacred liturgy and stories.

The tools of ritual are important and represent many things within the Wiccan belief system. The wand is the tool of air and is used to call up forces like the gods and other spirits. As a tool of intellect and the mind, the wand helps us to focus our mental powers for the work at hand. The athame is a black-handled knife and represents the element of fire. It's also used to direct energy but it directs personal energy that comes from the practitioner's own body and spirit. It represents our will and the ability of humans to hone our energy and send it forth for manifestation. The cup is a tool of water and holds either holy water for blessing or the ritual wine that is drunk at the end of the rite in thanks for the abundance that the gods bring us. The pentacle is a round disk with a five-pointed star painted on it and represents Earth. The pentacle acts as an anchor that grounds our energy into this world and helps us stay stable and grounded during ritual.

The Wiccan worldview is a simple one. We are interested in doing what will bring success and happiness to ourselves and our community. "Live and let live" is a value that most Wiccans ascribe to. So while we wish to stand in full power and personal authority of our lives, we do so with the understanding that we should cause as little harm as possible along the way. The only essential code of conduct that all Wiccans share is called the Wiccan Rede. The Rede says "do what ye will, an it harm none." While we acknowledge that our very lives are a product of birth and death, growth and destruction, it is considered unnecessary to intentionally cause harm to others along the way. Since Wiccans believe that all people and beings on the planet share an intimate spiritual connection, it's simply not in our best interest to harm someone else. After all, that would mean we're harming ourselves in the process.

The Wiccan Rede is most known for its role as a guide to the type of magick we'll work with. Wicca, coming primarily from witchcraft, is a magick-embracing religion. Wicca's acceptance and encouragement of magick (spelled with a "k" to differentiate it from stage magic) is probably one of the reasons why it is the most popular of the Pagan religions. Wiccans use magick to heal the sick, protect our home and families, draw in abundance, and to align our souls with the forces of nature and the will of the gods.

Wicca's rapid rate of growth isn't slowing down anytime soon. As Wiccans continue to become more out in the open and share more about the belief system, more people will become attracted to what it can do for our lives. Wicca is a religion of personal transformation and alignment. We acknowledge both the dark and the light parts of ourselves. We seek to integrate those things fully into our experience so we might come to better understand ourselves and our place in the world. Once we understand where we fit in the grand scheme of things, the bliss of a truly meaningful life will make itself known.

David Salisbury is Wiccan clergy within Coven of the Spiral Moon, a coven based in Washington DC and author of *The Deep Heart of Witchcraft*.

Lucya Starza

One question I often get asked is how being Wiccan affects what I do in my daily life and how I practise Wicca from day to day.

That is a very good question, because although Wiccans get together to celebrate the seasonal sabbats and the cycles of the moon – called esbats – in ritual, we aren't required to do any specific daily practices as part of our beliefs. We aren't instructed to pray each day, say grace before meals, wear specific clothes or jewellery, eat or abstain from particular foods or follow set behaviour apart from the general advice of the Wiccan Rede. This means in everyday life Wiccans can do pretty much what they want so long as their actions don't harm anyone.

However, many Wiccans do adopt what they call a daily practice. Some Wiccans might choose to meditate each day or do personal magic, but that's their choice. For my own part, my main regular practice is writing my blog – A Bad Witch's Blog (www.badwitch.co.uk) – and it requires discipline to keep this up. I started writing it because I hadn't been part of a coven or Wiccan group for several years and rarely even observed the sabbats. I thought of myself as a lapsed Wiccan – or a Bad Witch – hence my blog's name. I wanted to be better; I wanted an incentive to become more involved in Wicca and to develop a daily practice – to be a Good Witch.

It worked. These days, as well as meeting up with Wiccan friends to celebrate the sabbats and esbats, I regularly go to pagan talks and moots, read books to increase my knowledge, visit ancient sacred sites and frequently use magical and spiritual techniques – such as spellwork, meditation and divination – in my daily life. Blogging is a modern form of magical diary and I would encourage any witch to try writing one as a way of recording and deepening their practice.

These days I would say my spirituality – Wicca – influences pretty much everything I do, all the time. I believe everything is part of the web of life – which means everything is spiritual and connected. I sense the Earth Goddess alive beneath my feet and the Sky Father above me. I have been known to say hello to the trees in my local park as I walk through on my way to the shops or station, because I am aware that the trees and plants have spirits just as we humans do. I might even hug a tree if no one else is watching – which is perhaps a little embarrassing even for a Bad Witch to admit.

Katy Frost

For me the path of Wicca is followed as a solitary, albeit with support from my wider circle of sisters, close friends I can call on for support when needs be and with whom I celebrate the sabbats. The vast majority of the time though, I work completely alone, including esbats, and I follow a tenet that is instinctive and organic. This means I have no high ceremony or drama, everything is stripped back to the basics – the five elements, the circle, myself, the Lady and Her Lord. Simple. Profound. Beautiful.

The person who introduced me to Wicca practised this way too, as does the priestess who initiated me. I find that it is the best way for me to connect, and that devotion can be carried out whilst enjoying a simple walk in the park, a bath or preparing a nutritious meal.

I have got an athame, a cauldron and a chalice – they were all gifts and are much prized. I have herbs a-plenty, books crowding the shelves and statues of the Goddess who is my patron deity. But I can manage to practise my faith with my body alone – breath, passion, blood, body and spirit are contained within. The key for me is to meditate and visualise – this is how I connect with deity, and by focusing on web of life that links me to Her, nurturing me.

Naiara Sagarminaga

It's difficult to explain what it means to be Wiccan. The difficulty lies in that Wicca promotes personal work, in addition to group work, which leads us to have a personal understanding of our religion. In some way, we could say that there are as many "Wiccas" as wiccans. Even within the same tradition, being an experiential religion, not all individuals receive the same conclusion. If one hundred Wiccans sit one behind the other to explain what Wicca is, each one would say one different thing at least. Wicca is more than a religion, it is a way of seeing the world and acting in life. It's everywhere.

When someone asks us to explain that Wicca is, we all began to explain our history, the festivities, the God/dess, the different influences, etc. But the core of Wicca can't be explained. I participate in interfaith dialogue group, where everyone brings their vision on everyday issues from a religious perspective. Often, I see confusion on faces when I try to explain the point of view of Wicca. They don't understand how Wicca explains things and how we can fit this diversity. I always have the same answer: there are things that can only be understood when they are experienced and Wicca is one of them.

If I could believe that there is a tradition that reflects this diversity, which in turn is a great strength, it is the Universal Eclectic Wicca. Faced with an apparent tendency to rigidity, this tradition has taught me the importance of flexibility. It's a tradition based on groups or individuals, which masterly mixes a sense of group with individual empowerment.

So, who are we, the Wiccans? We are your neighbours, your doctors, your lawyers, teachers of your children, your super-market cashiers, the housewives/husbands, the waiters of your favourite bar … We are normal people with a spiritual restlessness and a strong commitment to our God/desses.

Monica Ferreira

Wicca has been become in these past years one of the most known paths inside Paganism and Witchcraft. TV, Radio, Cinema, Books and Press, all aspects of communication have, at one point, discussed and spoken about Wicca.

This communication, however, is not always positive. Much to the contrary; I've been watching TV shows and videos, listening to radio shows, podcasts and reading about Wicca and, in the end, I've noticed that Wicca is very badly shown and taught and even talked about. When starting to study Wicca, one finds two main roads: Traditional Wicca (which primarily comprises Gardnerian and Alexandrian lineages) and Modern Wicca (which involves more paths, such as Celtic Wicca, Faery Wicca, Dianic Wicca, etc.). These two main roads are very distinct from each other and there are a lot of controversial matters between both (initiation, coven participation, rules and laws, etc.), which will not be discussed here.

The fact that there are a lot of Wiccan traditions demonstrates that this spiritual path is, indeed, a very diverse and rich one. But, at the same time, this diversity can result in problems. When reading or hearing or even watching anything about Wicca, those who don't know this religious path, usually become confused. Mostly because one show says something, other shows say something completely different and, suddenly, you are in front of ten different opinions and you're not sure what's Wicca and what's not.

The main reason why this happens, in my opinion, is that since Wicca has gained such popularity in the media and in Hollywood, people have started thinking that 'Wicca' is an umbrella-term for all they might want. I've met several people, in my life as a Pagan, who believe that Wicca is whatever you want it to be. Just mix some things up and call it 'Eclectic Wicca'. Well... I don't think that is how it works. Or, at least, it shouldn't be. These mixes are the reason why Wicca, most of the time, is seen in a bad light and misunderstood in today's media and society.

Wicca has its roots and its foundations, which you can read in the introductory essay. But unfortunately, due to some people's bad usage of Wicca and its unique path, the media and all that it includes started seeing Wicca as rebel teens that are acting up against their parents or frustrated housewives that need something to fill their empty schedules.

That is not what Wicca is. Wicca is a religious and spiritual path, which brings to its practitioners a lot of happiness and spiritual stability. That is how it should be understood by the media in general. And that is what we, as practitioners and as fellow brothers and sisters of the Craft, must strive to do. Because when the image of Wicca in the media and in our society has improved we will reach a whole new level of awareness, respect and harmony within this diverse and multicultural world.

Shaman

Elen Sentier

All my life I've walked the Deer Trods of Elen of the Ways, the Ancestor. My mother's mother was a wise woman from the Isle of Man while my father was a cunning man from Lancashire who settled on the edge of Exmoor. My mother was a wise woman too, but she passed over into the Summer Lands when I was three years old; I remember her well and sometimes she still contacts me if there is a need.

I grew up in an ancient village where the church is dedicated to the goddess. In the village she's called Urith, or the Romanised Hieritha, but the old Brythonic spelling is Iwerydd (pronounced as *Urith*). It's a name for the Mother-goddess, found in the *Red Book of Hergest*, and her sacred well was in my aunt's garden; she was its guardian for over half a century and the cottage had been in her family for generations. The elder folk in the village (of which my stepmother was one) involved us young ones in the old ways, like blessing the bells and dressing the horses for the spring ploughing, back in the 1950s, so I grew up in the old shamanism of Britain.

The church itself had been built over the place where one of Iwerydd's priestesses was buried, on top of a natural hill at the centre of the village; the legend is one of the "wicked stepmother" ones, where the stepmother has the well-maiden killed because of her own jealousy. The well becomes a healing well, often for clear sight, as ours is. It's worth noting that the French word *clairvoyance* means *clear seeing*; it's about *honesty of the heart* as well as the more usual interpretations of the word. My first novel, *Owl Woman*, is constructed around the village legend. Our house was beside one of the two major leys that crossed under Iwerydd's grave. I used to walk it every day going to school, which was right beside the church. I'd often climb the triple-stemmed yew tree in the churchyard (all we kids would do that); the tree is older than the church building and is now one of Woodland Trust's ancient yews.

If you look you can see she has an eye at the bottom of the central stem. She was part of the triple goddess celebrations the women did and into which I was initiated at puberty. Many of the rituals and celebrations we all did in the village were tangled with the Christian calendar – understandably, as they had taken it over from us – but nobody worried, not even the vicar, and the traditions were so old they were an integral part of village life. We used to do our own mummers' play, the story of the well-maiden killed over the water, on her feast day each July. I've got a picture of my stepmother in it back in the 1920s. I was in the play myself for several years in the 1950s.

The Tungus word *shaman* means *one who knows*, but in the British tradition I grew up in we call ourselves awenydd rather than shamans – you pronounce it *ah-when-ith* and awenyddion is the plural. The awenydd is the spirit keeper; it comes from the word *awen* which means *spirit*. To be awenydd is to be inspired by spirit *and* to learn how to keep that spirit alive within the hearts of humankind so that they know to respect and honour all life, both seen and unseen. It's about doing what makes your heart sing which, although lovely and satisfying, is a deep and responsible job that requires a lot of *nous* (pronounced *nowse*), which is an old word for knowing what is true and real, the competent use of the intuition. It's about working with *the mind's eye* and with *body-knowing* … a whole different way of being and working than most of us are accustomed to.

Awenyddion, like shamans all around the world, work from this *inner knowing*. It's not in the least academic but about finding and knowing things for yourself, internalising what you come to know and making things your own, rather than quoting the book-learned opinions of other people. You learn from your own discoveries and from osmosis with the teacher you choose to work with, as we did in the village with the elders of whom my stepmother and my aunt, and the healer-woman next door , were a part. The healer-woman next door was also who I learned to help with the laying out of the dead, and rituals for them.

Awenyddion have been servants to the British folk for time out of mind. We've been walking the deer trods, following the ancient ways of the Deer Goddess in her many forms as our ancestors did from Palaeolithic times. Archaeologists have found traces of our work from the Mesolithic age at Marden Henge near Amesbury and in 2011 a drawing of a reindeer was found in a cave in south-west Wales that dates back at least 11,000 years, that's well before the end of the last Ice Age. And we still do the work … we journey to bring empowerment and wisdom and healing to all creatures, people, plants and to the land herself.

The shaman, the *one who knows*, is the one with the *kenning* in the British tongue. To ken something or someone means to know them. It gives us another of our names, the cunning folk; the family-name "Cunningham" is a contraction of "cunning man" and again means one who knows. The awenydd is the spirit keeper, the cunning one, the wise one; one who works in the ecstasy, one who has fire in the head, who stimulates, animates, motivates and electrifies others.

We honour the spirit of the Earth. Working *with* the spirit of the land involves us in all sorts of things; I find it in everything from growing my own veg to politics, as well as the better known tasks of spirit walking, journeying, power and soul retrieval, rites of passage and healing.

Learning to follow the deer trods involves a lot of what's known nowadays as bushcraft. The joy of living wild, even if only for a few days – is one of my passions. It brings me close to the Earth and teaches me how much she is my friend, my mother, teacher, mentor, and my companion.

One of my uncles was a woodsman. He used to take me out into the woods or up onto the moor as part of the spirit-keeper ways he taught me as a child. I first remember going out with him when I was about four or five; I started school the following autumn. We would go out at dusk and not come back until maybe gone midnight. There were special places we frequented, in clearings, under trees, beside brooks, hunched up in the heather, under rocks and in caves. We would go to just sit and watch. Field mice and dormice, bats, owls, stoats and weasels, badgers and foxes, rats and moles would come right up to us, sometimes even sniff my hand if I was very still and tuned in. Feeling the whiskers tickle and the tiny claws touch my skin was electrifying, I knew what they were saying inside my head; sometimes a fox or badger would come and lick or a deer stand and blow into my face. I could feel I was accepted and truly looked at and seen because I was taking full notice of them and acknowledging them as my elder brethren.

Uncle would whisper to me about them and, because he was a real *wild man*, they would come right up to him; they knew he knew them and they trusted him. I've seen him sat with an adder coiled round his wrist of a warm afternoon in summer, the pair of them, man and snake, dozing in the sun, doing each other no harm. Other times I've seen him call down a wild falcon or hawk to his fist; he would talk to the bird and sometimes, on occasion, the bird would allow me to stroke her before she flew off. I've called owls down myself.

I know other folk who can do this. And I know too that we, every one of us, could learn to do this if we wished; it's harder work if you weren't brought up to it as I was, from babyhood, but it's still by no means impossible to learn. It's part of what I teach now.

Uncle was one of those people who know the land and creatures and plants as intimately as his own family – indeed they *were* his own family, just as much as me and dad and the rest of the human family. To him, and to me, there is no separation. He was much like the hunter-gatherer people, able to live intimately with the land because he *knew* it and *knew how* to live with it. He, like the hunter-gatherers, was deeply and intimately linked to all of creation. Citification and easy transport have taken these abilities away from most people in the world today – some 85 percent of us, all over the world, live in towns and cities now. When many city-folk go out into the countryside they rely on book-learning, SatNavs, what other people tell them rather than *knowing* the natural world in their own bones. They are not friends with the world and some can find nature quite intimidating.

People no longer know that they can feed themselves very well from the hedgerows and the woods and the moors; that many of the plants are good medications for cuts, even deep ones down to the bone, and bruises and headaches and such. They don't know how to make a safe, warm fire, how to make stream water drinkable without chemicals, how to make a warm shelter from leaves and grass and branches. They can't see all the things the natural world lays at their feet to help them when they get stuck, when the car runs out of petrol or breaks down, but immediately rush for the mobile phone and the human to rescue them, ignoring and rejecting all the help nature offers. To spirit, this is all very disrespectful; as we all know it's really painful to be dissed and that's no different for spirit either. Being awenydd is about learning to see and respect and honour and live with what is not human as well as with our human brethren; honouring the spirit that is within everything ... animal, vegetable, mineral and human.

Living in cities, towns, villages, even being able to see another house, changes our relationship with the Earth and the natural world; we feel *safe* with other humans nearby, there's always someone we can turn to if things go wrong, we are not alone. We don't relate or commit to the natural world, we don't make friends with it and, in consequence, we don't really see it. If we find ourselves "out there" with nothing human in sight, many folk begin to panic, to search desperately for a signal on the phone, for a house, a barn, even the sight of a cow or sheep makes a difference. The cry of a buzzard or a fox, the sight of antlers on the horizon, the grunt of a hedgehog or badger in the dusk makes their hair stand on end and sets their imagination freaking out. They are cut off from nature ... and from spirit.

Bushcraft is about learning that nature is our friend – quite the contrary of the TV programmes that tell us the Earth is out to get us. It's about learning the multitude of things we are surrounded with when out in the wild that will actually help us. This works even better when we connect ourselves to spirit and learn how to ask both nature and spirit for help.

Being a shaman is about making connections ... and this is what following the deer trods does. Walking the paths you make the connections; the Earth gives you energy through your feet (if you allow yourself to feel and accept it) while, at the same time, you give energy from yourself in exchange. It's amazing what this energy can do in the physical world, including give you strength when you're flagging. The paths need to be walked; it's a way of honouring them, acknowledging them by noticing and exchanging energy with them.

These are ways our hunter-gatherer ancestors followed. If you give yourself the time and space to walk the deer trods, the animal trails, pathways, ancient roads and migration routes, the ways themselves will enable you to know the spirits of place.

Britain is part of the *boreal forest* although there are not many of the trees left now. The boreal forest is the largest forest on Earth, stretching all around the northern end of the world, everywhere from the tundra (latitude 70°) to the southern tip of Cornwall (latitude 50°). The Caledonian forest, the moors and wild places in Wales and England and the Highlands of Scotland are all that's left of it now. The ancient Greeks called the north wind Boreas and they called Britain *Hyperborea*, meaning *the land behind the north wind*; we British were the *Hyperboreans*. Reindeer were native to our land long ago and are now coming back through the wild herds in the Cairngorms. The boreal forest is the world of the reindeer; they thrive here. Our ancestors followed the deer trods of the antlered lady, Elen of the Ways ... female reindeer are the only deer to carry antlers. They are wild and still have the migration instinct so cannot be tamed as our modern cattle are; the folk who work with them, like the Sámi, the Caribou people and the folk of northern Mongolia, know this and *work with* the herds, following them ... following the deer trods through the seasons. My own people worked with the red deer who, with the roe deer, are one of the two native species still living in Britain since the reindeer were wiped out a few hundred years ago, along with the wolves. The reindeer are returning with the help of the Cairngorm herd; hopefully they will be given space in other high, wild places in this land.

The enchanted forest, the place of the deer – whether here in the physical or in Otherworld – is about the Earth-Song. Elen is also the Lady of the Dream-Paths, the Enchantress of the Song-Lines. Our dream-paths and song-lines are similar to the Australian ones, they are the paths of Earth-dreaming, dreamweaving, enchanting, singing. It is the way the Earth weaves everyday reality. The songs are the en-*chant*-ment of the land – to chant is to sing, to en-chant is to sing into life. Song connects us with the energy lines of life-force that run along all the forest tracks that the animals use. Walking and singing the deer trods deepens your understanding and brings you closer to Elen of the Ways.

Elen Sentier lives and works in the Welsh Marches. She is the author of *Shaman Pathways; The Celtic Chakras* and *Shaman Pathways; Elen of the Ways.*

Kenn Day

Post-tribal shamanism deals with the soul-level wounds and the situation of humanity in the current stage of cultural evolution.

Those of us who practice this form of shamanism do so in service to a community of individuals, most of them lacking any awareness of the myriad spiritual pieces that make up their whole self. We do so in service to those invisible parts that make up everything and everyone.

We offer this service while juggling apparently incompatible experiences of what it means to be here, to be human, to be a shaman, to stand between the worlds and work to awaken – both ourselves and others.

We are drawn by the wounds torn in the souls of warriors, of women, of children and the world. These wounds call us into being, into becoming, into the path of serving as shaman.

We may not always be able to heal these wounds, or ease the pain or bring the scattered pieces of self back together, but we cannot help but offer all we have to this calling. It is who we are.

How is a soul wounded? By caring for the person it inhabits. By protecting it from overwhelming odds. By choosing to break off a bit of itself to carry away the hurt, the pain the trauma of the moment, in hopes that the pieces will return – in time. Part of the shaman's job is to bring these pieces back together.

How is a soul awakened? The soul is not even asleep. It is our conscious part, what we call the ego, that is sleeping and dreaming that it is awake. Part of the shaman's work is to help the person wake from the dream, allowing the soul to enter more fully into the world.

The shaman dances with one foot in the everyday world and one in the world of Spirit, juggling the ordinary and the infinite, while riding the paradox beast through the underworld.

The strange and wonderful outcome is that we are blessed with ever greater opportunities to be of service and with a full and meaningful life. Not a bad exchange at all, and never boring!

Deb Shaw

Several years ago, when I first began learning the whys and

wherefores of shamanism, I went on a dreamquest. As I slipped into sleep, I asked for guidance.

"Great Spirit, show me the first thing I must do to be able to help people."

In the spirit world, I traveled over flat grasslands, then across a desert. I flew over snowy mountain peaks, and down into a greenwood. I descended to the forest floor, and walked. There, in a clearing, was a deep pool, fed by a spring. The water was very clear. In the depths, there were the silvery sides of the salmon, writhing in their watery dance.

I sat on the grassy edge of the pool, feeling the cool grass beneath me, the breeze lifting my hair, and the warmth of a mote of sun, breaking through the canopy. These things being the signs that I am in a Vision, I knew that something of importance would be revealed soon.

Some hazelnuts fell from one of the trees near the water. As the salmon swam to the surface to eat the nuts, the lesson became as clear as the waters.

Salmon is the most ancient of creatures. Salmon is the beginning. Hazelnuts represent wisdom. To be able to help people, we must first gain wisdom. Not superficially. We must take in the wisdom of the ages, assimilate it into our being, in the same way that Salmon digests his food. Once the knowledge of the Ancient Ones becomes a part of our flesh and bone, we can begin to teach others. In learning, we help ourselves; in teaching, we help them.

Angel Mathes

I've never liked visiting the zoo. When I reached out, as a child, to touch, my hand was smacked, and I was warned that these creatures were "dangerous", or carried diseases that would harm humans, or would somehow be damaged or outcast by my touch. From the safety of their enclave, it always seemed the monkeys were screaming anger and hurt toward us, insulting us, or making fun of us. School trips to the zoo left me sad, and it was never a place I took my own children.

I've never met a stranger when it comes to domesticated pets. Twice in my life, I've encountered violently aggressive dogs, who, I believe, were acting as they were trained, and neither was of a typical banned breed. As recently as yesterday, I visited a friend, whose aged barn cat came to sit with me, rub against my ankles, and nudge to be petted. I glanced up after a few minutes to see my friend staring in shock: "What did you do to her? She does NOT like people, and never lets anyone pet her!" When out and about, friends are constantly commenting on my tendency to speak to, offer my hand for a sniff, or otherwise interact with every dog or cat I encounter.

I've always had pets of my own. Many years ago, it took an unusual twist. As I lay in bed reading, I'd feel the thump of a cat jumping up to join me, but look to see nothing there, except perhaps a wallow on the blanket. It happened many times, in many homes, and I still have ghost-cats come to visit. Recently, at a friend's home, I commented on how beautiful his black cat was. He responded with surprise that they only had a Russian Blue, as the black cat had drowned the previous year. Several more times, I saw the black cat preening itself on the couch in his sun room.

I now live in a wooded hollow, surrounded by trees, with a pond out back, in a secluded cul-de-sac, in a town of 40,000, which is completely surrounded by one of this country's larger cities. Yet I have regular visits from deer, foxes, two dozen geese, woodpeckers, a particularly vocal cardinal, raccoons, a woodchuck, and countless squirrels, rabbits, and chipmunks. I share a home with four "rescued" pets – three cats and a dog – as well as the occasional ghost-cat visitor.

These things are absolute necessity for me. The connection to Earth, and to Life, in its infinite variety, are part of what defines who I am. Without the intimate immersion in the natural world,

I feel like I can't breathe. The need for connection, and willingness to pursue it, is a key component of the shamanic path.

Charlotte Rooney

I make myself comfortable and set off on my journey. I start to climb my tree, a treasured oak from my childhood. The going is tough at first but becomes easier and effortless as I speed up the tree with sticky tree frog feet.

Eventually I reach the crown and take a moment to enjoy this privileged view – peaceful, quiet except for a light breeze that lifts my hair, the landscape laid out before me. My oak tree has inexplicably transformed into an ash.

I hitch a lift with a passing friendly pelican that scoops me up into its bill pouch and carries me onwards and upwards. We pass through a cloud layer and my physical self starts to shake and clatter beneath my orange blanket. "Turbulence" I think, as my left arm seems to take on a dancing, jittering life of its own, but before it has time to become uncomfortable we have broken through into a glittering, silent world of ice and wide grey skies. I feel excited and uplifted – winter worlds have always pleased me. I play here for some time like a puppy, sliding and gliding about, until I notice a dot on the horizon and make my way to it.

It is a medicine man. I stand before him and respectfully request a healing. In response he adopts a warrior stance, punches his way through my chest and grabs my spine, grasping it as he would his hunting spear. He shakes it and shakes it until all my flesh has fallen away and I am left just a thought but somehow core, concentrated. He throws my spine, his spear, and it strikes a creature from this world – small, white and bushy, needle-toothed with eyes and a nose that are black, cunning and sharp.

With business-like compassion the medicine man washes the blood from my vertebrae. Using it as a frame he builds me a body from snow. I dance and spin, delighted with my new crystalline self, until I remember my sacrifice. I walk over to my brother snow-creature's corpse, then squat by it and urinate. I collect a good double-handed ball of the yellow-stained snow, and pack it into the creature's wound. It heals instantly.

I stand, complete. I am wearing the creature's pelt as a cloak. I dance some more, feeling the rightness of this time, this place, until it is time to return via pelican and tree to myself, beneath a blanket, in a warm hall lit by autumn sun.

Christo-Pagan

Mark Townsend

Rain patters loudly against the glass sky-light above. The room is small and simple, yet comfortable. My writing desk has a lamp to the left, a wash basin to the right and, directly ahead; an icon of Saint Brigid. She keeps me company, smiling down upon my busily tapping fingers. Saint of the holy fire she holds her eternal flame and I say a prayer to ask for the fire she holds to ignite my imagination.

For the last five days I've been staying in the little retreat house of the monastery of the Celtic Orthodox Church near Remmes, Brittany. Each day has been encircled by richly symbolic ritual and ceremony involving icons, incense, bells, chanting, sacred gesture and the taking into the body of the bread and wine of the Eucharist. It's been many years since I've experienced such 'rhythmic' Christianity and it's having a profound effect on me.

I've eaten breakfast and dinner with the brothers every day now and our discussions have touched many and various subjects including Arthurian mythology, magic, sacred geometry, reincarnation and Paganism. They are a surprisingly open minded and eclectically aware community. Their hospitality has been warm, generous and freely given. And some of the brothers, on top of being Eastern Orthodox Christian monks, are Druids! The druidic 'Awen' symbol can be seen on a few of the church's icon as well as on the large stone monument in the monastery cemetery. This druidic connection goes back to the very beginnings of the order, for the original founder (Saint Tugdol) knew the founder of my order The Order of Bards, Ovate and Druids (OBOD) Ross Nichols, and indeed ordained him as a Celtic Orthodox Deacon.

And so it seems more than fitting to be here as I write this essay on Christo-Paganism.

Of course to many the term Christo-Pagan is an oxymoron. It's like 'vegetarian butcher' or 'sexual celibate.' The idea that a person can follow both the Christian path with it's strictly monotheistic vision of deity and it's *'Christ as the one true way'* message, and also plug into the pantheistic / polytheistic and generally universalistic ethos of modern Paganism, seems utterly contradictory to both communities. However, there are a growing number of people who do indeed feel that they can happily combine parts of each path and walk between them, some of whom use the term Christo-Pagan to define themselves. Before I attempt to give a broad brush portrait of the kind of people I'm referring to, I feel it's important to define the terms Christian and Pagan independently. My feeling is that both terms are often misunderstood and (especially with regard to Christianity) narrowed to a point where 'mainstream Christian' means something that many thousands of 'mainstream Christians' would not necessarily relate to. So, when people (Pagan and Christian) assume that the two paths are incompatible, it is often these caricatures they use as their definitions, and not the reality.

So, what are the basic hallmarks of a Christian and, likewise, what defines a Pagan?

Christianity

To answer the question what defines a Christian is not as easy as one might first suppose. For the answer often depends on which particular denominational tradition. A simple example is the fact that while both churches believe in the post Nicene Jesus Christ as 'fully God and fully human', the Baptist understanding of what makes a person a Christian is more tied up with personal faith in Jesus Christ as saviour and Lord than baptism itself, whereas for a Roman Catholic (and high church Anglican) the moment of being made Christian IS baptism, even if performed when still an infant. The doctrine is known as 'Baptismal Regeneration.' So for the latter an articulated faith often comes *after* the sacrament, whereas for the former the articulated expression of faith always comes *prior* to the baptism, which is seen as a public declaration of faith.

However, leaving aside the denominational differences, is there a core of ingredients that most churches agree on as the very basic hallmarks of a Christian?

Let's list what some of them might be:

- Following the teachings and principles of Jesus of Nazareth.
- Having faith in Jesus Christ as Son of God.
- Being baptised in the name of the Father, Son and Holy Spirit.
- Believing in the Triune nature of God.
- Belonging to a worshipping community.
- Receiving the Sacraments, especially the Mass, Eucharist or Lord's Supper.
- Believing in the Bible as God's Word and (at the very least) using it as a guide for life.
- Attempting to live a life modelled on Christ and thus loving neighbours as self, feeding the poor and forgiving enemies.

Some of the above are more to do with orthodoxy 'right belief' whereas others are more orthopraxy 'right practise' and (from my three decades' experience of travelling through various denominations) they make up what I consider to be the most obvious likely answers, were I to ask the question 'what makes a person a Christian?' or 'what are the essential ingredients of a Christian life?' in an assortment of church traditions. The interesting factor is that I can find exceptions to every single point (above) of those who are members of Christian churches and consider themselves good Christians.

For example, there are two large and established churches that do not have any sacramental theology / practise in the usual sense. Neither the Society of Friends nor the Salvation Army baptise or share the breaking of bread as 'communion.' Yet many Quakers are Christians and follow Jesus's teachings devoutly, and no Salvationist would be happy if he or she heard their own Christian status being questioned.

There are also Christians who are non-Trinitarian. Many Unitarians, for example, and Jehovah's Witnesses claim to be Christians yet do not subscribe to the doctrine of the Holy Trinity.

Even the notion of Jesus Christ as the literal incarnate Son of God on Earth is not a fully universal Christian belief. Many liberal and progressive Christians see this language as mythic and metaphorical, and prefer to base their faith on following the human called Jesus, than worshipping the God-man we call Jesus-Christ. Also, before the great Creeds of the early church were hammered out to combat heresy, there were a variety of Christian understandings, some with far less emphasis on the divine status of Jesus and more on his humanity. The recently discovered gospel of Thomas is a good example of this, for here Jesus is a human who is transparent of God's light and, like a mirror, enables his followers to discover their own inner light. He is not the saviour they must believe in for salvation.

The reason I'm stressing all this before attempting to define 'Christian' is because many Pagan criticisms of Christo-Paganism have come from the point of view of an (understandable) caricature of Christianity that, while being the most dominant, is by no means the only version of Christianity.

My own notion of what makes a person a Christian is thus very simple. If you associate with the story of Jesus and find meaning within it, and feel comfortable wearing the label Christian, then you are a Christian.

Paganism

When it comes to defining modern Paganism we quickly discover that it is a similarly difficult exercise. Here's an example. In the UK The Pagan Federation (while in no way claiming to be the official voice of all self-confessed Pagans) defines Paganism as, 'A polytheistic or pantheistic nature worshipping religion' and Pagan as, 'A member of a polytheistic or pantheistic nature worshipping religion.' However, I've come across a number who identify with the label Pagan yet have issues with this description. Some do not warm to the first part of the statement and prefer a different way of expressing their understanding of deity other than pan or polytheistic (such as animistic, duo-theistic or monist). Others reject the idea of worshipping nature, feeling that this term conjures up false ideas of submitting to a superior and intelligent power. Reverencing nature might be a more acceptable term than worshipping in this case.

Saying that, in my experience it is a little easier to come to at least a very general consensus of Paganism than Christianity. This is partly due to it being far less riddled with denomination-alism, dogma and fixed practises, and it tends also to be a bottom up rather than top down way of expressing religious faith. In other words it is not seen as a 'revealed' religion of the book, like Christianity, but is an experiential path. And while this makes it broader with much variety, it also means there's more acceptance that what works for one group or community may not necessarily work for another, and vice versa.

And there do seem to be some themes that are common through most modern Paganisms.

In order to get some feedback from Pagans themselves I posted a request on my Facebook spiritual community wall, that of Hedge-Church. I asked for Pagans to define, as simply as possible, their understanding of paganism, and I also linked it to the PF definition, some of whom were very happy with it as it stood.

Wiccan author Gus DiZerega, who is also a member of Hedge-Church wrote three numbered points on a definition of Paganism:

1. Emphasis on the sacred as immanent (whether or not it is also transcendent).
2. Focus on restoring and maintaining harmony (rather than salvation or enlightenment).
3. Polytheistic.

He added, "I suspect everything else shakes out from various interpretations of those three points."

A few thought that the term 'animistic' should certainly be added to the PF's definition of Pagan deity, and one Pagan member of Hedge-Church called Luis A. Valadez broadened things ever further. He said:

Not all Pagans are polytheistic. Many are atheist and even monotheistic. The atheists are called Naturalist Pagans. They believe that the mythologies are just symbols and imagery that can be interpreted psychoanalytically via the methods introduced by Carl Jung. Man invents Gods as a way to help cope with life. They believe that everything is sacred, and that Deities are not necessary to understand that the world and the Cosmos are sacred. I personally define Paganism as the revivification or reconstruction of the pre-Christian religions of Europe, North Africa and the Middle East. I believe 'Pagan' is specific to these areas for a number of reasons, not least among them because it was in these areas that the word began being used to mean those who were 'non-Christian' and adhered to the faiths of their ancestors under the Roman Empire. So I believe it is a limited definition and does not (and should not, in my opinion) apply to anyone else including Buddhists, Shintoists or Native Americans. It also makes room for a variety of beliefs and practices, as Classical Paganism was wont to be. This applies today with the myriad beliefs and practices under the umbrella *Pagan*.

So, again, there is a breadth with regard to what's considered Pagan, but it does look like any definition must include some kind of reverence of nature as sacred, and a notion of deity that is usually (though not always) pan or poly theistic.

Christo-Paganism

What I find thrilling is that a growing number of people are finding they are more and more able to combine their Christianity with their Paganism. Clearly from the above attempts to define both traditions, and the near impossibility of doing so for Christianity, one can see how overlaps are more than possible. Of course, for a Christian who sees Jesus as the only true way to God, it would be very hard to see how they could be comfortable within a Christo-Pagan environment, but for those who're far more mystical, metaphorical and nature based in their approach to faith, it seems more than logical to make the connection to the Pagan path.

Though not all of them choose to use the term, this movement is generally labelled as Christo-Pagan.

Some of them have come from the Pagan world and are thus more characteristically Pagan in their beliefs and practises, and other are more Christian and thus more monotheistic. Here are some examples from Hedge-Church.

Elizabeth McNally says this:

I believe those who follow the Christo-Pagan path (myself included) would for the most part agree with the following (I've kept it to five for simplicity):

1. That there is the Goddess in Her threefold aspect, known

by many names. With all her names she is known as Maiden, Mother, Crone.

2. That there is a God most willing of sacrifice.
3. And it harm none, do as you please.
4. That as she is the Mother of all living things and we are all Her children, we seek to live in harmony not only with each other, but with the planet Earth that is our womb and home.
5. We follow the natural cycles of the moon and the sun and celebrate the esbats and sabbats.

The first time I entered a Christian church after choosing to follow a bridge back I was uncomfortable. I knelt down and to the left of the altar was a beautiful stained glass window depicting the crucifixion. There was the God so willing of sacrifice. At the base stood the three women, Mary the Mother, Mary Magdalene, the Maiden, and Sofia, the Crone of Wisdom. On the ground was a vessel (for me the cauldron). At that point, I knew I could be with this crossing of paths. I've been following it ever since.

And this is from Renee Ravencraft Bierbaum, a Christo-Pagan who clearly had a more monotheistic understanding of God/dess:

I am a follower of Christ, a Jesus FREAK. I love, love, love Jesus and all that he stands for. However, I find comfort and release in nature. Nature is my church. There is *no* cathedral ever built by the hands of men that can even come close to rivalling what the Creator has already made – a beautiful ancient forest, the thundering sea, a mountaintop vista. *This is divine.* I, a Jesus Freak, follow and love the seasons of the year, the turn of the wheel so to speak, the cycles of the moon. *All* is interconnected. I follow the old ways of healing and worship and there is nothing more worshipful than sitting in a Native American fire circle. I think Jesus himself knew this and respected it. If you study the miracles of Jesus, he was trying to teach his disciples how to heal as he did and he healed using very pagan methods and the power of prayer. Remember when he took dirt from the Mother Earth, spit in it and rubbed it on the blind man's eyes? Why would he do that when he could have very well just touched the man and healed him? Think about it. I believe the Creator has put energy and power in the earth, the skies, the waters, everything has energy and Jesus was trying to teach us how to tap into that Divinely created source of energy, but the people were looking for a king to come and rescue them, not a teacher, who came to teach them how to re-connect so they totally missed the lessons. I guess I see my 'God' as one god with many names and attributes. When I am in need of feminine strength and love I see my God as Goddess, Mother. When I am in need of male strength and love I see my God as Father God. Sometimes God is Great Spirit. Sometimes God is The Ancient of Days. So some would see me as worshiping several 'gods,' but in reality to me, *all* is *one*, it's my needs at the time that differ.

Conclusion

I suppose one of the more frustrating aspects of living between the two traditions of Christianity and Paganism is, for me, the lack of understanding and tolerance than can come from both sides. And I have to admit to being more than a little bit disappointed when it comes from Pagans. As a long term member of the church and an ordained member of the Christian priesthood for fifteen years I've come to expect a *lack of understanding and tolerance* from fellow Christians.

I have a large pile of unpleasant mail collected from Christians who've objected to me in different ways and sent their complaints. And sadly the modern Church in the eyes of vast numbers of the general public is often seen to be closed minded, blinkered, judgmental, superior and holier than thou. But Pagans, on the whole, claim to be (and do tend to be) much less dogmatic and far more open and eclectic. It's a very common experience to find in Pagan books and on Pagan altars influences and artefacts (including ritual words and deities) from many different religious paths of the world. This is generalising but there seems to be very little objection to drawing upon the wealth of global spirituality and intermingling Hindu chakras, Celtic and Nordic deities, Native American smudge feathers, Greek mythic stories, Jewish Kabbalah and more. Yet there seems to be a huge objection to the inclusion of anything that is the remotest bit Christian. Of course part of me understands that many modern pagans have a generally negative memory of Christianity, some have been profoundly hurt by it. Nevertheless I see this tendency as inconsistent and unjustifiable.

Mark Townsend is a combination of priest, magician and writer, who uses seemingly opposing forces as equal gifts in our search for the meaning of life. He is the founder of The Hedge-Church and author of *Gospel of Falling Down*, *The Path of the Blue Raven* and *Diary of a Heretic*. He lives in Leominster, UK.

David Kling

My spiritual life has been a long and sometimes arduous journey. I have learned valuable lessons of life while on this journey. One such lesson was to refrain from doing violence to parts of my life that have brought me meaning and comfort. At various times in my life I have identified as Christian and at other times as Pagan; however, what I have learned is the importance of integrating these two aspects of my life into my whole self. This process of integration has not been easy because embracing a Christo-Pagan mindset is often anathema to both Christians and Pagans. To embrace both Christianity and Paganism is to walk in the margins and is often alienating. Often you will find yourself not accepted by either tradition, as syncretism is frequently viewed with suspicion; although, this integration can also bring freedom and liberation.

One night back in 2006 I was walking a candle-lit labyrinth at a Pagan Festival and I was silently praying the Jesus Prayer, a prayer rooted in Eastern Orthodox Christian mysticism. The words of the prayer are, "Lord Jesus Christ, son of God, have mercy on me a sinner." During that labyrinth walk I had been thinking about the intersection of Christianity and Paganism and striving, in my head and in my heart, to reconcile the two ideologies. A new prayer came to me on my labyrinth walk, "Lord Jesus Christ, divine Logos, show me the way of non-attachment."

Over the years since that night I have reflected on the words of that prayer and their meaning for me. Focusing my thoughts on Jesus as the Logos has helped me link the person of Jesus with the Gospel concept of "Word made flesh" with the Logos espoused by the "Pagan" Stoic and Neo-Platonist philosophers of antiquity. The emphasis on non-attachment embraced a symbolic understanding of the injunction presented by Jesus to his followers to give up everything and "come follow me." By living in non-attachment I am giving up my attachment to material possessions and even creeds and sectarian causes and agendas. As Jesus found liberation from death through resurrection I too could find liberation from the bonds that hold me down, from the idols of my own darkness. I could be free.

I have found a sacred place within myself that no longer needs to be married to a strict definition of Paganism or of Christianity to feel whole; likewise, I also do not feel a need to divorce myself from either Christian or Pagan ideologies, sentiments, or culture. I have integrated the two and made them one within myself and I feel wholeness, connection, and freedom; a new Trinity residing within my soul.

Sascha Cooper

My path as a Christo-Pagan hasn't been an easy one. It has been full of emotional roller-coasters, both for the best and worst, but most of all it has been an amazing discovery of who I am as a person.

It started when I was 18. At the time I was a fully fledged Christian. I had never been forced down this path, but fully loved and embraced it. However... everything changed when I did a silly fundraiser for my school fête – as a fortune teller of all things! But when told that I was accurate and that the women on mum's side of the family were of Romani Gypsy descent, from here on in, my life was full of contradictions and discoveries. How on earth could I be Christian and have this kind of gift?!? Surely this was frowned upon by the church! I still continued with my gift to a certain extent, but always with guilt.

But when I moved to London, I discovered Wicca and Paganism and found a huge connection with that from the word go. Despite this though, I still felt guilt. I felt a huge resonance with God and Goddess, but I felt I was betraying my religious upbringing each time, so I considered myself for a long time as eclectic so I could discover who I was in my own time. It protected me for a while from the critics from both Christians and Pagans, but it wasn't long before I heard, "You cannot combine both paths! You must choose!"

Something inside me was telling me I had already made my choice, but I couldn't explain it. I still felt a resonance with Jesus; however, I was drawn still to the Pagan Goddess and nature generally. It haunted me for a long time and no one would give me answers to potential questions I had, so in the end I stopped asking.

A move to Brighton, however, finally clarified that my initial instincts were right. I found a group that enabled me to learn more about Paganism and Wicca. But when the time came to join the coven, again that feeling inside of dread made me stop going ahead with it. One night I did a search on the internet and typed in for a laugh 'Christo-Pagan'... many hours later, I discovered that I had been following my true path all along! It was to be a solitary one I have never regretted. I still have Jesus in my life as my chosen God and Mary Magdalene as my Goddess. They seem to work for me in my life and I hope to continue that relationship.

Elizabeth McNally

I was raised in a Catholic family and taught by Catholic nuns in convents all the way through high school. I began to ask questions about my faith and my religion from an early age. I felt something was missing. It was not until my early 30s, however, that I was introduced to Paganism while enrolled in a course in Religious Studies. My spiritual life was blown wide open when I learnt one of the lecturers was a Witch. That lecture inspired a decade of reading and self-study. I walked away from the Catholic Church and became a solitary practitioner of the Craft. A decade later I moved out from being a solitary practitioner and entered the Pagan community.

My core beliefs as a Pagan are as follows: There is a Goddess in Her threefold aspect, and many are Her names. With all of Her names, we call Her Maiden, Mother and Crone. As She is the Mother of all living things and we are Her children, we seek to live in harmony with each other and the planet. There is a God, Consort and Sun, giver of strength and most willing of sacrifice. Death is not an ending of existence, but a step in the ongoing process of life. Those who follow this path have no need of another between themselves and the Goddess.

While involved with interfaith work in the Pagan community, I realized I missed the old friends of my childhood faith. I had not walked away from Jesus or his teaching, but rather the Catholic Church and its exclusionary stance. I don't remember exactly how, but I began a dialogue with Father Mark Townsend within the social media of Facebook. As a priest and a Druid himself, he opened up the possibility that I could combine both spiritual paths, and so I began building a bridge back, to include Jesus and my other favorite Christian mystics. As I had nowhere physical at that time to worship, and it occurred to me I was not likely alone in where I was spiritually, I approached Father Mark and proposed an online church on Facebook. He recognized the need and Hedge Church came to be.

As I took my place in the pew of the Church for the first time in many years, I found myself uneasy. As I look around I noticed to the left of the altar a magnificent stained glass window, depicting the crucifixion. There was Jesus on the cross (the God so willing of sacrifice), the three women; Mary Magdalene (the Maiden), Mary (the Mother), and Sophia (the Crone). On the ground was a vessel (the cauldron, where all ingredients combine). I had traveled full circle.

Trevor Greenfield

I've always liked Jesus. There were pictures of him in my primary school, a guy in a white nightdress with a devoted and disparate array of followers. And I like Jesus the compassionate revolutionary, a zealot who takes pity on a centurion. I like Jesus the healer, unafraid of demons and disease and I pretty much like anyone who walks into a temple precinct and picks a fight with the authorities.

But I stopped going to church when it occurred to me that I didn't really understand Christian theology... if I believe that someone authorized the sacrifice of his son on my behalf then I'll be saved... OK, but what does that mean? More to the point, without Christianity, what was on offer, if not psalms and prayers and sermons interrupting my day? De-regulation maybe, a low-impact belief that let me do what I wanted and then validated it using a curious blend of ill-thought-out logic and faith in something I couldn't, or didn't have to, relate to; less of the Coptic, more of the Copout. It comes back to haunt me, this indolence, because despite my own well-studied argument I seem to still expect a certain level of respect for my higher calling from others.

So, cut adrift, like a pilgrim without a destination, I asked myself a question... what do I believe in? I resisted for a while because the only answer I could come up with seemed so trivial it occurred to me I'd actually missed the point of my own question. But in the end I just gave up trying to manufacture an alternative. Jesus is on the road to Emmaus; Moses is on a mountain looking down upon Canaan; Yahweh is loading the dice in favour of a Semite tribe in their coming battle with the Moabites and Allah is preparing for an austere and terrifying Day of Judgment...

But I believe in Cissbury Ring an hour after sunrise, my dog fifty yards ahead of me trying, forlornly, to catch rabbits, sheep bleating in the paddocks below, grey-sky breaking to blue and the soft earth beneath my feet. I believe in chalk and flint, white bones of the ancestors, wind and rain, and the sacredness of this place.

And Jesus? Well, we've all got our roads to travel. He was a good friend, and friends don't give up on each other. Maybe we'll meet again one day, where Gods and mortals wander silently awaiting recognition; lost, found and lost again in a mythical hinterland of miracle and rumour.

Goddess Follower

Jane Meredith

The waves crash against my legs as I stand in the edge of the surf. The sun is hot on my face and arms, though it is still early morning. The water is cold and filled with tiny pieces of seaweed, churning. Big clumps of it lie washed up on the beach. The salt in the water sticks to my skin, the sand under my feet shifts and shapes itself. As the waves rush out I see a tiny, rounded shell exposed for a moment before it burrows quickly downwards. I feel the power of the sea with the incoming wave; when it sucks out again I am almost pulled off my feet. In my body I feel my own tide, past ovulation and towards bleeding; it is particular, an exact resonance in my body. I fling my arms out and breathe deep. For me, this is Goddess. This shell creature, this tide, this fleshy, breathing, heart-beating body of mine.

People come to the Goddess from different directions. Some come from atheism, some from feminism, some from mainstream religions and some from the ecological movement. Some arrive at the Goddess from other branches of the occult, paganism and the New Age. Often these things overlap and there is no requirement that a devotee of the Goddess relinquish earlier spiritual affinities; instead these may support and strengthen each other. Many in the Western magic tradition and some involved in conventional religious movements such as Christianity and Buddhism also count themselves as worshippers of the Goddess. The Goddess appears in a dream, or a vision; people hear her voice or are fascinated by her myths and stories. When they explore these avenues they find her waiting for them. Artists, poets and dancers discover her through their creativity; women and men yearning and working for a sustainable earth find her in the forests they seek to protect, the gardens they grow and the life-centred and life-affirming values they hold. People find her in the body of a lover or a child, in the beauty of the world and in ancient sculptures, stories and symbols.

The contemporary worship of the Goddess, while it has been informed and inspired by archaeological, historical and mythological studies has evolved from lived experience; from the many women and some men who have met the divine feminine in their own lives and in unique ways, in degrees of such force and power that it rewrites their spirituality. When I ask a group of people what the word Goddess means to them there's a variety of responses. It's the earth, one says. My inner self, says another. Artemis; my mother; Kali; horses; angels; a knowing inside me… there are as many answers as there are answerers. And there's no argument over it, no debate; no one says, 'No, your mother is not the Goddess'. Instead we catch a glimpse of how, for that person, their mother is the Goddess and we, in that moment, add to and expand our own concept of Goddess.

There is no single or correct way of understanding Goddess and no core practice conducted by all of those who believe in or worship the Goddess. Several quite different concepts of the Goddess exist, although they overlap and intertwine and many people find themselves holding more than one view, or transiting from one to another. One approach is that of relating to pre-existing, named Goddesses, such as Kali, Ishtar, Persephone and Freyja. Another approach is understanding the whole earth and all of its components as the living Goddess, popularised by James Lovelock's Gaia Theory. There is also the approach of seeking Goddess internally, as an aspect or kernel of self. These three understandings are each part of the wider Goddess movement and Goddess spirituality; where they support and sustain each other.

We live at a very particular time, when we are not limited to the knowledge or practices of our own culture, heritage or era. We can learn about and – if we wish – worship Goddesses from almost any time and place in the history of the world. Hundreds, if not thousands, of named Goddesses exist, from cultures throughout history and from all over the globe. There are ancient Goddesses, from the first recorded history; such as Asherah, Inanna and Lilith. There are Goddesses from Greek, Egyptian and Celtic cultures; Rhiannon, Demeter, Aphrodite, Isis, Hecate and Epona are a few of them. In India Goddesses, including Kali and Lakshmi, are still worshipped. There is Kwan Yin, Chinese Goddess of compassion and the Japanese Amaterasu, the Sun Goddess. There are Native American Goddesses; Grandmother Spider and Changing Woman are two whose stories have made their ways across to our own culture. From the Christian mythos come the Marys – the Virgin Mary and Mary Magdalene – actively worshiped by millions across the world. There are volcanic Goddesses and deep sea Goddesses and butterfly Goddesses.

Many of us have one or several of these named Goddesses that we feel a particular relationship with. This relationship might include having the Goddess appear to us in visions, dreams or path-workings; journeying with or praying to that Goddess in magical or devotional ways; dedicating ourselves to her; working with the archetype she represents and seeking to have her energy or influence touch our own lives. These relationships are very personal. Although they may be informed by myths or evidence of ancient worship they are not confined to that, or ordered or overseen by any authority. For some of us these Goddesses may take the place of the sisters we long for, the mother we never had or the ancient wisdom and guidance of elders that we miss so painfully. They are also avatars of feminine power, beauty, unconditional love and the affirmation of the divine in the shape of a woman that is so missing in our mainstream culture.

It is impossible for us to entirely know what Inanna meant to an ancient Sumerian, or Freyja to the ancient Norse people; but with the enormity of their life-and-death giving powers these Goddesses surely meant something far more vast, numinous and immediate to them than they ever can to us. Nonetheless these Goddesses inspire and guide us, speak to us and offer meaningful spiritual connection. When we invoke them, sing their praises and invite them into our lives we experience them as alive and for many people relating to a particular, named Goddess is their introduction to Goddess work and Goddess spirituality. These named Goddesses have answered a huge hunger within many of us, starved in our culture for images and concepts of the divine feminine but they are far more than archetypes, ancient myths or collections of historical data. We literally hear their voices, feel their touch and know them as distinct beings.

Rather than – or as well as – experiencing Goddess as an external being, archetype or spirit some of us also experience Goddess-within. This form of Goddess may not have a name at all. She is a sense, a feeling, an understanding. She may be that part of ourselves unashamedly embodied as we dance or create, make love or give birth. She may be the part we call upon for healing; for inspiration, courage, compassion, strength or insight. We may experience her as an inviolable inner core, the inner light, our essence or kernel that is both uniquely ourselves and yet also somehow part of – one with – the entire universe; that part that sprang into being with our individual existence and yet mysteriously has always existed and always will. Recognising this inner core as Goddess has given many people – and most especially many women – an avenue into their own empowerment and spirituality.

And yet what makes Goddess distinct? After all, ancient deities from different cultures, inner voices or embodied knowledge of the divine come in masculine as well as feminine forms. The Goddess and Goddess spirituality are distinct because she is life-giving, not in an abstract or impersonal way, but because she gives birth. She is life-centric. This understanding is an intrinsic part of both the named Goddesses and the Goddess-within. Many ancient Goddesses also hold powers of death and destruction; but one is always part of the other. Life and death are two sides of a whole; something that today we might call the life force. The Goddess gives birth not as the Gods of many stories do, through the shaping of mud, through breath or through words, but through her body. She gives birth as our mothers gave birth, as animals give birth and as the earth gives birth to all its forms; to mountains and rivers, to forests and volcanoes, to foliage, flesh, fur, feather and fin. From the Goddess' body, from a woman's body, another body is formed and comes into existence.

The concept of the earth as Goddess has at its core the living life force. Scientists have theorised there is an impulse towards life. We know that life is programmed above everything to survive and reproduce. The Goddess-as-earth embodies this; the earth exists as one being and humans are just a part of that. We are a part with consciousness and self-awareness; possibly a brilliant part and certainly a dangerous part but not more essential or valuable than any other part. From this under-standing springs an eco-feminism based in reverence for the divine feminine not as a nurturing mother who fulfils our needs but as a planet desperately in need of sustainability as a core value. She does not exist for us; although we exist because of her. For this Goddess the seas literally are the waters of her birthing and her blood, the winds are her breath, the earth is her body. She is utterly present in each part of herself, whether that is my own body, a bee or a stalk of grain. Stretching out from the earth she can be seen as even more vast; she is also the glory of the night sky, she is the moon and the expanse of the cosmos.

In our journeys with Goddess we may begin by hearing an inner voice, which later we identify as Artemis, Hathor, Inanna or Ceridwen. It may be that the myths and stories of the Goddess fascinate us, which leads us towards a relationship with the earth as Goddess. It may be that we have always felt a deep affinity with the earth, we know her as a part of ourselves and we choose to explore different aspects of the divine through a variety of named Goddesses. There is a sense of gateways; that inner knowledge of the divine feminine can lead to the exploration of outer forms, which leads towards a Gaian-consciousness; yet for myself, it happened in the reverse order. Or rather, it was all jumbled together, but the order in which I unpicked it was first at a planetary level, then later through working with named Goddesses and finally as understanding and naming of my inner core. Naming an inner experience as Goddess encapsulates meaning. Giving that Goddess a name creates dynamic relationship. Seeing the multiplicity of those named Goddesses as facets or impressions of the life force running through everything gives the largeness of the generative divine, the Goddess.

There's an experience that every one of us has and it's the earliest experience. It's the bodily experience of coming into existence; of being conceived, being carried in our mother's womb for nine months and being born. In this way we have all had the real, immediate and direct experience of Goddess; of coming forth from a woman's body. This existence we are born into, this life, carries with it equally a death, our own death. Each child that I bear I give life to, and with that life comes the necessary death. I cannot give one without the other. This Goddess we are discussing is the force of life and death; she is not mysticism but primary, lived, embodied knowledge. To place this at the centre of religion, of our concept of the divine – this being carried within a woman's body, and being born from it – and to recognise this as divine is to create religion that respects life before authority, obedience or faith. Goddess creates a religion of creating and nurturing life and accepting and honouring death.

The earth gives birth to us; our bodies are made up from her substances, which return to her when we die, just as with the redwoods and possums and rocks and trees. Our mothers give birth to us. The universe has given birth to us; to our planet and our individual lives. Our lovers and our teachers give birth to us. And we give birth to our children, our ideas and creativity, to consciousness, to our students and friendships, to ourselves again and again and to the earth itself as we create her form. We participate in the life of these things and also the death, as parts of our lives die, fall away and transform. In participating in the life and death process we are actively part of Goddess and in any moment we can become aware of this process. There are the waves of the tide, the tiny sea creatures and our bodies; there are the stars and moon, ancient myths and songs; there is art and relationship, love and breath, and there is the great, shared, body-knowledge of being held within the womb.

For me, the Goddess is the Sumerian Goddess Inanna and inevitably her dark sister, Ereshkigal. She is Isis and Aphrodite and Persephone. She is the snakes who live on my property, the changing faces of the moon and the depths of the night sky. She is my woman's body. She stands behind me as I work ritual and magic, and occasionally she speaks and acts through me. She is my understanding of life and death. She is the earth; the rocks are her bones and the living things her heart's blood; all of the stories of the earth are the thoughts that play through her mind. The moments of my life I treasure most deeply are when I have been in her presence; the birth of my son, moments in dreams and rituals and love-making when I held and was the whole world; moments of reverence and revelation as I stood in her temples or observed the beauty of the river, the clouds, a white cockatoo, a tree. This is Goddess.

Jane Meredith is a Priestess of the Goddess and regular presenter at the Glastonbury Goddess Conference and the Australian Goddess Conference and holds workshops worldwide. She is the author of *Aphrodite's Magic* and *Journey to the Dark Goddess*.

Johanna Lawson

The Goddess lives in my very own backyard. I can see Her there in my garden from my kitchen window. She is there every day, every night, through every season, come rain or shine, always. She is everywhere in the garden, in all that grows there and all that inhabits it.

In winter, She rests beneath a sparkling white blanket, insulating the life to be reborn. The dormant perennials, the hibernating creatures, and the scattered seeds all slumber within Her, in Her nurturing soil. She brings me inspiration on her chilling winter winds. During those cold days and nights, I sit by the window and wrap myself in the comfort of herbal teas and gardening catalogs as I await Her glorious awakening.

As the days grow longer, She begins to show herself in small buds on trees and shrubs, the unfurling seedlings, and the familiar song of returning birds. I spend countless hours in the garden, talking to Her as I revel in playing in the dirt, dancing in Her spring rains and revelling in Her sweet scents and colorful blooms. She is full of life, lush and green.

With the turn to summer, She is beginning to tire with the weight of ripening vegetables and abundant herbs. I help to lessen her load by picking tomatoes, snipping herbs, and cutting flowers and, in return, She sings to me through the buzzing bees or the rattle of cicadas and sends butterflies to dance around me. At night, I sit under Her stars and gaze into her silvery beaming face.

In autumn, She is beginning to fade and She allows me to take the bounty of summer indoors for drying and storing. I blanket Her in the fallen leaves of the surrounding trees, all the while thanking Her for all She gave me through the spring and summer. The last days of October arrive and She lingers there in the garden, aged and weary, until She begins to fade into sleep, ghost-like, and I can see the apparition of what once was and dream of what is to come. She retreats into the depths of the garden where I watch Her in Her rest through the darkening days. No matter where I go, wherever my backyard may be, She will always be there, for I nurture Her and She nurtures me.

Samantha Marks

The road I walk is an antlered one; a Path of hoof, antler, blood and bone. Of ancestor spirit and an utmost respect for the land. Honouring the ancient energy of an Antlered Lady swathed in the golden colours of autumn, elusive as the deer themselves. I'd catch a glimpse of an antler out of the corner of my eye, or hear the snap of a twig in the forest glade, but never did She give me Her name.

My journey began back in the nineties with visitations, coming from this Antlered Woman, in meditations and ritual. She came alongside the Green Man, whom I'd be working with for a long time. When I asked or searched for Her name none would be given, and I knew She was no Cerridwen, Isis or Brighid. I began to realize I just had to accept, to be and to follow. Trust and acceptance became second nature along this Path, as long as I stepped with opened heart and love. So I would honour Her as my Lady, until a time She gave me Her name.

The Lady played Her hand with the fateful meeting of a wonderful artist, who made me cry with his image of the Lady who had visited me so many times before. He formally introduced me to 'Ellen' and listened to the experiences I'd had and shared with me those of his. That day was like the missing piece of jigsaw falling into place for me. From that point forward Her voice became louder, Her images and presence stronger.

Places I had visited and made offerings at, with further research, showed links or name references of Elen (or St Helen, Her Christianised form). Threads weaved and I met fellow sisters and brothers, pilgrimages to ancient sites and track ways were made in Her name. A dream saw the creation of a retreat in Elen's honour, now an annual gathering of the Antlered Clan. A whisper of magic and the Temple of Elen was born, which the whole community have had a hand in building. I cannot speak highly enough of those that proudly wear invisible antlers on their brow! Such love, support and community they bring.

My walk along the Antlered Road is taken in love, trust and honour. A love for my Land and all that tread upon it, Trust in the Path I walk and where it takes me and the utmost honour for my antlered Lady. Elen of the Track Ways.

Dyan Hammercheck

She is the mother of all mothers. She is with us from the moment our souls are placed into our earthly bodies, and she stays with us when our earthly bodies return to the earth. We hold in ourselves a precious piece of our Goddess's heart; we are never alone. Our mother is ever-knowing, ever-flowing, and ever-growing. She is with us through our heartaches, heartbreaks, and when our heart skips a beat. She is the mysterious dark side of the moon, shining with the radiance of the sun. We are surrounded by her loving and endless embrace, as she lives her infinite life through the flowers, the trees, the nature that is held near and dear to our hearts. A mother is someone who will push her children to the brink of failure, and then watch as her children take off and soar above all expectations. She pushes her sons and daughters to be the best people that they can be; that we can be. It is possible to succeed without a mother's blessing, but life is a whole lot easier when our mother is there with us every step of the way. The Goddess is not overbearing, she is not overprotective, nor over-restricting. She encourages her children to use the greatest gift she has given them, free will. Our free will is ours alone to do with it what we will; our mother will not take away her gift from us. As we, the Goddess's precious sons and daughters use the gift of free will to live out our lives, we must remember the one we should hold closest to our heart, our loving and accepting mother, the Goddess.

Jessica Colonell

I have practiced eclectic Witchcraft since my teen years. I love the freedom to choose which parts of the craft work for me while discarding the parts that do not.

This absolute freedom hampered my personal discovery of the Goddess for years. Which Goddess, if any, speaks to me? I began my own process of discovery by identifying with The Lady as a general term in my rituals and daily practice. This approach felt impersonal and detached. I tried working with several different Goddesses, but none felt quite right. It wasn't until I was in my late twenties that I discovered The Morrigan.

Of course, I had heard of her before, but only as a Goddess of War and for her part in the Arthurian legends. I didn't realize she is so much more than that. She is her own trinity made up of Anu, Macha, and Badb. The crone aspect of The Morrigan, Badb, is the part of her that is most often mentioned in texts, and reading about her maiden and mother faces, makes her so much more complex and relatable.

Discovering The Morrigan as my Patron Goddess required looking within myself. Her many facets speak to who I am deep down inside. I was shocked to discover she was there, within me, all along. She resides in the deepest, darkest part of my soul. I needed to be brave enough, and honest enough to look there and find her waiting.

This discovery brought my personal practice of the craft to a new level of understanding. I believe the Goddess is within all of us. We just have to turn out focus inward to see for ourselves.

Eclectic Pagan

El Bee Kanobe

I cast this circle in the names of the ancient Gods and Goddesses. Here may they manifest and bless their children...

All across America, Pagans are gathering in small groups and large assemblies. They are gathering in homes and basements, in church basements and coffee shops and in the all-welcoming large circles of outdoor festivals. They are coming together to celebrate the Seasons and Harvests and the Incestuous Sacred Dance of the God and Goddess. Many will even celebrate the phases of the Moon. American Pagans will be of every stripe and color but for the most part, they have one thing in common. They may celebrate in their own fashion as small groups following a specific Tradition but they will gather together under one banner of fellowship and worship. That of Eclectic Paganism.

Ask most American Pagans what their religion is and you will hear them say, 'Pagan'. For these people, it doesn't matter that scholars will say Pagan cannot be a religion. It is an 'umbrella' they say. The American eclectic Pagan could also be thought of as a 'generic' Pagan. Yet more precisely, an Eclectic Generic Pagan. One who thinks that just about everything is acceptable and will circle up with just about any group out there. The glue that holds these generic Pagans together is a common worship format. Also, standard acceptable ethics. Both the worship format and the standard ethics are indistinguishable from those of most Wiccan traditions. Yet, these folks tend to call themselves Pagans, not Wiccans.

American Paganism took a turn somewhere in its evolution. It became very earth bound and the emphasis moved from ritual to celebration. Ritual Celebration, I like to call it. We generally make a lot of noise during Ritual Celebration. We beat drums, sing songs and chants and dance around backyard fire pits and large bonfires into the wee hours of the morning. There are wine bottles being passed as well as a drinking horn full of mead. This turn took it away from being very ritualistic to being a tradition of fewer bells and whistles. There are still some bells and whistles but they stay because they resonate with the earth-focused folk in our midst. A chalice might be a wooden cup. The athame might be a sickle. There could be almost anything on the altar. This attitude of inclusiveness makes Pagan circles very inviting and welcoming.

For the most part, everyone knows what to expect regarding setting up the circle. The circle is cast and quarters called. The God and Goddess are evoked or invoked and blessings given. After that, anything goes. The body of the ritual can be anything the priest and priestess want it to be. Most often it is celebration centered on the Sabbat or lunar days such as full moons and new moons but that celebration can take many forms. Ritual Celebration can take many forms, the American Eclectic Generic Pagan is exposed to many expressions of faith. They become accustomed to participating in generic Pagan circles everywhere. It becomes an Eclectic Pagan gathering.

Eclectic Pagans are allowed to hold differing concepts of Deity. Some may think of Deity as being transcendent while others can only see Deity as permeating. Eclectic Pagans also include Polytheist, Pantheist and Animist as well as Deist, Henotheist and others who have yet to experience how they relate to Deity. It's a testimony to the degree of fellowship these people have that allows them to circle for common benefit. My personal circle of friends include Wiccans of every persuasion, Druids, Ozark Witches, Christo-Pagans, Native Americans, Luciferians, and many others. It's amazing all these people can gather under one banner to celebrate life.

Eclectic Paganism is the 'melting pot' in America. Even before modern Wicca was introduced to the Americas, there was a thriving Pagan culture present. There still is. We have Voodoo, Hoodoo and Root Magic that came up the Mississippi River. Oriental railroad workers took their magickal culture cross country. As a child, I remember the Gypsies coming to my town twice a year sell their skills and wares. They worked a lot of Root Magic for the Ozark Pagans back then. We had the Protestants of New England and a sizable Irish/Scot/Celtic folk settling all over the country. There has been a thriving Spiritualist group here for the last one hundred and fifty years. All these and more shaped the Eclectic American Pagan.

With the exception of the varied Native Americans, America doesn't have an historical spiritual heritage like the rest of the world. America's entire spiritual heritage is either from conquest or importation. America's Eclectic Pagans are taking the best from many sources and are creating traditions. These traditions are becoming widely acceptable across a wide spectrum of American Paganism. Some of these traditions are borrowed from the Native American spiritual traditions. The Sage Smudge and sweet grass, the sweat lodge and Spirit Quest are a few of the borrowed traditions. Depending on where you live in America, your expression of Native American culture will not be the same experience as that of someone from another part of the country. The same is true of the massive influence of Irish/Scot/Celt culture, history and spirituality felt in America. Irish culture in New York is not the same as the Irish culture of the Ozarks. The Traditions being created from all these varied cultures and sources will evolve into something recognizable as a distinct Magickal Tradition in its own right. That is already happening to some extent. There are several established Eclectic Traditions.

The two that come to mind are American Eclectic Paganism and North American Eclectic Wicca. They both have been around and active since at least 1989. They both are still evolving but each will take what it has found works best for itself and what resonates with it. In the case of North American Eclectic Wicca, it has developed established Liturgy using many sources. These Traditions are what you will generally see at outdoor camping festivals. It begins with a procession, a smudging/cleansing and a blessing. A circle is cast and the quarters are called, "Hail to the Spirits of the East, Spirits of Air, bring your sweet cool breezes with you as you stand in the East and guard our Circle." Deities are seldom invoked at large circles. It is much too difficult to maintain the energy required. Most priests and priestesses will just evoke the God and Goddess to attend the rite. Can you imagine the energy required to maintain the God aspect as well as face a hundred or more petitioners because you invoked Pan? It's better to just evoke when in large groups. "Hail Pan, God of the wild wood. Come pleasure us as you bask in our worship of you. Bless these, your children of the night, with the sensual sounds of your pipe. Attend us now at the height of your season".

As mentioned, the body of the ritual can be anything you want it to be. Here is where we often make music, dance and play in celebration of a turning of the Wheel. Here we also get creative. Not bound by the fetters of any one tradition, the priestess is free to let her imagination fly. It's a magickal mix-n-match of ideas. Sometimes the ritual may be a celebration of praise and honor to a particular God or Goddess. Other times magick might be the focus which, of course, could lead to all kinds of misbehavior. Ritual can be Shamanic. It may include a ritual drink that helps facilitate a trance. It can mix pantheons, which is a major infraction according to traditionalists. It can be somber and joyful at the same time. Eclectic ritual can be a time when the priest and priestess celebrate traditional aspects of various Pagan paths as well. There might be a Five-Fold Kiss or a Great Rite included. We might make sigils or color eggs or plant flowers or weave baskets or make candles. Energy is raised and thrown into the intention of the ritual, usually by some ecstatic drumming and dancing. Spells are spoken or chanted. Magick is made and sealed.

We generally let this aspect of our ritual last as long as needed and when the energy is at its height, send it forth and ground out the excess. Some form of the Rite of Cakes and Ale is often used to help ground out the excess energy. Sometimes platters of sweet cakes or fruit are passed around, as well as a cup of wine or mead. Often more than just one cup. We often take this time to share with each other what we have been doing, new loves, new children, new jobs. Someone may have a chant to share or a new song they wrote. People might speak petitions to their God or Goddess. We will let this sharing time progress as needed and when it has run its course, we thank the God and Goddess for attending our rites and ask them to stay and play with us.

We don't always take down the circle right away. We will leave it up for hours and sometimes close it the next morning. All the while the circle is up we play in the space we created. More drums appear. Dancers emerge from the shadows... more food, more wine, more firewood. Let's build that fire. There are always fire tenders more than willing to keep it going even in the heat of July and August. Some clothes will come off. Fire spinners may entertain us and stories are told. This celebration can last for hours and generally does. In the winter months, pot luck suppers become part of the celebration. Houses are crammed with people. Coats and hats are piled in a corner. Beds are made available for folks who just party too hard.

Many of you reading this will think it's not much different from what you do all the time. Good for you. This format is what you will have gravitated to after you have studied a bunch of different traditions but can't fully immerse yourself into any of them. You probably identify as a Pagan when asked. You are an Eclectic Pagan.

El Bee Kanobe, also known as Larry Brown, is the long-time Elder and Priest of Yarrow Coven of St. Louis and the Dean of

Religious Studies at the College of Occult Science. El Bee has been an active public Pagan, teaching and writing for the past forty years.

Suzanne Reynolds-Alpert

Eclectic General neo-Paganism is so prevalent in America today due to the "melting pot" aspect of our country. The individual-istic, somewhat non-conformist attitudes the country was built upon certainly play a role. Our religious freedoms have allowed ideas from elsewhere to infuse the Traditional British Wicca that was imported and the homespun folk magicks that grew here. What distinguishes Eclectics from Traditionalists is that they are comfortable borrowing, substituting, trying out, or making up ritual elements. Deities are mixed and matched. Sacred Space is created one way this month; another the next. The Eclectic shies away from conformity – and there's conformity to be found in both traditional religions *and* many neo-Pagan ones.

Kanobe does well describing what he calls *Eclectic Generic Paganism* as it exists in the United States. In particular, he calls out the influences of pagan and magickal practices from elsewhere (i.e. Voodoo, Hoodoo); Root Magic, and Celtic-based folk magicks that spread and evolved variously throughout the U.S. The influence of various Native American beliefs and spiritual practices are noted. Wicca may have initially galvanized a community of witches in America, but Eclectic neo-Pagans on this side of the pond possess the decidedly "American flavor" already described.

I believe that Kanobe missed calling out two very important influences – the roles of Unitarian Universalism (UU) and second-wave feminism – and how these worked to further disperse the beliefs and practices of the millions of Americans that self-identify as "Pagan."

Many UU churches have supported their neo-Pagan community members by allowing them to use church spaces and resources, and by welcoming them into their congregations. The Unitarian Universalist Association (UUA) adopted as one of their seven Principles, "Respect for the Interdependent web of existence of which we are a part." Further, the UUA cites "Spiritual teachings of earth-centered traditions... which instruct us to live in harmony with the rhythms of nature" as one of the sources from which UU Principles are drawn.

The influences of second-wave feminism on neo-Paganism are many—notable examples include the ecofeminism of Starhawk, and books by Zsuzsanna Budapest and the late Shekinah Mountainwater. Budapest and Mountainwater in particular infused many Dianic (women/Goddess-only) ideals and spurred the creation of countless covens, making the cauldron of American neo-Paganism even more female- and Goddess-centric.

For the past fifty-odd years, many women have found sanctuary from the patriarchy inherent in most religions. Men and women alike longed to honor the Divine Feminine along with the Divine Masculine, and neo-Paganism provided answers. Both feminism and Unitarian Universalism possess frameworks for these explorations.

Many witches – those trained in Gardnerian or Alexandrian Wicca, for example – initially found their adopted religion liberating. However, in both traditions there is a fairly strict belief system and means of doing ritual. Many American neo-Pagans want more freedom to decide which Gods to worship or invoke, and how they want to use tools (if any) during their rituals. The continuing influence of both feminism and Unitarian Universalism on American neo-Paganism should not be overlooked.

Freeman Presson

If you're a Pagan in the modern West, you're eclectic. Let's break this down. If you are involved in Witchcraft or Wicca, then the sources of your tradition are Arabic, Greek, Italian, Saxon, Celtic,

Qabalistic, Masonic, Thelemic, and modern-visionary. If you are a devotional Pagan, you're likely drawing on Archaic, Classical, Renaissance, Romantic, and modern-visionary views of your Deities (if you are lucky enough to have a variety of sources).

One of the most important things is to understand how different those world-views are. The Archaic, the Classical, the Hermetic, the Enlightenment (so-called), and the modern mindsets do not understand each other without a titanic effort. *Un*learning the mechanical world-view is as important as anything you can learn.

In my case, I became explicitly Pagan along with my wife, as she had experiences that (as we jointly worked out) were traceable to Gods of Mesopotamia. Why them, why us? Past-life connections, if that's not using a greater enigma to explain a lesser. We did a lot of trial and error, including joining a group or two, but nothing would do except that we found a few kindred souls and started our own Temple. People, and even some of the Deities, have come and gone, and we have settled into relationship with a handful of members and six Deities.

This is really enough, but we are also fortunate to have a fairly low-drama Pagan community where we live, so we also participate in local activities, including seasonal feasts with our local ADF grove and lively Pagan meet-ups and potlucks at the local "Pagan store." In the last two years, I have broadened my interests to include Hermetic studies with the Church of the Hermetic Sciences (Order of the Temple of Astarte), in which I took the Pastophoris degree (Fellowship of the Grail) last year. This is giving me a deeper reach into certain parts of Western Magic, and a few lifetimes' worth of study material.

Nikki Shields

It has been said that a sign of genius is being able to hold two opposing thoughts in one's mind without difficulty. So, how can you create traditions in eclectic Paganism? How do you design a calendar of events that works for such a diverse group of partici-pants? My answer: be flexibly consistent.

Here in Maine, we celebrated our 30th annual Beltane on the Beach gathering. Every spring more than 200 Pagans of all ages and traditions gather for a potluck lunch, a ritual, and the dancing of five or more Maypoles. In an area of low population spread out over many miles, plus the rugged individuality New England is known for, it's amazing that so many people gather in joyful celebration year after year. Yet there is that solid consis-tency: it's held at the same state park on the ocean, on the first Sunday of May. Everyone knows. New families are invited as they join the collective Pagan community.

Recently a Druid who is active in the community had the idea for a counterpart event, an autumn ritual where Pagans gather to go within in search of visions both personal and collective. The first event attracted about 30 people, and is being talked about widely. He expects the attendance will double each year. Again, consistency is important: this event is held on private land up in the foothills, and takes place between Mabon and Samhain.

On a smaller scale, my family has hosted an annual Winter Solstice celebration for more than 10 years. We usually have about 40 people in attendance, sometimes fewer due to the wintry weather. We are consistent: it happens on the evening of the Solstice, with a bonfire, a ritual, and a potluck. Those who wish may stay up all night to keep vigil. As our kids have grown, this tradition has attracted a terrific group of teens who love the idea of staying up all night around the fire together.

There is some truth to the saying, "build it, and they will come." When you offer a consistent time and space for community celebration, it will attract the eclectic Pagans in your area. You can't expect the rituals to be as tightly-knit as in a coven, for the celebrants will change for each event. They might not all be Pagan: our Winter Solstice ritual was once interrupted by a young teen arriving with a friend, who upon seeing the bonfire, the circle of oaks, and the archway lit with faerie lights and luminaries, exclaimed loudly, "Oh! This is just so pretty! Wow!" She didn't realize we were in the midst of our ritual, but her joy was so genuine that no one minded the interruption.

When planning and hosting such events, consider yourself a facilitator for the group's experience. By being flexible and allowing your gatherings to unfold as they will, you'll be helping build an incredibly creative, supportive, and empowered community of people brought together by a common love of the Earth.

Hayley Addis

Eclecticism can be wonderful, in an ideal situation folks bring together the deities and practices that they have deep relationships with. They share them to create something that works for all involved. Each person holds the context for their practice and brings the depth needed for it to make sense and hold weight. This is very different to grabbing whatever you fancy from books, throwing them all together and seeing what happens... although that can have some great effects, the result is often a strange creation that doesn't quite work magically.

My tradition, Reclaiming, illustrates positive magical eclecticism perfectly. Born out of a desire to bring magic into activism, to create manifest change in the world around us as well as our own individual lives, it is an anarchistic community around the world. In each gathering people come together with different magical histories and specialities. These combine and are used to create something new which can become part of that particular gathering's lineage. The keys to this process working are twofold: 1) each person knows their practices intimately and 2) the creative spirit is at play to blend them into the work *within the spirit of the tradition*. Activities are not transplanted wholesale but are integrated into the ethic/energy of Reclaiming so they become the foundation of something new. If eclecticism is a patchwork quilt, then Reclaiming is patchwork in shades of one colour.

In terms of celebratory paganism, eclecticism works well. If you are celebrating the yearly cycles and connecting with community, any form which feels good to all involved will suit the purpose. If you want to make magic (i.e. cause change energetically in accordance with will), however, the energy you are connecting to has to be clear and understood. In that case, the form of the practice, its history and context are vitally important. Without knowing why one starts in the East, for example, the intention does not join up with the energy and this disconnect causes blockages to clean manifestation of change. You can do it and get results, but you've just made it harder for yourself. Jumping around between forms confuses the subconscious and sends out mixed messages, using techniques just because they look nice can attract attention from energies historically linked with them which you might not want and so on. If someone fully understands the practice they bring to the group they can make sure that it energetically fits with everything else, if they don't then they can't.

Many people are very happy with the celebratory aspect of paganism and perhaps the occasional spell-working and this is as it should be. If you want to be making magic, however, it works best to be either deeply immersed in an established tradition that has clear patterns which you can use as your foundation, or to tap into the magic and follow your intuition and guides in forging your own path that is in alignment with you and itself, integrating those practices you fully understand.

PART 2

WHAT WE BELIEVE

DEITIES

NATURE

ETHICS

AFTERLIFE

ANCESTORS

PAST & PRESENT

Deities

Robin Herne

Not all pagans believe in deities – there are modern pagans who regard themselves as atheists. However, the purpose of this article is to examine the nature of gods from the viewpoint of those pagans who do believe in them. Ancient ways of viewing the gods often had marked differences from some of the beliefs common amongst modern pagans.

The ancient world was almost solidly polytheist, which is to say that they believed in a multitude of gods, goddesses and other potent spirits that could be contacted, communicated with, and might prove benevolent, indifferent or hostile towards humanity. A lot of modern pagans, heavily influenced by the writings of Carl Jung, speak of deities being aspects of a greater, overarching presence (such as a Lord and Lady). However, few ancient peoples regarded their deities as aspects of anything.

The Roman writer Quintus Symmachus wrote:

Everything is full of gods. Whatever men worship, it may fairly be called one and the same. We all look up to the same stars; the same heaven is above us all; the same universe surrounds every one of us. What does it matter by what system of knowledge each one of us seeks the truth? It is not by one single path that we attain to so great a secret.

Whilst Symmachus was primarily striving to make diplomatic overtures to increasingly militant Christian sects, there were probably a fair number of fellow pagans who felt that whilst different cultures had different names for deities, they may well be worshipping the same entities.

Are all goddesses of the hearth one and the same being, just known by different names in various languages, perhaps clothes in different guises according to who is looking at her – or are Vesta, Hestia and Gabija quite distinct beings? Whilst it's outside the scope of this article to answer such questions definitively, I hope to look at some of the issues surrounding it.

Much like historians, pagans tend to classify deities by their cultural affiliations – we speak of Greek, Egyptian, Chinese etc. deities as if they had passports and paid taxes. Whilst a matter of historical convenience to use such terms, it is debatable how genuinely useful concepts of divine nationality are. Judaism gives an example of a deity who has, apparently, made an exclusive pact with a particular genetic lineage of people. It is difficult to think of any similar covenants, though I have heard that other people have encountered deities who have insisted on being addressed in a certain language.

A difficult issue that surfaces within modern paganism is that of cultural imperialism – cherry picking bits from a culture which one is not part of. Whilst this can often lead the cherry picker to make mistakes (lacking an in-depth understanding of the culture they are plundering), where the culture that is being plundered is one that has suffered historical oppression by the culture of the picking pagan, then accusations of arrogance and exploitation can arise.

I have no reason to suppose that Gods indulge in some sort of racial purity where only Greeks can worship Greek deities or anything of that sort, however, people exploring the spiritual world would benefit from a degree of sensitivity towards the humans whose cultures they are dipping in and out of.

To some extent the argument about whether there are fifty gods, one god or no gods is all a bit pointless without being able to define exactly what it is that we mean by a deity in the first place. It's a remarkably hard question to answer, and clearly different religions have varied notions on what they consider their respective deities to be. I suspect that one of the problems faced in this exploration is that many people feel obliged to find a unifying theory that incorporates all possible perceptions of deities as if they were all the same thing, when quite possibly there are a number of quite distinct types of entity that get labelled under the catch-all of 'deity'.

We could consider 'deity' as an almost zoological category, a particular type of entity distinguishable from other beings and with its own cycles and habits. Alternately we might consider it more of a job description, a deity is a being that must do X, Y or Z and any being capable of those functions might qualify. In terms of who defines the job requirements, presumably the worshippers would be on the interviewing panel. A diseased person might expect their goddess to heal them, and if She cannot do so then they might well try another till they find one that can. In this respect, people can often (in the author's experience) seem quite fickle and only willing to espouse an allegiance to or belief in a given deity whilst they are getting whatever it is they feel to be their dues. When life suddenly hits the rocks and the deity fails to deliver what was expected of them, it is far from unknown for worshippers to go elsewhere or jack religion in entirely.

Or we may look at the notion that deity is a status conferred by worshippers, but not intrinsic to the thing that is worshipped. If a being is treated as a god then to all intents and purposes it becomes one. This may seem a variation of the previous point, except that not everyone expects a great deal from their deities. Plus there are many people who, when they don't receive what they asked for, will tend to assume there must be a wise reason for this and remain in the relationship.

There are doubtless other ways of conceiving of what a deity may be, though all such discussions may seem a trifle strange unless the reader is starting from an animist perspective. Animists believe in the existence of a world filled with spirits (or, if you prefer, consciousnesses) – human, horse, oak tree, granite, river etc. In such a world any one of these conscious minds might find the status of deity conferred upon it, and may either embrace or reject or be utterly oblivious to that perception.

The Ancient Romans, Egyptians and Taoist Chinese all considered (or continue to consider) that all people have a divine spark that could flower through ritual offerings, self-reflection, great accomplishments and so forth. These "little gods" could grow to become notable demigods, usually after death. We still treat celebrities as if they were beyond the level of normal humans, decorate our houses with pin-up posters or calendars or autographed photos of them. If this does not border on a form of worship, I do not know what does.

As well as lavishing attention upon the living, we are also quite given to devoting ourselves to the dead. Ancestor reverencing is nothing new, of course, and again there is a lot of blurring of boundaries between where an ancestor ends and a deity begins.

The Ancient Romans believed in the indwelling spirits in all sapient beings, spirits which were gendered, with the male spirit being called the genius and the female juno. In early Roman religion, the genius seems to have been an important shared ancestor who watched over his (or her) descendants. Later on, the genius came to be seen as a more personal, individual guardian watching over a specific individual rather than a whole clan. In Sweden there was a widespread belief not only in the three famous Nornir, but also that each person had their own individual guardian norn who should be given offerings of a special porridge, the nornegrautin. The idea seems to be essentially the same.

Most Roman families made regular offerings to the genius of the paterfamilias, much as the whole Empire dedicated temples, sacrifices, rituals and so forth to the genius of the Emperor in his capacity of Father of the Roman family. The reasoning behind this would appear to be that the guiding spirit would be able to advise and steer the mortal mind of the individual, and under Roman law the paterfamilias was the chief decision maker and legal guardian of the family. The Gods of China were all once human beings translated to holy entities after death, the Egyptians revered the living and dead Pharaohs as sacred incarnations.

The last known mortal to be apotheosised within Western forms of paganism was the beautiful Greek youth Antinous, in life the lover of the Emperor Hadrian. During his two decades, Antinous evidently captured the middle-aged emperor's heart. Prostrate with grief, Hadrian heard reports that the Egyptians had taken to making offerings to the lost lad – because his demise echoed that of the god Asur who also drowned in the Nile.

Was Antinous born a god or did he become one? Is he a "real" god or was his elevation more a matter of politics and a lonely emperor's whim? These are as much questions that speak to the philosophical starting point of the questioner as they are avenues leading to objective or readily verifiable answers. A pragmatic approach may be to try communing with Antinous and see what he says (assuming you get a response at all).

A small tribe with Iron Age technology dwelling on the banks of a river may view the spirit of that river as a goddess, given that they depend upon Her for food, fresh water, travel, all manner of resources swept down from upriver etc. To all practical intents and purposes, She is their goddess. To the technologically advanced travellers wandering past and observing all this, the spirit of the river may be classed as "just" a naiad, a localised river nymph and scarcely on a par with their deities who are worshipped across the expanse of a vast empire. Who is correct? This is where the issue of whether godhood is a quality intrinsic to the entity or more something conferred from outside becomes relevant.

This is armchair philosophising, because we are essentially talking about concepts so vast our brains may simply not be developed enough to properly grasp what we are just skirting the edges of. To paraphrase an analogy that I have used elsewhere we may be like ladybirds looking at a gardener. A human could outlast ninety generations of bugs, is gargantuan in comparison, and behaves, thinks, and feels in ways that must be utterly mysterious to it. Would it even comprehend that this immense force is a single being? Those colossal columns may appear to move about independently of each other, rather than seem to be limbs of one creature. If the bug did guess that the legs eventually joined, it might assume that the shovel was also somehow part of it. Would this vast and seemingly eternal force be a god in the eyes of the insect? There may be beings in the universe that are as far removed from us as we humans are from ladybirds. They may be so long lived and strange and unlike us as to appear to be gods, wights, angels etc. Without getting too Doctor Who, it is worth considering that humans may not be the only intelligent entities in either the cosmos at large or upon Earth specifically. There may be other things out there and some may want to talk to us. Why they should do so is another question. Some of their motivations may be beyond our comprehension, but others may be ones familiar to us – familiar because we also take an interest in other creatures whose communication systems are so different from ours that half the time we have to guess what is going on in their minds. We keep pets, we farm some things, eat others, we experiment on animals, use them for sport, torment them for sadistic pleasure, some we put in zoos, and others we actively preserve in the wild simply because we find them beautiful and want to see them pursuing their own courses.

Several species enjoy symbiotic relationships, so why not suppose that deities also bond with humans or other creatures?

The concept of immanent deities present in the material world also raises interesting possibilities. Beekeepers sometimes talk of hives exhibiting a sort of 'group mind'; maybe the collective consciousness of a forest – all those trees, shrubs, rocks, rivers, badgers, deer etc. – coalesces into some kind of group sapience which we humans then envision as a deity (such as Cernunnos, Mielikki or Silvanus) when it impinges upon our own awareness? This, in itself, raises the issue of what is capable of having a consciousness in the first place. Present day science normally favours consciousness as a product of brain activity, and therefore requires a creature to have a brain first (and many scientists seem to feel that only certain creatures with brains have awareness, rather than all those things with brains). Animism surely implies that sapience is not actually restricted to animals with brains, or even necessarily to things that current science regards as alive in the first place.

Many Pagans these days believe that all goddesses are aspects of One Goddess, and likewise with the male gods (this idea is usually called duotheism, or duolatry by academics). This is a perfectly valid belief, though not a particularly common one in ancient times. In some respects it could be compared to the notions of multiple identities as espoused by such psychologists as John Rowan, as individuals we are all quite used to becoming a multitude of people in response to varied situations. Mr Jones the bank manager behaves and dresses and thinks in one way at work, but becomes Bob to his wife and behaves in a different way, Dad to his kids, Robbo to the rugby team on a Sunday, Bobby when visiting his dotty old aunt, and so forth. As humans we have different names for different modes, and often different styles of dress, speech patterns, and topics of conversation etc. with each of these selves. No surprise if a deity ends up with even more selves than a human does.

Just as humans are complex creatures, so are deities (regardless of whether you see them as individual forces or aspects of something greater). A lot of books greatly oversimplify their characters, tending to give a cardboard cut-out feel to them where one Moon Goddess is much the same as any other. Greek mythology books talk in terms of Zeus being the god of thunder, Apollo the god of the sun etc. This is fine up to a point, but it's a bit limiting. Gods have lots of interests, just as humans do. Jane may be a nurse, but does this mean she is interchangeable with any other nurse? Clearly not, and there is far more to Jane than just her job description – she may be devoted daughter, a skilled gardener, a brewer of excellent wines, an athlete, a tap dancer, and any number of other things too. Getting to know any god or goddess is getting to appreciate their full range of interests and quirks.

Robin Herne is an educator, poet, storyteller, poet, artist, dog-owner and Druid. He is the author of *Old Gods, New Druids*, *Bard Song* and *A Dangerous Place*. He has also written numerous articles for Pagan magazines and has appeared in television documentaries. He lives in Ipswich, UK.

Ferdiad Selkie

The sky is shading gently from dusk to night as I walk my circle, say my prayer, light my candles. Amber flickering light plays across the face of the familiar figure seated before me, cross legged and straight backed, gazing implacably ahead. His entire appearance is both meditation and lesson: large wide eyes stare through me, beyond the physical and into the deep forest paths of the Otherworld; proud antlers reach skyward from his brow, symbols of power, divinity, sovereignty; the torc at his neck confirms his authority. Wrought by the alchemy of smithcraft it shows he is master of his realm. I know him as Cernunnos, Lord of the Wild and of Beasts, guardian of the gateways that lead to the Sidhe, into the wildwood beyond the village, to that tangled briar of the unconscious, unknown spaces of dreams and fears and deep soul learning.

I offer resins and herbs to the censer before him and watch the sacred smoke rise. He holds aloft a torc in one hand and a giant, ram-horned snake in the other: further symbols of his divine status and also of the challenge he poses to those who would learn from him. The snake is powerful, potentially deadly, with curling horns displaying its Otherworldy nature. Horns and antlers, magic and majesty, Cernunnos is a true master of beasts to hold such a creature. The torc he holds, a power matched to the torc worn at his neck, is the symbol of the secrets he guards, the paths through the wild, the dark gateways into the unknown.

It is not a choice of instinct over will, or of knowledge over death. We do not choose what the gods will give to us, for who would not choose the torc and be spared the serpent? Instead he offers us challenge, and these are the symbols both of his godhood and of the secrets he guards. Knowledge of the Otherworld is not granted, as simply as one might be handed a torc; it is rather a goal, earned through exploration, walking the pathways and being open to guidance. Nor is death something to be avoided or defeated. The challenge of the snake is not that of a monster to overcome in primal combat, it offers rather a challenge to the fears we hold in our life. If we can embrace and master a creature that can defy death and shed its skin to be reborn, and hold it in a way that causes harm neither to snake nor handler, then we can accept our mortality and walk through life, unafraid, in the clear knowledge that we will die.

Those scant shards of knowledge of the Old Gods handed down from antiquity can only be breathed into life by seeking a personal relationship with those gods as unique deities. The simple act of sitting with my gods, contemplating their nature, offering sacrifice and prayer, are my ways of developing a gentle but profound connection and opening to what I can learn from them.

Bracken Setanti

I sit down, close my eyes, take nine deep breaths, and...

There once was a woman who was in deep need of healing. It was the custom amongst her people to go down to the sea when in such need, to ask for help.

At the mouth of the Ribble occurred a potent mixing of fresh water from the land and salt from the sea, and the wise people of Lancashire knew that in those flat, land-tides was powerful magic.

So, she went, down to the sea and she asked. She knelt by the sea side and she asked for the healing that she needed. The sea rose up and anointed her and she gave thanks.

Again she asked for the help that she needed, and the sea rose up and poured down upon her head. Again she gave thanks.

A third and final time she asked for the deep healing she craved in her blood and bones. The sea rose up and crashed down upon her head pulling her out and down, down into the deep, dark ocean.

Tossed and buffeted by the sea she was, but she felt no fear as she was drawn deeper and deeper into the dark and the icy cold.

The deeper she went the calmer and colder became the waters surrounding her, until she stopped, bumping up against something hard as ice and cold as marble.

All fear had fled some time before. The woman felt only curiosity. She propelled herself gently backwards and…

Oh, an eye. A huge eye opened. It looked so deeply into her. It knew everything she was.

She felt recognition, deep contentment, but she was disturbed to see that the eye looked out from a gargantuan living stone statue in the form of a mermaid too heavy and weed bound to swim. The mermaid and the woman bore a close enough resemblance to be sisters. The woman resolved to clean the weeds from the living rock.

The woman grabbed her mop and her scrubbing brush and she set about the task with gusto, cleaning until she could clean no more and she had to return to the surface.

On her second visit she was surprised to see that the job looked easier than it had the first time. Was it her imagination or had the statue shrunk a little?

She scrubbed the huge eye, the crown, the shoulders and

spine where the weeds grew the thickest.

By her fourth visit the statue and she herself seemed round about the same size. The great fish tail looked much more like human legs.

By her seventh visit, the statue was no bigger than a tiny baby-doll which she held in her hands, lovingly soaping until it was spotless, and it vanished.

Swimming up to the surface was an easy thing by now. As she hauled herself out of the waves to sit and sing to the sky on a craggy rock, she untangled her flowing hair with her nails and admired her own beautiful, glistening tail.

Willow Mooncloud

When I first began my path and was avidly learning about the Gods and Goddesses and the many pantheons they belonged to, one seemed to resonate with me more than the others I was reading about, Arianrhod, Goddess of the Silver Wheel, a Goddess of reincarnation, Karma, the Moon and the Stars. From the Celtic pantheon, she represents the Mother aspect of the Triple Goddess and is linked to fertility, death and rebirth. I don't know why I feel drawn to and feel closer to this Goddess, I just do! With her guidance I am able to achieve more in my magickal workings. I do not 'Worship' the Goddess, but revere her, and I know that when I write a ritual or a spell, that she is with me, guiding what I do.

I also believe that we as a race are re-awakening our spiritual selves and are more able to accept and understand what is needed of us and for us at this particular stage and time in our evolution. That is why we are more receptive to other forms of communication, such as within meditation or trance. Some may say it is hallucinations or daydreaming, but as a practising Pagan/Wiccan I can personally say that I have experienced something whilst in a meditative state that I cannot explain, and really don't have to, as to me it was a gift given. I think over thousands of years we have forgotten how to use our sixth sense, our third eye and psychic abilities. I really do think life would be so much less hostile if we were able to use our 'inner' powers as it were, and perhaps this is why our Dieties are 'speaking' with us now, our minds are developed enough to be able to comprehend what they are trying to teach us?

Irisanya Rainbow
Let us be silent, that we may hear the whispers of the gods.
Ralph Waldo Emerson

Courting the divine. I didn't know what to think when I heard this phrase for the first time. I couldn't decide if it was too casual a thought to flirt (?) with a deity, or if it was a possibility that I could consider and even explore.

Then the rainbows came. I remember the day clearly, sitting down with the registration form. I remember sitting there, not knowing how to fill it out, or whether I was ready to jump into studying magick again. My past experiences had been dull, even off-putting. But Reclaiming felt different.

Still, I hesitated on that December afternoon. I looked out my apartment window and saw a rainbow descending from the sky. My heart swelled, tears formed, and my body filled with an energy I had not felt before. I was not alone. I closed my eyes and felt something, someone hold me and tell me it was going to be okay.

Because I am a child of the Internet (and then, a woman with few mythology books) I looked up 'rainbow' online. That's when the feeling with no name became Iris. I met Her. I met Her few stories, and I saw Her messages for me. Every page revealed another phrase I'd heard from someone in my life. Every page showed me that Iris was more than just a paragraph in a book. She was already a part of my story. A courtship began, with care, with sincerity, with reverence.

This is not a one-sided relationship. In my training, I've learned to have tea with deities – sometimes with tea, sometimes with other devotional practices. I've created altars for Iris, spontaneous and permanent. I've stood under rainbows and given thanks for Her messages. And I've made sacred pledges to Her under the light of the moon and the warmth of the sun.

She is the one that carries messages to and from the Gods, and the One who can willingly travel to the underworld and back again. In Her, I have found strength to know that I too can make those journeys and that I too can carry messages and share them. She is the one that shows up as people you already know to tell you it will be okay. And I have heard Her again and again. *You are not alone.*

When I stopped to listen, a beautiful relationship began. And isn't that what courting is all about? Those long nights where you can't hear enough from the other person. Those long hours of talking until you see the dawn.

Relationships often challenge and reveal your true self. Iris led me to my spiritual home and to my beloveds. She led me to the river where I continue to drink and make sacred vows.

Nature

Joanna van der Hoeven

We are Pagans – we are the country folk. Nature is at the very heart of our religion, our spirituality and our way of life. It was the Romans who called us paganus, meaning "country dweller". We hold the wild places, the cycles of the earth that provide us with food and all things that inhabit the earth, in reverence. Many sects of Paganism hold the secrets of their spirituality within their names – Druids, the Oak-Knowers; Heathens, the people of the heath; Wiccans, those that bend and shape like the reed. All of these and other aspects of Paganism hold the same values in common. The earth is sacred. The Earth is sacred.

We see ourselves as part of a great cycle of life and death, and celebrate this according to the seasons in what is known as the Wheel of the Year. We honour that which is happening in the natural world around us, and yet just what is this natural world? What is our place in it? What makes something natural and something else unnatural? These questions start us on a quest to discover just what is our own nature, and the nature of all things.

As Pagans, we see ourselves as a part of nature – we are not separate.

Within Dualism, theories of hierarchy became prevalent thanks to Aristotle, who extrapolated upon Plato's theories of multiple souls. Dualism has been the predominant theory in both religion and culture for many Western countries, and has had profound effects on how we view nature, and our own place within it. The theory of Dualism, in that mind and body are not one, was at odds with the Materialists, who stated that there can be no separation. The Dualist's separation theory spilled over into other ways of thinking, hierarchal ways that differentiated man from nature, and even from other men.

Many, many Pagans are at odds with the theory of Dualism,

for we see ourselves as not separate to nature, and certainly not above other flora or fauna as some of the great Western thinkers would have us believe. This way of thinking, sadly, still continues today. Even the Oxford English Dictionary's definition of Nature seems to exclude us in certain ways – humans are not a part of Nature. How on earth (pun intended) could that be?

Let us look at the OED's first definition of nature.

1. *[mass noun] the phenomena of the physical world collectively, including plants, animals, the landscape, and other features and products of the earth, as opposed to humans or human creations: the breathtaking beauty of nature*
   - *the physical force regarded as causing and regulating the phenomena of the world: it is impossible to change the laws of nature.*

This definition states that humans are not part of the physical world in the collective sense. To the Pagan, this is nonsensical. Are we humans not part of the animal world, mammals specifically? So why does the belief that we are separate from nature persist? Encouraged by philosophers and opposing religions, this belief has seeped into our everyday lives and is so entrenched that it can be demoralising to the Pagan who sees herself not only as part of that cycle, but playing as vital a role as any other within it, from the pollinating bee to the field of wheat ripening in the sun.

Yet I am as guilty as other Pagans at forgetting that I too am a part of nature. I use ritual, meditation and creativity to help me try to remember this on a daily basis. All too often I will find myself walking down a busy London street, craving the "natural world" over this human landscape. Yet this human landscape is also a part of the natural world. There is nothing that exists that can be separate from the natural world.

A university professor of mine once posed this question –

what does "natural" mean to us? We all responded with ideas of flora and fauna, of "natural" things. Then she said, "What of the plastic lawn furniture that the spider spins her web on? Is this too a part of nature?" Yes, indeed – for the spider, this plastic thing is a part of her world, and it is a part of our world too. The chair has not arisen out of nothing; it required our ability and the resources to make it, all stemming from things available on this very planet.

I am a part of the collective world. I am a part of the landscape, along with the plants and animals, the spirits of place, the furniture. I am not opposed to nature, I am nature. I cannot be separate from it.

It is the idea of separateness that has caused so much devastation to our planet, both in ecological terms and also in terms of human suffering. The environmental crisis is due to our thinking of ourselves as separate, with no forward thought for the world that we, and our descendants of the future, will have to inhabit. For the creatures that call themselves "homo sapiens sapiens" (the beings that are aware that they are aware) we sure know how to avoid thinking ahead.

This separateness is not only with regard to the flora and landscape around us. This separateness from the animal kingdom, from the grand scheme of things, has led to horrible acts such as genocide within our very own species. When we see another being as different from ourselves, like the generations of Africans who were denied any rights and taken as slaves due to their "non-human nature", we can commit travesties of epic proportions.

Paganism seeks to heal the wounds that separateness causes. Like the spider, seeing that the threads of its web have been damaged, we seek to rebuild those threads so that the whole web gains its inherent integrity once again.

If nature is regarded as the physical force of cause and effect that regulates the phenomena of the world, it becomes separate from us. I would posit that even though we may honour deities of nature, Mother Earth, Sabrina the River Goddess, Grandmother Spider – we are not separate from these deities. We are all made of the same star-stuff that created this universe. Indeed, if nature is the physical cause and effect that regulates the phenomena of the world, then just what are we doing when we make changes to our environment? Are we somehow affecting an inalterable law of nature? Not in the least. Mother Nature is described in the OED as *nature personified as a creative and controlling force affecting the world and humans*. This description could also be applied to my next door neighbour who grows his own vegetables and has his own chickens.

The second definition of nature is less acrimonious to the Pagan, and has a policy of less exclusion.

2. *the basic or inherent features, character, or qualities of something: helping them to realize the nature of their problems e.g. there are a lot of other documents of that nature*
 • *the innate or essential qualities or character of a person or animal: it's not in her nature to listen to advice; I'm not violent by nature*
 • *[mass noun] inborn or hereditary characteristics as an influence on or determinant of personality.*

The first part of this definition mentions basic or inherent features. These features are those which define us and which also bring us together. My genetic history defines my physical body, with the colour of my eyes and hair, my height and arthritis, linking me to all my past ancestors. This makes me distinct from my husband, and yet we still share an ancestral bond that binds us together, both being human.

The second part mentions innate or essential qualities or character of a person or animal. Leaving aside the fact that humans are animals, we can explore nature not only on a genetic and physical level here, but also on a spiritual level. What is the nature of a Pagan?

There are so many different branches of Paganism, and yet they all stem from the same tree, that of a deep sense of honour and respect for nature. This manifests itself in a myriad ways, each specific to a person, or even a tradition. Yet there is an overarching sense of the sacredness of everything, the sacredness of nature that defines the nature of the Pagan. This can manifest itself in deities of the landscape, or of the elements – but it can also manifest in deities of our own nature.

We have created many Pagan deities of human nature – deities of love and lust, of war and of death, fertility deities and gods of travel, music and poetry. Within Paganism, we have taken these aspects of human nature and deified them in order to better understand them. It is difficult to have a relationship with something as abstract as the notion of love or death, but if we deify this we can relate to it as something that is both within ourselves and also external, so that we can talk to it, pray to it or simply honour it for something that is "bigger" than ourselves.

What is our nature? Within Buddhism, Buddha nature, or true self, otherwise known as "original or pure mind" is the nature of all beings. It is their current state – and all beings may achieve enlightenment. It states that Buddha is not separate. In fact, a common Zen saying is that when you see Buddha on the road, you should kill him, for he cannot exist outside of our selves. It is the inherent nature of *all* things.

In Zen, the goalless goal is to achieve "pure mind", that which is not dualistic, something that is completely and utterly at one with the rest of nature. This integration is a simple philosophy, and yet can be terribly hard to achieve after so much time has been spent in our human history divorcing ourselves from nature. This state of pure mind is achieved by looking at every-thing with "beginner's mind". Beginner's mind is always open, never closed – it is always looking at something as if it were the first time. It is an anathema to say, "Oh, I know all about that," with beginner's mind. It is the wondrous mind of the child. By using beginner's mind we can achieve Buddha nature, where the sense of self dies every moment in order that we can become aware of our oneness with the universe.

Pagans often notice that sense of wonder in the natural world around us, and within us. The exquisite sunset over the ridge; the soft caress of a lover; the power and beauty of a horse running free. We see ourselves as a part of all of that, and know that it is something to be cherished. We are watching the sunset and we are the sunset.

So, what is the nature of all things? As a Pagan, student of Zen and a Druid, I would posit that the nature of all things is simply to be – to let the song flow freely and to both hear and allow others' songs to flow. Where a song is discordant, no longer natural, we can work to make it harmonise once again with nature, through whatever means we have.

What is the natural world? The natural world is everything, us included. It is the beautiful field that has just been ploughed, the towering clouds of a thunderstorm. It is also the computer in front of me that I am currently using to write this essay. It is everything that we see, hear and feel. Human nature is also Nature. There are some glorious aspects of nature, and there are some horrific ones. As Pagans, we celebrate the glorious aspects of nature, and work to resolve those that are not in harmony with the continued cycle. We protest at clear-cut logging camps, we write letters to our MPs on the badger cull and we volunteer at a women's shelter. We dance in the light of the moon, we write poetry whilst sat on a city park bench and we meditate in the stillness of twilight at our altars. We acknowledge that we are a part of the cycle of life and death, and find our place in that cycle. It is, quite simply, the nature of our way. In seeing the divinity within nature, we also see the nature of the divine.

Joanna van der Hoeven is a Druid, the Director of Gypsy

Dreams Belly Dance and author of *Pagan Portals: Zen Druidry*. She was born in Canada and moved to the UK in 1998. She enjoys horse-riding, hiking, camping, singing and reading. She lives in East Anglia, UK.

Rebecca Beattie

In 1917, the author and poet, Mary Webb, wrote that in life:

> We need no great gifts – the most ignorant of us can draw deep breaths of inspiration from the soil. The way is through love of beauty and reality, and through absorbed preoccupation with those signs of divinity that are like faint, miraculous foot-prints across the world.

Webb believed that both healing and inspiration were to be found in Nature, and that a person who connected to nature, connected to the 'cosmic life'. The essay from which this quote is taken was entitled *Vis Medicatrix Naturae*, (the Latin translates as 'The Healing Powers of Nature'). Webb was well qualified to comment on the healing powers of nature. All through her adult life she suffered from Graves' disease, a condition of the thyroid, and at that time, there was no effective medical treatment. Webb, like most patients with Graves' disease at the time, was prescribed peaceful time outdoors.

Webb lived much of her life immersed in nature in her home county of Shropshire. She practiced meditation in nature, and used the practice of nature mysticism to draw inspiration for her writing, as well as to connect to the divine. But lest we think that her philosophy would exclude those of us that dwell in cities, Webb also said that 'nothing need cut man off from nature – even in the town there is the window box, dogs, city birds.' Webb also spent some time in London, and wrote her most famous book, *Precious Bane*, whilst living in Hampstead.

As a person who connects to the divine in Nature whilst

living in the city, there is much wisdom to be found in Webb's words. I was recently asked, 'How do you maintain a nature-based practice living in the city?' and the question took me by surprise. While the idealised image of the crone's cottage in the woods might be very appealing, the reality is quite different for many of us who follow a nature-based path. The practicalities of modern life mean a large proportion of the population lives within the metropolis, and yet this does not deter most pagans from following their practices.

While my childhood was spent in a very remote, rural setting where nature was hard to miss, even in the city there are the signs of nature wherever we go. We can find healing and a sense of peace and connection to something much bigger than we are, in the smallest details of nature all around us. At the time of writing, spring feels as if it will never come this year; the sun still has the cold chill of winter, the hawthorn hedges in Bloomsbury are still tightly budded, and the sap sleeps deep within the plane trees that line the streets. And yet the promise of spring is still there. Amidst the noise and chaos of the city, there are sanctuaries found within the wild places that sit between the worlds; those liminal spaces that are not quite the city, and yet not the countryside. There is peace to be found in the smallest of city gardens, and healing found amongst the birds and the flowers. Crocuses carpet the grass, a woodpecker drills for a home amongst the trees in the square. The robins and blackbirds still sing joyfully in the mornings, and foxes can still be seen slinking through the night. The city parks are full of dog walkers, enjoying the fresh air, the grass verges sprout camomile in the summer, and squirrels are busy touting for attention all year round.

Sometimes one needs to be attentive to the smallest details, because therein lies the common connection to the divine in our multitude of paths. True connection and peacefulness happens when we see those beautiful details, and stop to pause, and be mindful.

Ngatina Purnell-Webb

The wheel stands between Samhain and Alban Arthan, daybreak is just a breath away from icy so I brace myself as I step outside for some water. While the kettle is filling I notice that the gate has been left open, so in the walk to close it I open myself to my surroundings, allowing myself to feel totally present.

The view this morning in the desert is idyllic; the last two days have been blessed rainy, grey, wet affairs and now, as the sun rises over the horizon, the day dawns clear and bright. A mist rises from the damp ground, twisting around the legs of the horses grazing in the distance and contrasting against the inky black of the ravens flying in front of ruined chimneys. The river red gums in the distance are silver silhouettes in the haze and the ranges of ancient mountains glow softly behind them.

As I breathe in, the cool crisp air clears my lungs and mind and my thoughts flow to the sounds of the magpies warbling their joy in the sunrise and then a raven's caw echoes out, reminding me that even in this land far from her ancestral home, The Morrigan walks with me. Flocks of galahs call in raucous chorus and draw my eye to the patterns they create with their seemingly choreographed aerobatics, holding my attention until they disappear into the misty distance.

The gate is closed now but I feel centred and almost meditative so I continue to circle my yard, sunwise, and inspect the results of the rain on my gardens and contemplate how as a Druid and permaculture gardener, I am weaving the magic of nature – shaping the world around me in a physical sense by planting the garden and returning trees to this parched landscape but also growing my own roots through that immersion in my environment.

My mind wanders to the time I spend travelling in the city, wondering how I can keep this deep, soft spiritual calm alive amongst the rush and hard edges of millions of people living together. Then I recall an afternoon in a park, sitting with an old jacaranda... with my back pressed to the rough bark and the neat blades of grass beneath my feet I slide into its calm as cars streak past us and the noise of the city falls back like a wave retreating from the shore. Time seems to become thickly fluid, like honey, and I feel us a slowed focus in the time-lapse image of urban life...

This then is today's lesson – that no matter where you are, you can find the deep peace of nature if you choose to seek it.

Beverley Price

When asked what first brought me to paganism I always answer that it was the film The Craft that first got me interested in paganism. However, when I sit back and truly think about what first got me into paganism, it was not the film, all that did was give me a name for something I already was, a believer in the power of nature.

I did not have a happy childhood, as was bullied, so I lost myself in nature. She never hurt me, she never ganged up on me, she did not tell me to be quiet, that I was a nobody. In fact, I always felt like a somebody in her presence. I eventually found a place of solace within nature from these terrible bullies, and that was by a river that had a huge stone on its bank, with no rhyme or reason for it being there.

So many a broken hearted days were spent with my tears, and sometimes blood mingling with the waters of the river, as she soothed me like a mother, like the Great Mother. I would go there on "good days" and share with the river, food, drink, flowers, and badly written poetry, yes I did that even then. I did not understand or know about the concept of offerings. I just had these things and I want to share them with the river spirit. I knew the river had a "life" to it, this River Bran, named after the eponymous hero of the Welsh myth, but to me the river did not feel male, it felt female. I made the leap to the river being a Goddess.

An old people's home was placed in the bowl in the land, right next to the river. Of course, being Wales and the amount of rain we have, it was not long before the river bursts its banks, threatening the lives of many old age pensioners. Chaos and madness always happen. After this had happened half a dozen times, the council decided the best thing would be to change the course of the river, and then it would not burst its banks at that point any more. No one thought to move the people, or more sensibly to not put them there in the first place.

So over the next year or so, the river's course was moved. After they had finished the work, I returned to the river, and the energy that I had known was gone, part of this was due to the fact that "my spot" no longer existed, but more importantly the river was "dead". What had once been a river of substance and speed had been reduced to a mere trickle, and the trout that had always been aplenty in that river died also. The bureaucrats got what they wanted, the river never did burst its banks again.

Marie Strang

I lived out in the country when I was a little kid. Our neighbor was a grandmotherly woman who had forty acres of red pine trees with paths among them. I would go out there by myself and wander among the trees. I swear they were my friends. Beyond the pines there was a hill and more paths and other trees and a marsh. One day I sat on that hill and was still and quiet for a long time. I felt a presence, something special, something divine coming from the trees and plants and land. I went home and told my mother that "the woods was my church" and I have felt that way ever since.

There is something special about oaks, too. I remember there was a stand of woods by the village church and all of us neighborhood kids played on these two ancient oaks that we called the Grandmother Tree and the Grandfather Tree. They were huge and easy to climb. There were books and toys stashed in them by who knows how many kids. I don't think the adults knew about them at all. The grandparent oaks were a special, secret place only us kids knew about.

When I was eight, we moved from the country to the city and I've had the feeling that I left a big part of me behind, out in the woods. I never adjusted to city life. I was miserable there. I "pined" away for my trees! I live in a small town now and we have an ordinary sized lot. I have a garden, and a few trees (including maples, which I also love) but I wish I lived on several acres of woods. I will always find my spirituality in Nature.

Ethics

Emma Restall Orr

A principal justification for many a religion has been the issue of ethics. It is stated that without God, divine scripture, or the interpretations of such writings by the initiated and wise, a human being will stumble, blind and unguided. If a religion, however, is defined and validated by its having a clear code of ethics inspired by its understanding of deity, at first glance Paganism doesn't appear to fulfil the criteria.

To start with, Paganism is not a single religion. The common categories of Wicca, Heathenism, Druidry, are easy distinctions to make, but in reality Paganism is an umbrella term for a vast number of traditions, each one the accumulation of countless years and stories, formed by particular places, people, events and memories. These traditions are further subdivided into groups, groves, hearths, covens, for which the acknowledgement and celebration of local heritage, the stories of a town and its surrounding landscape, are a crucial part of what forms and identifies that group, whether it meets for ritual, for teaching or purely for social purposes. The history of that group is often equally important, its priests or teachers having a known line of heredity back to priests or teachers of note, all these elements making each group distinctly unique, that uniqueness adding to its value and apparent standing.

Not only each tradition, then, but each group in Paganism may present the sacred in its own particular way, according to the context of its evolution and its immediate reality, influenced by what is abundant or scarce, threatening or comforting, in its political and social circumstance, its geographic locality. As notions of sanctity are honed, so are values agreed, those values ordering priorities that then inform and fuel each decision that is made and accepted. So ethics are crafted, rationalising and justifying those choices, uniquely.

With no centralised point of authority, what is considered ethical within Paganism as a whole is consequently enormously diverse. Indeed, the diversity of Pagan practices is a large part of its attraction for many, encouraging as it does the idea of personal exploration and self-expression. The notion of individualism now so fashionable within Western cultures is enthusiastically seized upon by Pagans. The rights of the individual are seen as fundamental, providing the opportunity for personal empowerment, the permission for self-realisation. A person's bloodline and life experience, their own visions and insights, are widely accepted as potent influences, often regarded as no less important than the consensus, or the views of elders within the group or its broader community.

This relativism may be extended further: to ideas of truth. Without a transcendent deity, a creator God who exists outside of nature, little thought is given to the concept of a universal truth. Instead, many Pagans acknowledge that each subject, each individual, perceives the world differently, and that it is through one's own perception that one's own truth is formed. To the animist, who deems soul or mind to be present throughout nature, this relativist truth may be augmented: if mind – perception, sentience, experience-ability, however it is languaged – is fundamental to the nature of the universe, truth, or reality, may be both insubstantial and subjective, while being metaphysically essential.

Polytheism, another core philosophy within Paganism, may also encourage a relativist perspective. Leaving aside the need for a distinct definition of deity, the polytheist accepts the existence of many gods, his devotional practice typically honouring a fair few. When in the 1990s I was working as a priest leading public rituals with hundreds in the circle, one of the joys was the recognition that within each gathering so many gods were acknowledged. It wasn't tolerance of others' theologies that allowed for peace at such events, but the celebration of what is Pagan religious heterogeneity. Yet, the study of and devotion to different gods has the effect of differently weighting priorities: a goddess of love, a god of growth and virility, the goddess of a certain river, the god of a specific tribe or landscape, gods of light and knowledge, gods of darkness and mystery, each fill the mind with particular thoughts, motivations, energies, altering or emphasising ideas of value, and drawing the individual to assess situations differently, to choose accordingly. Ethics become even more personal.

With pluralism such a fundamental premise of Paganism, many are more than happy to champion the notion that each distinct path, each group, or even each individual, might feasibly have its or their own code of ethics.

Twenty-first century Pagans, however, are quite different from those of thirty years ago or so. Numbers are growing, to the extent that many are now seeking acceptance within society more generally: Pagans are expressing the desire to take holy days as holidays from work, wanting their children's faith to be recognised in schools, hoping their spiritual needs will be taken care of in hospitals, and so forth. Proffering an understanding of Paganism that is broadly comprehensible, and valid for the majority of Pagan paths, may now be advantageous. If that understanding were to encompass a general set of values, those values could be presented as the basis for a code of ethics, and as such Paganism may be more easily appraised and accepted.

Seeking commonality for this purpose, if there is a single belief that underlies a large proportion of Paganisms, that belief is usually acknowledged to be a profound respect for nature. This may be expressed as a devotional reverence for nature as deity, or as a more secular appreciation for nature as order and chaos, or indeed anything in between. It may include human nature, or may seek to understand nature as that unsullied by humanity. Yet, however it is approached, nature is always merciless. Discarding the anthropomorphised sentimentality and poetry of 'mother nature', in its actuality and totality nature is neither gendered nor caring. It does not judge and it is not fair. Even with an embracing goddess at the centre of a pantheon, few Pagans would dismiss the reality of nature's brutal amorality. Nature, then, cannot provide us with an ethical compass.

For most Pagans, however, nature is not an authority that must be obeyed. Nature is instead a teacher, and one of its crucial lessons is that of context. Everything exists within an ecosystem, ecosystems being layered within ecosystems, each a complex pattern of interaction, influence and relationship. Nothing is isolated, nothing is alone. Every atom, organism, sentience, is connected within the whole, unfolding through time and space, moment evolving into moment.

Upon this foundational premise, not only is it accepted that every thought and action has an effect, but every decision that is made consciously must take into account its specific context. Different circumstances, available resources, language, culture and comprehension, different biological and emotional states, all suggest that our actions may result in different effects, different consequences. What can be reasoned as ethically correct in one situation may not be justified in another. What may be life-threatening there may be harmless here.

As the Pagan's primary teacher, nature appears then to sanction ethical relativism.

However, if Pagans are to proclaim the relativist argument, any scepticism about it must also be addressed. There are many thinkers who vigorously argue against the stance, presenting a good number of different reasons for doing so. I shall offer just two, the key criticism being in itself both compelling and comprehensive: relativism can be used as a way of justifying almost any behaviour at all, with any negative judgement being rebutted with an accusation of prejudice, dogma or ignorance.

For example, many in the West deem the female circumcision

practised in some African societies as the abhorrent and abusive genital mutilation of young girls, but its proponents argue that such claims are arrogant expressions of cultural prejudice. Reversing the perspective, one living in accordance with Sharia law may feel allowing young girls in our culture the freedoms they have is no less than abusively negligent parenting, putting them at risk of sexual predation or worse, while the Western youngster may feel she is perfectly entitled to dress and roam as she wishes. If relativism is a truly valid ethical framework, the challenge is to accept that what is understood as *right*, or indeed *real*, across the human world is extremely diverse.

A further criticism levelled at relativism is that it risks the mistake of drawing an imagined perimeter of cause and effect around an action. The consequences of a particular event are in some way seen to be limited by the isolation of the event, but such an attitude denies nature's principal teaching: that everything is connected. The demand for cheap products in the West is encouraging environmental and social devastation in the East, for example. Domestic violence within one family affects a whole community.

Yet, if we were to put relativism to one side, what would be the alternative?

An interesting possibility could be presented as the opposite premise: what if every choice we made were only valid if it were valid for everyone?

As I turn off a forgotten light, I might ponder that if every household in Britain used just five minutes less electricity every day, in one day the accumulated saving would add up to 230 years of continuous electricity use. That is thinking nationally; taking it globally quickly produces inconceivably large numbers. If every person consumed as much as the average American, we would need five planets to resource the consumption. To dismiss the challenge with regard to equality can seem painfully arrogant and selfish: as I have the resources for a hot bath every day, why shouldn't I have one? What does it have to do with me if billions of humans don't? Yet what resources would be needed for every person to have the same?

Determining ethics with a universalising perspective is also interesting if we consider the decisions we make that are founded on emotional states of mind. Being in company with someone who is miserable with self-pity, who is bitter with unresolved issues, who acts aggressively with misplaced frustration, can be very unpleasant. Universalising, asserting our own right to be angry is to sanction a very angry world. Making the effort needed to find peace may feel excruciatingly hard, but if everyone were to make that effort the world would be quite different. Others may not follow, but what if we were to begin?

Thinking universally beautifully inspires charters of global ethics, such as those promoting human (and other) rights. Yet the weakness is indisputable. A universal ethics risks being irrelevant, inappropriate, its imposition seeming dogmatic and prescriptive. In Paganism, any form of absolutism is treated with rank suspicion: the authoritative voice of a single God is broadly rejected.

However, if we were to consider the notion of a single universal deity from a Pagan perspective, using Pagan language and values, what emerges is far from the feared autocratic overseer. Earlier I mentioned the belief systems of animism and polytheism common within Paganism. A third is pantheism. For some, comprehensive animism rationally entails pantheism, but for others pantheism is the foundation of their theology: simplistically put, god is nature, nature is god, nature being the term used to denote the limitless entirety of everything. The reason for using the word 'god', or even God, is to emphasise the gloriously incomprehensible totality that is the actuality of the universal whole.

Common to most religious and spiritual paths, for the majority of Pagans, the practice of their tradition is neither complex nor demanding. Living busy lives, working hard, bringing up families, the crucial element is the sense of being a part of a social network of like-minded people, the community providing support for the individual as he builds a coherent and healthy sense of who he really is, developing self-confidence, self-expression, self-responsibility and creativity.

As within any other tradition, there are some for whom this is not sufficient. They are not only not satisfied with this level of spiritual study, but they are willing to make the necessary compromises and put in the considerable work required to find what is beyond the apparent. It is not enough for the unknowable to be an abstraction, a mere idea: the sincere seeker craves experience and understanding of what may just be beyond the ability to perceive, or indeed beyond perception.

The problem with such journeys is that they can only be taken alone, each traveller using their own language to describe what is beyond the scope of words. Across the board, what is most commonly alluded to, however, is an otherwise unimaginable experience of wholeness, a sense of complete integration, beyond separation, the self's edges eroding until there is no individual self at all.

The motivation for such a journey may be articulated very personally. For myself this level of seeking is not just a desire to experience and to be in communion with deity: it is also an ethical compulsion, an investigation of how we make decisions, the search to understand the nature of free will.

Such ideas have been investigated by philosophers and theologians for millennia. From a Pagan perspective, the reverence for nature inspires the study of the forces of human nature, exploring the surging powers of emotion, the perpetuating currents of habit, the self-reflecting mechanisms of human consciousness, all of which put into question the notion of free will within the comprehensive fabric of nature as a whole. Even somersaulting through the mental acrobatics of reason and logic, the self quickly disintegrates. Stepping beyond theory, diving into the mystical adventure, the layers and patterns of the self are revealed, the edges of the individual at first blurring, then fully dissolving. The selfless state is not one within which we can function. Time and space, as perceptive tools, produce the sense of separation which creates a subject and object, a you and me, allowing for the relationships that make up our human reality. However, this very real and personal experience of complete integration can inspire profound human ethics. When the *I* becomes *we*, decisions begin to reflect a wish to co-operate, sharing resources with care. Needs are whittled away, desires showing themselves to be wider forces of nature's will. When the *we* further dissolves into the ocean of *being*, the effect on our ethics is far deeper than empathy. Indeed, the more of the self that is lost into the wholeness of being, the less the self is used as a guide in the world of form and separation, and the more fundamental is the effect of that complete and formless whole.

In Paganism, then, the authoritative voice of a single God as loving father or judge is not the source of ethics. Returning to the question and definition with which I began this piece, I would suggest that it is nonetheless a potent understanding of deity – god as nature – that may provide Paganism with its code, nature being not a dictator but a powerful teacher. As such, Paganism can indeed be seen as a set of related religious traditions.

Such an ethical code is in part relativistic, requiring that each decision be made with a comprehensive and wakeful acknowledgement of the immediate context, with all its layers of ecosystems and interwoven relationships. However, its code also requires deference to the fact that every aspect of that context is essentially rooted deep within the *totality* of nature, and the effect of that moment's decision will shimmer through every part of the whole.

Yet such an understanding only goes so far. Where the

practice of Paganism is truly ethical, it is because the *experience* of that divine wholeness is also present, flowing into the teachings together with an understanding of will, and influencing each decision with the wisdom of selfless responsibility.

Emma Restall Orr (aka Bobcat) has been one of the most well-known Druids worldwide for over a decade. She worked for the Order of Bards Ovates and Druids, was Joint Chief of the British Druid Order for nearly ten years, and in 2002 created the international Druid Network. She is celebrated for her uncompromising views on ethics, environmentalism and personal responsibility, challenging the Druid and Pagan community with her writings, talks and other public appearances. She is the author of a number of books including *Living With Honour*, *Kissing the Hag* and *The Wakeful World*.

Heather Artfich-Staniszewski

As with beliefs and practices, Neopagan ethics can vary. But most Neopagans share the same ethic of doing no harm and the basic values of religious freedom, reverence for nature, equality of the sexes, and openness to forms of sexuality. Below are some more specific ethical guidelines given by the Wiccan path.

The Wiccan Rede

Wiccan morality is ruled according to the Wiccan Rede, which (in part) states "An it harm none, do what thou wilt." ("An" is an archaic word meaning "if".)

Others follow the slightly adapted Rede of "An it harm none, do what ye will; if harm it does, do what ye must." Either way, the Rede is central to the understanding that personal responsibility, rather than a religious authority, is where moral structure resides.

A common belief amongst Wiccans is that no magic, even of a beneficent nature, should be performed on any other person without that person's direct informed consent. This stems from the understanding that it would interfere with that person's free will and thus constitute "harm". So-called "love spells" are very much frowned upon by the greater Wiccan community for precisely this reason.

The Law of Threefold Return

Many Wiccans also promote the Law of Threefold Return, or the idea that anything that one does may be returned to them threefold. In other words, good deeds are magnified back to the doer, but so are ill deeds. In other words, if you cast for someone to sprain their ankle, you might break your leg and have to be in a cast three times as long as necessary.

The Threefold Law is sometimes stated like this:

Ever Mind The Rule Of Three
Three Times Your Acts Return To Thee
This Lesson Well, Thou Must Learn
Thou Only Gets What Thee Dost Earn.

Wicca Basic Code of Conduct

1. **IF** no one is harmed by your action (physically emotionally or spiritually) then do as you Will to do in Life, in accordance with your Higher Self. Seek your identity and your purpose.
2. **WHEN** someone does something good for you, then repay the kindness by doing something good for another person, so that the seed that was planted will bear fruit.
3. **KEEP** your word and your oaths, when you give them.
4. **DO NOT** kill anything except when food or protection are required.
5. **ACKNOWLEDGE** and give due reverence to your gods, observing all of the sacred times and festivals.
6. **BELITTLE** no one's belief, but simply offer what it is you believe to be true.

7. **STRIVE** to live in peace with those who differ from you.
8. **STRIVE** to be aware of those around you and seek compassion within yourself.
9. **BE** true to your own understanding and strive to turn away from what is opposed within you.
10. **HELP** others according to their need and according to your ability to give of yourself.
11. **RESPECT** nature and strive to live in harmony with Her.

Rhiannon Knott

For me ethics come naturally in living a pagan life.

The connection with spirit, be it of the land, elements, animals or humanity, becomes a whole, and with that deep connection comes an ethical code that emanates from within, from the heart. For example: The connection with the land promotes the desire to live lightly, to protect the land and preserve its sovereignty for future generations to learn from it, to carry on protecting it. Environmental issues and the need to become actively involved grows.

As the connection with the animal kingdom develops, so does the recognition of animals as equal spirits. There is a natural progression towards vegetarianism/veganism, and the desire to campaign and highlight animal rights.

With the expansion of the heart that paganism has brought me, the empathy and love that flows from my heart to the rest of humanity is undeniable. This has developed into the sending of love and healing to individuals, and also to the people of the world as part of daily practice. To become involved in human rights and to be available to others in any way I can offer help. This is my personal experience; it came from a place deep within, from the heart or maybe from a soul level.

So although paganism does not come with a text book or any other "code of ethics", it doesn't need to. What it has done for me is wake something at the core of my being that has enabled me to grow and expand in a way I could not have imagined.

Lisa Spiral Besnett

The most important thing about ethics is figuring out where you personally stand. In exploring Paganism your personal ethics will be challenged in many ways. Some of these will be really positive. Some will require you to make a choice between your ethics and working with a particular teacher or system of Paganism.

For many people the issue of working skyclad is the first challenge of their personal ethics. Most Pagans find that their issues about being skyclad are based in a culture of humiliation about body image that they work actively to reject. However, there may be other reasons skyclad work is a challenge. People with gender identity issues may find being skyclad casts them in gender roles they no longer find acceptable. Likewise victims of sexual abuse may find being skyclad too vulnerable, or being with others who are skyclad too challenging.

These are all personal challenges, but when you are looking to work with a group how those challenges are met can become ethical issues. As a leader in a group that often works skyclad I have been confronted by these issues many times over the years. I am aware that these issues come up at other Pagan events like festivals and even public rituals. Knowing when to face your personal fears and when to walk away can be very confusing. The line is different for everyone. Where do you think you stand?

Another place where people are often confronted with issues of ethics is in understanding the necessity of maintaining oathbound secrets. A good teacher can help you find an appropriate line that is respectful for the tradition and for you. Oathbound is necessary to respect the privacy of the others in the group. It allows for a level of intimacy in spiritual work. It also protects the integrity of the tradition. Oathbound also makes it ethically difficult to deal with a teacher who is abusive. It can be enough of a red flag for a councilor to encourage members to leave a group. It can isolate you from your friends and family who are not practicing in the tradition you have chosen. Again, knowing where your ethical boundaries are is key.

I am a firm advocate of choice. Be aware in your explorations that you always have choices. They may not always be pleasant choices to make, but they are yours. You can choose to face your fears and adjust the ethical boundaries that have protected you. You can choose to acknowledge your ethics and walk away from what you perceive to be unethical behavior. This is your personal spiritual journey and where questioning your ethics may be a big part of your path, maintaining your personal integrity is also important. Make your choices well.

Mary Caelsto

As a pagan, one of the most empowering things about my belief system is that each of us creates our own relative truth. We view each experience in our lives through the filter of our own past experiences and beliefs, arriving at the truth of the situation. Other individuals involved in the same scenario can view the situation through their own lenses, sometimes coming up with a completely different explanation for events. Along with relative truth, the phrase "personal responsibility" comes up, for each of us must take responsibility not just for our own actions, but for the effects they have on other individuals. This is the whole of the three-fold law. That what we do—for good or ill—comes back to us three times as strong as when we sent it.

If we cannot take personal responsibility for the entirety of our actions, including how they affect other individuals, then we are failing to live in accordance with our spiritual laws. Though the intent to not cause harm is a noble one, if our actions do cause harm, then we must take responsibility for that fact.

It is there, at the intersection of our laws and relative truth that many pagans fall short in practicing the very ethics in which they believe. Clergy may defend their actions by saying that they cannot be responsible for what they do when they teach certain lessons. Allegations of abuse brought to senior priests and priest-esses may fall on deaf ears, with the individual being told that she or he created the reality, thus, there can be no responsibility on the other side for the abusive actions. These two examples are many where the relativism discussed in the earlier essay, is used to justify very hurtful and harmful behavior.

As pagans, it is easy to look at a situation from the outside and believe that we see very stark black and white contrasts between the behavior. We then apply our own relative truth to the situation. We state that someone is, or isn't, taking responsibility, and we declare someone right in the situation. That's easy to do when we're not involved.

When we are, however, it's more difficult, because we always want to be the person who is "right". It's human nature. We want to claim that we are taking responsibility for our actions. Only a thoughtful and careful scrutiny of behavior can determine if that is the case, and such scrutiny, if not done by everyone in the situation can lead to a piling on or mobbing scenario. In a church or coven situation, the results of such a scenario can be catastrophic.

In order to live the ethics to which we subscribe, pagans don't have to get rid of the doctrine of relativism. They do, however, need to understand that all parties in a situation have personal responsibility and when malicious or unethical behavior occurs, it needs to be called out for what it is. If someone does so, then they should not be shamed or treated as if they were the wrong doer. Instead, a careful examination of the situation, including the actions of all parties, will reveal the truth. It is up to every pagan, especially those who wear the title of priest, priestess, or clergy, to understand this and not to use relativism to justify behavior which under any other circumstances would be considered hurtful and wrong. Due to its continual mainstreaming, we have a responsibility to represent paganism in a strong, positive light. Ensuring our belief in relativism doesn't go unchecked, is one way to do so, and to continue to portray the strong ethics as defined by the three-fold rule and "harm none".

Afterlife

Mabh Savage

Of course, and you will tire of hearing this, Pagan is an inexplicably broad term; an umbrella not large enough to keep dry the hordes that shelter beneath its holey and perhaps even holy material; stretched thin to breaking point as more and more non-Abrahamic religions, spiritual paths and ways of life huddle together under this catch-all term. So is there a 'Pagan Afterlife'? There really is no simple answer to this question. Through my own views, the views of those close to me and others I have interviewed, plus research done online and from books, it is clear that like most aspects of Paganism, you may get twenty different answers though you ask twenty Pagans who all claim to follow the same path. Some Pagans devotedly follow the ideas set down by their ancestors, or by those who penned the myths that led to the traditions they follow. Others, though they follow a path that is widely associated with ideas such as reincarnation or the Summerlands, have no belief in an afterlife at all and simply believe that their energy will flow into the universe once expended upon death. The universal truth is that the definition of afterlife becomes more and more personal and individual the closer a person holds their spiritual path to their heart.

Death. Instantly you feel something. Fear? Curiosity? Uncertainty? Death is a constant; something that will happen to us all. A transition from one state to another. The end of a journey. The ultimate apex, or the lowest trough. What is not constant is our understanding of what happens next. The uncertainty about death has, since man began, led us to wonder about what is next. Where do we go? Do we go anywhere? Are we simply ended, or are we transformed from our fleshy bodies to another state of being? Most religions have spent a great deal of time trying to answer these questions. An afterlife that rewards actions in this life is obviously a keen selling point for many Abrahamic religions, but what about those of us on a different path?

The term 'Pagan' often goes hand in hand with 'Wiccan', but this is incredibly inaccurate. Wicca is a hugely popular religion (apologies to those Wiccans that don't view themselves as religious) but it is certainly not the be all and end all of modern Paganism or Neo-Paganism. I myself am a member of the Covenant of Hekate, a group that seeks to understand the mysteries of Hekate as not just a goddess but a Cosmic World Soul; a force of nature. Various forms of Hellenic (ancient Greek) religion, worship and belief are followed today. The first thing we may think of when we look to the ancient Greek afterlife is Elysium, or the Elysian fields. This is a place akin to Paradise for those related to gods, heroes, righteous men and warriors of the people. This is a theme that crops up many times: the afterlife as a reward for excellence in life. And why not? When you live a life fraught with danger, disease and the daily risk of death, the idea of a wondrous place you will enter upon your demise is indeed comforting. The idea that you must prove yourself worthy though; what better way to motivate your fellow man to strive above his station, than to fill him with the notion that his gods will reward him for his achievements? I think this is one of the many areas where the Abrahamic religions differ from most polytheistic systems; certainly in every deviation of Christianity I have come across, *every* man is granted access to heaven as long as he is good, kind, follows the ten commandments, repents of his sins and so on and so forth. There is no extra reward for being a great person; no motivation to strive to succeed. Perhaps this is a good thing; should one really have to be a better person than one's fellow man to be rewarded by the gods? By only rewarding the great and the strong, are we belittling the daily gifts of the kind and gentle soul? A debate not soon to be finished, I feel.

Modern day Hellenic Polytheists, like most Pagans, believe a variety of things about the afterlife. One lady believes that the

Chaldean Oracles hold the answer; upon death her soul will cross the rivers of the underworld, to meet the Goddess Hekate at a triple crossroads. There she will either be reincarnated, go to Tartarus for punishment or rest peacefully in Elysium. She also believes that the soul never resides permanently in these places, but may evolve and move; for example from Tartarus, the soul may be reincarnated to learn more. Another follower refers to Orphic teachings that tell us that the soul travels through the underworld and has a choice to drink at two fountains; one fountain will make the soul forget what it has learned in the last life, and the other will enable it to retain the memory of all that it has achieved.

Ideas of paradise and reincarnation are certainly not unique to the Hellenic systems though. Reincarnation pops up again and again throughout various Pagan paths. The idea that you will return, with no memory of your former life, but with perhaps some inner wisdom gleaned from your prior experiences; this is a popular belief and one that is perhaps easy to identify with, as none of us remember what came before we were born and none can say for sure what happens after, so the idea that we have been here before and are simply taking a different journey across the same landscape is interesting indeed. Are we instantly reincarnated upon death? Opinions certainly differ on this. There is a place mentioned among Wiccans, and others on a similar path, called The Summerland (or Summerlands), which is very similar to the Celtic Tír na nÓg; a resting place of peace or rejuvenation before reincarnation. Similar themes appear in modern Heathenry, and also on eclectic paths that take aspects from many religions.

When asking a few of my peers what they feel will happen to them when they die, often this has surprisingly little to do with their religious path. One lady, who is on a Wiccan path, wanted very much to return as a tree; *not* in the sense that she believes she will be reincarnated as a tree. She wants the full physical transformation of her body decomposing and being absorbed as nutrients for the natural world. Specifically she would like to become part of an Oak tree, as this is a tree she feels a close connection to in her life, and on her spiritual path. Companies such as Bios Urn are realising this wish while encouraging the sustainability of the planet by providing burial urns which literally transform your ashes into the tree of your choice. Another belief is that our consciousness itself is a form of energy and as such cannot be destroyed; only transformed. One lady who simply describes herself as 'Pagan' said she believes consciousness continues after death, depending on what level of awareness has been attained. One's consciousness may cling to illusions of individuality and personality, lingering in a self-created reality, the shape of which has its source in one's own beliefs. She believes that ultimately though, all consciousness will return to one higher, universal state of divine consciousness that we may call God or Goddess. This is not an individual consciousness or being, but the culmination of all consciousness; it *is* consciousness itself. She describes this as 'a creative moving shifting quantum field from which everything is made'.

So perhaps it is possible that we create our own afterlife, based on what we believe in hardest; what we cling to most desperately, and only by letting go of these beliefs do we become one with the universe.

Many Pagan paths have their roots in Celtic tradition, but the Celts had confusing ideas about life and death. They had many objects that could both kill *and* restore life to those fallen, with no mention as to where the victim had resided before rising again. Those of us who still follow the legends and stories of the Celts believe that when we die, we go the way of the Tuatha de Danaan; slipping sideways to the sun, moving out of sight but never out of mind; still a part of the world, but unperceivable to those who consider themselves 'alive'. This could be Tír na nÓg, the land of eternal youth, where years pass by in an instant; a physical island, but with no sickness, hunger or pain.

We don't think of travelling here as a death; it's another stage of existence. The pain, the loss and the *end* of the previous life, certainly that is a death. And we rail against it, like all mortal beings. We *want* to live. We know we are where we are meant to be right now, and by our gods and ancestors, we want to carry on being there! But when our time comes, though fear and pain may walk with us, we know that once we come to the end of the path, we will exist again in another world. We will walk side by side with our ancestors; we always have done, but now we will be able to see them, speak to them and learn even more about this amazing universe we live in. And when we have been here a while? If we feel the world of the 'living' has more to offer us, more to help us grow and change and evolve, we can return. We will be reborn, or reincarnated, as another normal person, perhaps even one of our own descendants. Or, because time has no meaning beyond the veil that separates the realms, we may return as one of our own ancestors. What happens if we do not return? Do we stay forever in the otherworld? Or if we feel we have learned all we can, do we simply become a part of the universe; a gear in the endless machine of life itself?

Another ancient people, the Norse (another umbrella term), had the well-known Valhalla and the less famous Fólkvangr, specifically for those that have fallen in battle. But what was there for the common man? Well, when one died, one 'went to Hel', which of course is a common enough phrase within many mainstream religions today. But the Hel of Norse mythology was the daughter of the 'god' Loki. Hel guarded the underworld at the base of the world tree Yggdrasil. Those who died in everyday circumstances, from among the nine worlds Hel has authority over, found themselves in Niflheim; a cold and icy world on the edge of Muspelheim, the world of fire. Niflheim is the realm and halls of the dead alone, but where the frigid ice meets the intense heat of Muspelheim, life is supposedly created from the steamy drama of the clash of these two worlds. This seems to me to be a perfect symbol of the continuity of life: although we die, and go to rest, in our passing there is the chance for something new to be born.

Generally we coin the term Ásatrú to describe a current faith or veneration of the Norse pantheon. Other followers of Norse beliefs refer to themselves as Heathens. The original meaning of this was simply 'not Christian or Jewish'; while accurate, the word 'heathen' has taken on, for many, a much more specific and personal meaning. Within groups of Heathens there are also groups and individuals that follow very specific aspects of the Æsir or Vanir, and so we see coined terms such as Odinism, Forn Sed and The Northern Tradition. All these paths stem from the same Norse roots, though there may be as many branches as Yggdrasil itself. But do they all end in the same place? Where do modern Heathens believe they will end up when they are parted from this mortal coil? According to 'The Asatru Community', an online information portal and place for Heathens and Pagans to meet, Helheim, the Realm of Hella (Hel) is still widely believed in as a place of peace and rest. However, there are many other beliefs too. If you worship one god or goddess in particular, your spirit or soul may reside in their hall for eternity. Another concept is the aforementioned belief in reincarnation, although it seems in Heathenry it is more common to be reincarnated in your own bloodline. If you name a child after an ancestor, the child may inherit that ancestor's soul. As such it is considered bad form indeed to name a child after a living relative, as it is tantamount to encouraging the death of the namesake.

Listening to accounts by modern day Heathens, there are different versions of the ancient beliefs. One Heathen voiced the belief that Hel is a place of rejuvenation before returning to this life, and that Niflheim is just one small part of this. This reminds me of the Wiccan idea of the Summerland, and also the Irish Celtic idea of Tír na nÓg. How many similarities there are, though the roots of these beliefs stem from all over the globe. Time and again though, what I have found in all my conversation with other Pagans, Heathen and otherwise is this: it doesn't matter. The afterlife is a fascinating subject, yes, and many people on a Pagan path have their own ideas about what will happen at the end. But what matters most is *life*: what you do with your life, how you live it, and the impact you make upon this world while you are alive.

I was stopped once in the street by a Mormon preacher; really nice guy: friendly, well-spoken and a good listener. He asked me about my religion and told me about his. He said the best thing about his religion was this: when he died, he knew he would go to a place where he would be with his loved ones for eternity, and so he had no fear of death. He asked me if I too would not want eternal life. Would I not want to see my son again one day, after I died? I replied that if I did the best I could while I was alive, and was a good mother to my son, and was kind, giving, honest and true to myself, then I was already ensuring my own immortality, because I would live on forever in the memory of my loved ones. They would pass that memory to their children, and so I would become eternal. My Pagan path teaches me to have responsibility for my own actions, rather than basing my ethics on the teaching of some great god or one ancient book. So at the end, my afterlife is the sum of my own actions and teachings. I couldn't ask for more than that.

Mabh Savage lives in Yorkshire, England, and was raised by Wiccan parents who had a passion for Celtic history, both mythological and actual. She is now involved with several Pagan groups and is exploring her heritage as a way to get closer to the world around her, and understand her ancestors more. She is the author of *A Modern Celt*

Hennie van Geel

Afterlife. Still life in whatever form we can imagine, so there seems to be nothing to worry about. Dying is a job we must do first. Somehow, though there is only life, life is broken into pieces and bits; one big bit being death.

We seem slowly to have forgotten what impact our death has to the people who are with us; even if you are just found years after dying, there will be a shock. When dying presents itself, the pain of saying 'fare thee well' is there. The goodbyes that are inevitable and saddening; worrying about funerals, coffins and after-funeral-meals. And oh, yes, your fear, suffering and not wanting to die just yet. One more day, please...

Afterlife, even my atheist friends somehow cannot grasp that someone who has died, is really gone, out of touch, never to be met again. The dying person knows all too well that they will never be the same person again after dying. At least, your body will be gone forever, at highest, there will be nothing to be aware of, which is somehow a comforting possibility.

Dying is hard labour. All day and all night. Someone fetching you a glass of water is bliss; being able to sleep a whole night long, is bliss; crying your eyes out without feeling ashamed is bliss. Perhaps sudden death is most blissful, who can tell?

no more thinking
no more brooding
on life's uncertainties

no more reality
no more illusion
of immortality

no more words
no more rhyme
the hush of sensibility

Sarah Carvey

Death is irrefutable.

We are designed to age, wither and cease to function. Physicality is finite. Once dead, burned or buried, we return to the bosom of Mother Nature. Biodegradable. The original recyclable. One again with Earth or atmosphere. To quote Max Erhman I am, "a Child of the Universe, no more nor less than the trees or stars."

My body shall rot and I shall become part of the plants and sod, sustenance and shelter for smaller creatures. Were this world to be destroyed, remnants of me shall be dispersed in the Universe; carbon atoms and matter. Reincarnated.

My 'immortality' is only guaranteed in the memories and impressions I leave with those in this world when I am gone; for them to filter down to future generations – to bind me to a family tree as my mortal shell becomes part of the Tree of Life.

What is stated above I know to be fact. Whether I have an immortal spirit or soul or if there is an afterlife is, for me, less certain. My personal view is that what happens once my body dies I simply do not know. I expect no Heavenly Home, nor Hellfire and Damnation. My only reward for a life well lived is the hope to die with an easy mind and few regrets. An 'afterlife' in spiritual terms is not a concept I can relate to nor claim to understand. My rational brain struggles with what I cannot perceive on this mortal plane.

I am not afraid of death. Death is natural. It defines our humanity and fragility. And if there is nothing more when I pass on I shall not be fearful. If I have a 'soul,' some energy or spirit that lingers after my earthly time is done, will it join with a greater ethereal, esoteric eternity? Eternity itself is beyond comprehension; indefinable, infinite, akashic – without beginning or end. If such a plane exists, perhaps on occasion it dips down into our present, revealing a glimpse of what is to come or what has gone before or perhaps what has always been there? Ghosts, angels, Gods; the supernatural by definition. For these occurrences I have no answer; but no question either. I am secure in what I understand and content to leave what is beyond my reason.

Should some Paradise or Purgatory exist – name it what you may – it is beyond my imagination. And should I be granted enlightenment in this inconceivable state, I shall be in awe. In wonderment. In trepidation.

Death is irrefutable.

Jay Cassels

The concept of dying terrifies us, for some it is a fear and for others it is an unknown which creates a fear. As a witch, a pagan and a spiritual medium, I tend not to be phased by the whole dying concept just the method on which I get to the other side, but I don't dwell on it. I would say that until I sat with my father and helped him cross over, this whole concept of dying didn't sit well with me. It wasn't fear or something I needed to be fearful of, I just didn't know.

It started me thinking about the concepts and ideas that we have, not just as pagans but as a culture and a society. There are degrees and levels in everything, but in this there are those who see death as the gateway to heaven and hell, those who see it as the Summerlands, those who see it as the spirit world and then those who see nothingness, that once the eyes close for that last time we cease to be.

What if, and bear with me on this, what if it is all of these things? What if the afterlife is the Summerlands, the spirit world, heaven and hell or perhaps nothing? Speaking with those who have passed over and walking with my father to the threshold between this life and the next, has made me realise that for those who pass, the next life – this afterlife – is whatever they need it to be to help them transition.

Death is not some six foot robed being, nor is Death a pretty young woman with a swirl; Death just is, if it helps think of it as a room; silver and grey with a light somewhere within it. This light is white and cosmic, beyond it is not for our mortal eyes to see. It is only for the eyes of those who are passing over.

No matter how we pass into the room, there is peace; no fire or brimstone, no meadows or gods; however, you are not alone. At that threshold between this life and what comes next, is family all those who have gone before us, and it is not limited to just the people; when I walked with my father, I saw not only his family, but also those from my mother's as well along with the animals that had been our companions. It is only after we cross into that light do we go where we belong. However, there is no need to take my word for it, you can find out for yourself when it is your time to pass.

As I stated at the start, the concept of dying terrifies us, but maybe, just maybe, having a little perspective and a belief in something that little bit bigger than the confines of our humanity may help to gives us hope that there is life after this one and we can continue and progress.

Andy Jaeger

Honouring my ancestors is an essential element of my practice as a pagan. It reminds me that I did not spring, fully formed and independent, into this world. I come from my ancestors. I am born from their bodies and I am inspired by their souls.

My mother died when I was a child. The loss was devastating. But in truth, being visited by death at a young age was a privilege and a gift. Death showed me that the life in my body is temporary, but that the life in my soul goes on.

I have often thought about what will happen to my body when I die. My mother's body was cremated and scattered in a rose garden. If there is any goodness left in me, like her, I want my organs to be used by someone else. Anything that's left over can go back the earth. Either way, I know that nature will recycle every atom of my body.

As for my soul, how the cycle of life continues after death is a mystery. I know that the wheel of the year turns and moves from the death of winter to the rebirth of spring. And so I sense that death and birth are two sides of the same door. I can never know with certainty what lies beyond the door of death. All I know is that when my time comes, I will pass through it.

Whether or not I carry my life through the door of death and am reborn elsewhere, I want to live this life well, and leave a treasure trove of memories behind me. Whatever else happens, once I die, my body will be taken back by nature. But I hope my soul will be remembered, as I remember my ancestors.

Virginia, my mother, who raised and nurtured me and founded a nursery school that still bears her name, so that other children could be loved and cared for. William, my great, great grandfather, who lied about his age so that he could enlist to fight in the Great War. Ann, my great, great grandmother, who passed her father's trade as a watchmaker on to her new husband, and changed the life of a man destined to work in the mines. Hannah, my great, great, great grandmother, who married the boy next door and raised five children, living in a simple farm labourer's cottage. John, my great, great, great, great grandfather, a blacksmith who taught his sons to work with fire and metal.

My mother, my grandparents, my unknown ancestors. Their souls live on in my memory, my imagination and the stories I tell. Their bodies live on in the air I breathe, the woods I walk in and the companions I meet on my journey through this life. And when I pass through the door of death, my body will once again become one with theirs, and my soul will join with theirs, in the great story of all our lives.

Ancestors

Brendan Myers

When thinking about one's ancestors, and the role of ancestors in a spiritual tradition, it can be helpful to look back at what ancient people did with the bodies of their dead. In Paleolithic times, from 2 million years ago to 10,000 years ago, people tended to dispose of human remains as far from the community as possible. They may have wanted to prevent the spread of disease. They may have worried that the soul of the deceased might still be nearby, and might have malevolent intentions. But by the Neolithic age, from about 10,000 BCE to around 2,000 BCE, people began building elaborate tombs for their dead, and those tombs were built much closer to the community. People had changed how they thought about their dead. Perhaps they simply made different precautions to prevent diseases. Or, perhaps they were producing enough surplus wealth to allow the leaders to display their power by building monumental architecture, starting with burial mounds and grave markers. It is also possible that the construction of burial monuments, itself, prompted the change in human thinking.

I'm thinking of Irish monuments like portal dolmen, passage mounds, and stone circles, because I happen to be familiar with them. The most famous of them, Poulnabrone, in county Clare, was built around 4000 BCE, and the bodies of around twenty adults and six children were interred there. When it was finished, it became a permanent feature of a landscape, alongside the natural stone that surrounded it. And this sense of the potential permanence of certain human works may have prompted a change in the way people contemplated time and history, past, present, and future. But whatever the reason, Neolithic people began to think differently about their relationships with the dead.

With this changed way of thinking, it became possible to

imagine that one's ancestors had a new role in one's life. They might not be nothing more than lost and possibly dangerous spirits who had to be propitiated or tricked into leaving the community alone. Instead, the ancestors could now become helpers, allies, teachers, or intermediaries between the living and other spiritual beings. And this would make it very important to know who one's ancestors are, and also very important to know what one owed to them, and what one could reasonably ask from them.

Another way to understand the role of ancestors in a spiritual tradition can be found by leaving out the supernatural element, and looking at the simplest facts. The egg and seed from your parents forms the first cells of your body. And your parent's bodies were first formed by the egg and seed from their own parents, who were, in turn, formed from the egg and seed of their parents. Your relationship with your progenitors takes the form of a line of connectivity that reaches across long distances of time and space, like a chain. And every link in the chain is a person, who is parent to her successors and child to her predecessors. Each person receives a genetic code from parents who received it, in turn, from their parents, who in their own turn received it from their parents, and so on. Everyone receives from his male line a code of DNA that goes back to the very first men; and everyone receives from her mother's line a code of mitochondrial DNA that goes back to the very first women. This inheritance gives each of us our various genetic predispositions, possibilities and limitations which make us who we are. Indeed, the importance of this relation is so great that other relations in our lives are modelled after it. Teachers, elders, political leaders, and even the gods are spoken of like parents; students, young people, a leader's followers, and a god's worshippers are spoken of like children.

The line of your ancestors is not just biological. It is also cultural. Your parents, and any other influential adult in your childhood life, taught you a language and a world view, and various ideas and practices about religion or sports or food or politics, or anything else that they thought you should know, so that you could participate in the community. They, too, were taught the same by their own parents and influential adults in their childhood. Acknowledging that every generation modifies or contributes to the culture they inherit from their predecessors, this chain of connectivity also goes back to the very foundation of one's nationality, ethnicity, and language.

One handy and simple way to understand this is through the model of storytelling. When you tell a story, you arrange the events and experiences of life into the form of a narrative. Or to put it another way: when you tell a story, you lend to the events and experiences of your life qualities like the sense of a beginning or an ending, the sense of dramatic tension building up or resolving away, the sense of identifiable characters who play meaningful roles, and so on. These qualities help make the events and experiences of life intelligible. Now this is not to say anything new: this has been said already, perhaps better, by philosophers like Barbara Hardy, Paul Ricoeur, and Alastair MacIntyre. What I would like to add here is that the story you tell of your own life overlaps with the story of other people's lives. It is simply not possible to tell the story of your own life without also telling at least part of the story of a few other people's lives. And among the people whose life story intersects your own the deepest are your parents, predecessors, and ancestors. Without them, a complete account of your story could not be told at all. (The same can be said of friends, by the way: the friend is the person whose life story is so intertwined with one's own that the two stories become almost the same. But I digress.)

Now, one could debate about how many of one's predecessors and ancestors should be included in the story of one's life, or how far back in the past you should define the beginning of one's story. (Think of Tristram Shandy, unable to write his autobiography, because he gets too caught in the events leading up to his own birth.) But even granting that point of contestation, it remains the case that one's life story overlaps with other people's life stories, and those stories overlap with other people's stories, and those stories overlap with still more stories, and so on, and so on. Again, like links in a chain, or like a stretch of knotted rope, narrative storytelling is the instrument that grants intelligibility not just to human life but also to human relations, on a scale that can reach back in time to the foundation of one's language, nation, and culture.

Storytelling, as a kind of social bonding instrument, is important here not just because, as Ricoeur says, human life is already of a nature that lends itself to representation in narrative storytelling. It's important because storytelling is also a pedagogical instrument too. It is precisely through storytelling that our predecessors teach the culture that we inherit from them. So the bonding power of storytelling is not simply theoretical. It's also deeply practical. It's how we understand our relationship with our predecessors, but it's also how the relationship is actually accomplished. It's something you can observe happening in the real world.

What does this have to do with our ancestors? What makes it spiritual? It's not simply that this knotted rope can reach back in time to the very beginning of things. It's also that the social bonding power of storytelling can, in principle, connect you to the gods themselves. For, as various literary sources attest, the gods of European mythology were the biological and cultural progenitors of ancient tribes and noble dynasties. In *The Conquest of Gaul*, Julius Caesar, who claimed to be a descendent of the Roman god Venus, observed the following about the Celts of Gaul: "The Gauls claim all to be descended from Father Dis, declaring that this is the tradition preserved by the Druids." An old Irish text called the Lebor Gabála Éireann says: "...every princely family that is in Ireland, save the Eoganacht, is of the seed of Nuadu Airgetlám." An Icelandic text called the Prose Edda states that Odin, the All-Father, came from the city of Troy (the same Troy as in the Illiad, and that he travelled north when his wife, who was a prophet, foresaw that his destiny lay there. He and his people had many adventures on the way, and "wherever they went on their travels, tales of their splendour were told, making them seem more like gods than men." When Odin reached Norway, "he placed his son in power. This son was named Saeming, and Norway's kings, as well as its jarls and other important men of the kingdom, trace their descent to him…"

Irish mythology, for example, describes how the tribe of the gods, the Tuatha de Danann, fought and won two battles with a race of monsters called the Fomhoir. But however long they ruled Ireland afterwards, they were eventually displaced by a tribe of mortals called the Milesians. The two tribes negotiated with each other in various ways, until they finally met in battle. And the mortals defeated the gods, and forced the gods to retreat to hidden places under the hills, lakes, and mountains of Ireland. However, the gods were not entirely banished, and indeed the two communities intermingled sometimes. In Lady Gregory's literary re-telling of the stories, which she published in 1904, it's said that certain kinds of people are the descendants of the three races described in the stories. You can tell them by the qualities of their character, as follows:

> It is what the poets of Ireland used to be saying, that every brave man, good at fighting, and every man that could do great deeds and not be making much talk about them, was of the Sons of the Gael; and that every skilled man that had music and that did enchantments secretly, was of the Tuatha de Danann. But they put a bad name on the Firbolgs… for lies and for big talk and injustice.

These lines always struck me as deeply important. It seems to be saying something more than that our ancestors are the trans- mitters of our cultural and biological heritage. It seems to suggest that our ancestors also, in some sense, still live with us today. A scientifically-minded person might want to deny that they live on as disembodied spirits, like ghosts or demigods that one could speak to in some kind of ritual. As an alternative, we could say that they live in the form of a discernible presence embodied by the habits and characters and stories of their living descendants today. This alternative requires no supernatural element to be intelligible. Yet it seems to me no less spiritual. For its implication is that every person you meet is the bringer of an enormous and rich treasure of knowledge, culture, creativity, and possibility, whether he or she knows it or not! Her story runs deep, certainly deeper than any single occasion of storytelling, on its own, could reveal. And so, however much of that story she tells, there is always more to tell. That last point is what makes it spiritual: for the endlessness of the story is an immanent immensity.

Furthermore, you yourself are also the bringer of such a fabulous story! You also embody part of a story that is perhaps thousands or maybe millions of years old. This lends spiritual force to one's own selfhood, that is, one's presence to oneself. And this also lends a kind of moral responsibility, too. For now you have to decide what to do with this huge inheritance. Will you use it wisely or poorly? Will you draw power and inspi- ration from it, or will you ignore it? Will you contribute to its greatness by doing great things, or will you bring disgrace upon it, by doing disgraceful things? What story do you wish to bequeath to future generations, who will look upon you as one of their ancestors?

Brendan Cathbad Myers's interest in mythology and ethics was inspired by Celtic storytelling and culture, taught to him by his Irish parents as a child. His Ph.D. doctorate is in ethics and philosophy. He has appeared on many US radio stations and podcasts, and writes a regular column in several Pagan magazines. He is the author of a number of books, including *A Pagan Testament*, *The Other Side of Virtue* and *The Earth, The Gods and The Soul: A History of Pagan Philosophy*. He lives in Gatineau, Canada.

Annette George

As a child I felt the reassuring presence of my ancestors daily, knowing that many generations had walked the same country lanes, climbed the same trees and sat in the same hard pews in church. I loved to look at old photos and wonder who I resembled physically, but with red hair and flashes of temper, I looked no further than my pink-haired maternal grandmother of Irish decent.

Our family were part of the village landscape then, as we always had been. In later years when tracing my family tree I found no scandal, only a long line of agricultural workers who had never strayed too far from home, only a village or two away at most.

As an adult with a family of my own, I started questioning my links with the past in a way I hadn't done before, partly triggered by the sudden death of my paternal grandmother. She hardly talked about her childhood, only life after marriage. She went into service at fourteen to a big house in the village where she met my grandfather. Living in London as a youngster then moving to the country must have been a shock to her. But what shocked me was learning that she was Jewish. She never admitted it, venomously denying it if the subject was raised. For her own reasons she turned her back on her ancestors. It was as though her marriage marked the start of her family tree.

I was so eager to hear stories of my family, to put flesh to the names I'd seen on gravestones. Gran was desperate to put space between herself and ghosts from the past. How could you deny your roots, your heritage, your family like that?

However, now I'm older, I feel I've turned that corner. Denying my ancestral religion, I started on a new path. We may have shared genetics, but not a faith any longer. This new direction has seen not only my spirituality change, but also marrying outside the village of my birth and moving hundreds of miles away.

In days of old, families remained close distance-wise, they shared the same beliefs passed down through the ages. Now, in the 21st century we have lost touch with that. Families are fragmented, through distance or divorce. Religious beliefs have changed, we no longer feel pressure to be as our parents were. We experiment with various faiths, various homes and sometimes various partners.

Cat Treadwell says in her book *A Druid's Tale*: "It's easy to forget the reality of the past, and how quickly we are moving into it. We are all ancestors."

After reading that I realized we are all leaving a legacy for generations to come, we will all be someone else's ancestors in time, a name on a gravestone or a familiar face on a faded photograph.

In this age of computers and mobile phones, perhaps the graveyards are less visited, the family trees left untended. We make our own history, not looking to the past to find out who we are, instead looking forward to what we may become.

Todd Fashion

To followers of "the Way" of the Craft of the Wise, our ancestors were participants in our traditional practices, having held the knowledge and secrets of our wisdom often through great trials, whether one adheres to the belief that their Craft is an unbroken line having remained intact over centuries and millennia or not. Because of this established community outside familial and even most common social constructs referred to above, we honour our forebears within our specific lineage as well as our Gods, since it is they who have known death and continue to interact with other worlds. Adhering to the principle: "Once a Witch, always a Witch," one might say that our ancestors take on greater significance.

The spirits we honour as ancestral are not restricted to family and culture, but embrace a larger field of reference. This is also not necessarily restricted by cultural inheritance and observations, whether ritual or seasonal, but to the outlined teachings as passed down to us through our initiatory line(s). In honouring the dead, a witch often recognizes spirits of familial, cultural, traditional, (regarding magical lineage) spiritual, (spirits who may or may not die or be dead but who seem to govern elements of nature) and those the reader might refer to as Gods (demi-gods/angels/demons /genii /Fair Folk etc.). As pointed out, most peoples of the world trace their entire "tribal existence" from the issue of a God; witches are no different but likely pay greater observance toward such spirits, entities and deities than institutionalized religions.

Being that our God is the Lord of Death and our Goddess, She who journeyed forth to seek Death out and solve the mystery of disease, suffering and the sorrow that accompanies it; it could be said that we pay extra attention to those of our ancestral heritage of all types. We often regard them as continuing their lives in another form than within a fleshly body of the material plane of consciousness. Therefore, we tend to recognize their influence throughout our lives and honour them regularly as progenitors of our path, guides and keepers of sacred wisdom or "the mysteries."

Honouring our dead takes on many forms, starting with acknowledgement within the construct of our rites as well as specialized communion with them at specific times of year. These are such times as Samhain/All Hallow's Eve, Twelfth Night and other sacred dates of the "wheel of the year," feast days, anniversaries and whenever we feel a greater need. We may ask boons, blessings or guidance of our ancestors or simply their continued presence in our lives. Often, we may make offerings to them, sometimes through ritualized practices or through "inner plane" contact(s) making our connection and commitment to them that much more relevant and pivotal to our practice than popularly understood.

Perhaps more important, being that we believe we will "...meet, know, remember and love (them) again," our ancestors are considered our extended family with whom we are regularly reunited through the wheel of reincarnation.

Rosie Weaver

Many years ago I recall seeing an evocative picture; it was of a seated woman, her mother stood behind her resting her hands on her shoulders, and behind her mother stood her grandmother, in the same pose, backing her up, and behind her stood her great grandmother and on and on it went....

Through the mists of time we all evolve from one genetic mother, our shared genetic ancestral line can be followed back to her. The strong significance of the feminine influence permeates the being of us all, not only through succession through the ancestral line, but also from conception itself. We are all, it's scientifically proven, female in the womb of our own mother until either the X or Y chromosome factor kicks in, to determine which sex we will be.

Our natural tendency by its very nature of femaleness is one of nurturing, yielding and providing unconditional love for our children as most mothers do. Yet we live on a planet wrought with war, destruction, cruelty and suffering.

Throughout history we see that a patriarchal force has governed and steered us into this cataclysmic void. Male dominated politics coupled with religions have relegated both Mother Earth and all that is feminine into lesser beings. Seeing only the male counterpart as a good guiding influence, whose laws dictate that it is okay to exploit all other beings for personal gain.

Pagans are well aware of the female counterpart, The Great Goddess, understanding that we must honour, respect and take care of Her. The Goddess is seen to be manifest through all women, which in turn are respected, not exploited as the 'written word of God' seems to suggest.

The respect of Mother Earth/Mother Nature is central to Pagan philosophy. Druidism can also draw many parallels with Eco-feminism. The correlation between the two upholds that the Divine feminine is inherent throughout all women and Mother Earth/Nature. All women reflect the glory of the Goddess as does the Earth. We learn that we greatly respect such a wonderful blessing, which brings forth procreation upon every conceivable level of being. She inspires artists and great minds alike. Druids refer to this process as 'Awen'.

Much of the wisdom of our ancestors has been lurking in the shadows, hiding from a patriarchal mindset in order to survive. At this critical point in history we've come to learn that we can no longer exist with these outworn draconian ideals, which treat so many beings in a cruel, unfair manner. The imbalance between the sexes is being highlighted like never before, the Goddess spirit is rising in woman to reclaim Her power back. It comes at a much-needed time. The feminine force can restore all that is fragmented, as did Isis, when She picked up the pieces of her dead husband, Osiris, and breathed new life into him.

Kenn Payne

Ancestor Worship is by some viewed as an intangible obligation, restricted to the hallowed festival of Samhain where our relatives and loved ones are able to bridge the gap between the worlds and visit us in spirit. However, just as how Love should not be restricted to honouring come Valentine's Day, neither should we set aside the honouring of those who have contributed to what and who we are today to a solitary night on the brink of winter!

Cultures globally have rich and varied traditions surrounding the veneration of their ancestors, such as the ancient Roman festival of *Parentalia* during which a family visited its ancestors' graves to share cake and wine, both in the form of offerings to the dead and as a meal among themselves. Asian cultures have always – and still very much today – honour their dead and ancestors such as with China's "Ghost Festivals", Korean *Charye* (tea rites) and the Japanese Buddhist Bon festival to honour the spirits of one's ancestors. And, of course, there is the iconic Mexican Day of the Dead (*Dia de los Muertos*) containing its striking, colourful imagery, which in itself has an ancestor in ancient Aztec customs.

Western modern viewpoints today have sought to exclude death and the past from the mindset of the individual. It's a fast-paced, materialistic, shallow world where you have to very much live in the Now and only look to the Future; little to no time is given to reflection on the past twelve months, let alone anything that has come in the years, decades or centuries before. Children are brought up with little to no respect for their elders. Even as adults we tend to deposit our old and infirm in "homes" where they can be forgotten and their legacy fades away. As such we are also led to view death and anything related to it as unsavoury and "secret", spoken of in hushed tones, with imagery such as skulls seen as "evil" by the misinformed.

As a result, there is a great and saddening forgetfulness that without these people and all those who came before, we ourselves wouldn't be here. We should be respectful of those people who make up our ancestors – both known and unknown, living and dead. Everything we do and are able to do is because of everything done and able to be done by our parents, their parents, and their parent's parents, ad infinitum.

We owe our great debt of gratitude to our past generations. Every day we walk the shadow of the steps of our ancestors; it pays to be mindful of that. One day we ourselves will be the ancestors. How would you like to be remembered?

Past & Present

Morgan Daimler

The modern pagan revival grew out of individual ideas about what ancient paganism was; each of these individual ideas grew into a different neopagan tradition creating the stunning diversity that exists today. Modern pagans rely on history, inspiration, and innovation to create their paths, but each tradition will take a unique approach to finding a balance between them. Someone exploring neopaganism will find him or herself emerged in an overwhelming array of different groups and traditions that form the complex tapestry of the larger pagan community. One of the less well known threads in this tapestry is that of Reconstructionism, a newer method of approaching the worship of the old Gods. Although it is not as well known yet, Reconstructionism has much to offer the wider pagan community as well as those seekers for whom the past is an irresistible puzzle.

Many people have not heard of Reconstructionism yet and this can be a good thing because it means that the person has no preconceived notions about what this path is about. Unfortunately, among the people who do have a passing familiarity with Reconstructionism, or more to the point with Reconstructionists, there can be misunderstandings about this approach that cast it in a bad light. Instead of a living, breathing spiritual path, some people mistakenly think that Reconstructionism is only an academic exercise, full of people who like to argue over minutiae. This is not the reality in practice, but can be the impression people receive in online discussion groups, which is unfortunate. There is also the inaccurate idea that Reconstructionists are spiritual re-enactors, rather like a religious Renaissance faire, who only look backwards to the past. People interested in learning more about this spiritual path are often challenged to find resources and even to gain a solid understanding of how the type of Reconstruction they are interested in is practiced. Much of the time a beginner will be forced to start from scratch in creating their spiritual path, although online communities are becoming more common and there are now a few books out there to help guide people. So, then, if it isn't those things and can be hard to find resources on, what is Reconstruction and how do people practice it?

The basic premise of Reconstructionism is a simple one, although it is an endless process. Reconstructionists use every available reliable source, including mythology, folklore, anthropology, archaeology, and linguistics, to understand the ancient pagans who practiced the religion being reconstructed. Once the beliefs and practices of the original pagan culture are understood, even on a basic level, the person uses that knowledge as a springboard to envision what that particular pagan faith would have been like today if it had never stopped being practiced. This involves both an appreciation of the living non-pagan culture, if there is one, and the individual's own inspiration; sometimes people may also choose to study other closely related cultures to fill in any gaps. The reliability of any source may be debated and in some cases a source, such as Caesar for example, may be accepted by some and rejected by others.

The result is an overall similarity between Reconstructionists following the same culture, but with individual variations in belief and details of practice. Reconstruction of any pagan culture hinges on using an understanding of the past as a solid foundation to build a viable modern faith. Critical thinking is a vital skill in this process, not only to discern reliable source material, but also to sift through the ancient beliefs and practices to decide what to keep as it is, what to modernize, and what to possibly leave in the past. For example, most cultures practiced one form or another of human sacrifice, which is definitely something modern Reconstructionist pagans choose to leave in the past. But other aspects, like fostering out children, being a warrior, and tribal communities are all things that different Reconstructionists seek to modernize in order to keep. Just as ancient pagan groups varied even within one culture, so too does modern Reconstructionist paganism offer diverse interpretations of the spirituality being reconstructed.

Unlike most other neopagan traditions, Reconstructionism is not so much a religion in its own right as it is a methodology that people use to create the structure of their religion. In this way it acts as the framework on which any modern pagan religion can be built, which allows Reconstructionism to be applied to any ancient pagan religion that a person wants to follow. Reconstructionists can be found in Greek, Roman, Norse, Germanic, Celtic, and Egyptian paganism, to name only a few. It is generally not used with living pagan faiths because there is no need to reconstruct anything; however, there has been at least one book that approached Wicca from a Reconstructionist viewpoint.

The flexibility of this approach is both a strength and a weakness as it allows for anyone to reconstruct a pagan faith, but at the same time creates an endless variety of personal visions of a faith within that community. There can also be some disagreement about how much traditional material should be followed without being altered at all and how much personal innovation should be accepted, which creates a constant tension within Reconstructionist communities. This dynamic tension, while uncomfortable at times, is often the fertile ground from which new ideas and practices grow. This is essential to any community, Reconstructionist or otherwise, because without growth the religion will stagnate and be at risk of fading away. From the outside it can make it appear that the community is contentious and some people dislike what can seem to be unnecessary disagreements. However, valuable insights have often come from this that benefit everyone in the long run.

Reconstructionism is often said to be orthopraxic, rather than orthodoxic. What this means is that Reconstructionists may have varying beliefs, but they tend to have similar practices, at least in the broad strokes. This is especially true of the many European cultural paganisms which all share a common Indo-European root culture. Put another way, different groups which share the same culture may have different beliefs about the Gods, worship different Gods, and can even have different cosmology and holidays, but will generally have the same approach to ritual. In the many Reconstructionist groups this can include invoking the Gods or spirits of the rite, making offerings, blessing participants, divination, and feasting. Similarly the philosophy behind the actions taken in ritual have a commonality, as most Reconstruction strongly emphasizes reciprocity and connection as the core of ritual action. It is this shared ritual structure that holds the larger community together when the beliefs can differ so widely.

Making offerings is a practice found among all Reconstructionist groups in some way. Who the offerings are made to and why can vary, but the idea that we offer in order to receive or to nurture a relationship with powers beyond ourselves seems to be a universal one in the old pagan cultures and so is a practice that has been brought forward in Reconstructionist groups. Reconstructionists strive to make offerings that would be traditional in a historic context, and this can include everything from jewelry to weapons, food to alcohol; modern pagans may also choose to offer less tangible things such as poetry and song. The most important thing is that what is offered is the best that the person is able to give, and that it is offered with a genuine heart. The method of offering depends on what is being offered, as much as the culture being reconstructed, so that physical objects like silver might be given to water while food could be burned.

In some cases food may be offered to the Gods and then eaten by people or animals, which is believed to bless them. We can see an example of this in the Greek rite of Hekate's Deipnon, where a meal is prepared on the dark moon for the Goddess Hekate and left at a crossroads; such meals were traditionally eaten by stray animals or the poor. In the same way in Irish paganism, food was left out on Imbolc in honor of the Goddess Brighid and could be eaten by the poor people of the area or by animals. In some Norse Reconstructionist groups an animal may be dedicated to a deity and then ritually killed and eaten by the group, although it should be noted that not all Reconstructionists agree with the practice of modern animal sacrifice.

The view of the Gods among Reconstructionists can vary widely, usually based on the individual's ideas about the nature of deity, but most will be strict polytheists. This is because Reconstructionists look to the past as a guide for how to understand the Gods and most of the source material that exists about the old pagan Gods supports a view of them as unique individuals with personalities and preferences. Reconstructionists look to traditional mythology and folklore to understand the Gods of the culture they are reconstructing and tend to be very hesitant to rely on modern innovations or views. Usually a Reconstructionist will honor gods within one pantheon, and often from within one specific culture within a wider pantheon. For example, a Celtic Reconstructionist pagan may honor only the Welsh gods. Some people even go further and study a very specific geographic area and only honor the gods of that place; on the other hand some people may honor Gods within a wider cultural pantheon and in rare cases even honor Gods of different pantheons, although this is a controversial practice.

Researching the Gods can prove to be a very tricky challenge for Reconstructionists as the Gods are not static beings, but rather are fluid and flowing personalities that change throughout the collected mythology. There is also the difficulty of deciding whether a God from one culture who is related linguistically and has a similar mythology to a God in a closely related second culture is the same God or a different one; this is something that each individual will choose to approach differently. In addition to honoring the Gods in some way, most Reconstructionists also include the veneration of Otherworldly spirits and the ancestors. Honoring the ancestors in particular is seen as an important way to connect to those who have gone before and to connect to our own roots.

Holidays celebrated by Reconstructionists will be based on the holy days of the culture being reconstructed, resulting in a wide variety of holidays between different Reconstructionist groups. Even groups within the same culture may choose to celebrate different holidays based on what each group feels is important. For example, some Celtic Reconstructionist groups only celebrate the four fire festivals of Imbolc, Beltaine, Lughnasa, and Samhain, while others celebrate those as well as the two equinoxes and two solstices. Within Norse and Germanic Reconstruction the number of holidays celebrated as well as the dating of the different holidays can vary widely between groups. Roman and Greek Reconstructionists may pick and choose between the multitude of possible holidays in deciding what to celebrate. At its core though, all Reconstructionists take the same approach to holidays, which is to understand why the ancient pagans celebrated the festival in order to be able to truly bring that sense of celebration forward. This reflects the desire by Reconstructionists not to merely recreate a long dead practice, but to connect in profound and meaningful ways to the traditions of the past to create modern practices rooted in that past which have the same value for modern pagans as they did for ancient ones.

Reconstructionism is a minority within modern paganism, but one that is slowly growing. In many ways all neopagans have a little of the Reconstructionist spirit within them, as uniting past and present is an inherent part of neopaganism. Like other pagans, Reconstructionists seek to honor the Gods, celebrate holidays, and nurture connection with things beyond themselves; unlike other pagans, Reconstructionists tend to reject modern beliefs about the Gods that contradict ancient pagan ones and often prefer to stick to a single culture, or a few closely related cultures, rather than incorporating from diverse sources. As the pagan community grows and moves forward Reconstructionism will hopefully find its voice within the larger community, becoming less elusive and more of a presence, available to those who seek this difficult but rewarding path.

Morgan Daimler is a blogger, poet, teacher of esoteric subjects, Druid, dedicant of Macha, wandering priestess of Odin and Author of *Where the Hawthorn Grows*. She lives in the USA.

Elli McDonald

The interplay between the past and present in the Neopagan movement can be confusing. Are we reviving a long dead past? Are we pinning old names on new religious practices? Who has the authority to decide which historical sources are valid? How do we sort through these questions while still honoring our ancestors? And how do we tie it all together into something that has the power to support us in our modern lives? These issues are both a challenge and fertile ground for spiritual growth.

Individual Neopagans may answer each of these questions differently. The information we have from archeological, anthropological and literary sources is fragmented, impacted and incomplete. In addition, we have no universally recognized authority figure—no pope or Dalai Lama—to determine which sources we should accept. Neopagans have the right and the responsibility to research and draw their own conclusions. While this lends itself to a certain lack of unity, it also empowers each of us to build a spiritual practice that is uniquely suited to our own needs.

177

As a whole, we take this process seriously. Most Neopagans have a deep respect for those who came before us. Getting the history right becomes – in itself – a religious practice. We connect with the root of who we are by seeking out the wisdom of the ancestors – especially the wisdom that was left behind in the sweeping religious and cultural movements of the past two thousand years. At the same time, we realize that our modern lives are quite different from our Paleopagan ancestors.

In general, Neopagans are not seeking to recreate the past. We are, however, looking to our ancestors to guide us in building a meaningful spirituality in the present. We are transforming prehistoric religious ideas, values and practices into something that is relevant and powerful to the modern mind. The work we do today reflects both ways. It honors the ancestors, but it also leaves something for our descendents to build upon in the future.

Linda Sever

Before the coming of Christianity, the various peoples of Europe, such as the Greeks, Romans and the Celtic, Germanic and Slavic tribes, practised their own indigenous religions. All these religions were polytheistic, recognising the many gods and goddesses as individual beings, as well as honouring the ancestors and the spirits of place. With the coming of Christianity, following the conversion of Emperor Constantine in 312, many pagan societies converted to the new religion, sometimes voluntarily but often through coercion.

However, not all the pagan traditions were lost completely and, in particular, the rise in interest in nationalism in the 19th and early 20th centuries led many people in Northern Europe to look towards their own native mythologies. This resulted in the rise of a number of mystic movements, spiritualism and magical traditions. This, in turn, has led to many of the neo-pagan, Wiccan and Druidic movements today.

However, unlike many neo-pagan traditions, reconstructed

pagan religions are based firmly in the historical pre-Christian practices of a specific culture and are adapted, where necessary, for the 21st century. Reconstructionist pagans base their religious practices on those described in ancient manuscripts and texts, like the old Norse or Icelandic sagas, such as those found in the Prose and Poetic Eddas. They look to the latest archaeological or art historical evidence, which can help to enrich or add a new angle to their religion. Where there is no historical information, reconstructionists seek guidance from their patron gods or ancestors, or through extra-ordinary experiences. In the case of heathenry, this is known as Unverified Personal Gnosis (UPG), although there is a debate with reconstructed movements over how much UPG should be relied upon within one's practice.

Writing as a reconstructionist (aka recon) Heathen, I am a polytheist and honour (not worship) a large number of gods and goddesses, although I do have particular patron gods, all of whom are distinct and real individuals. I celebrate three main festivals and some other minor ones. Our ceremonies consist of making offerings to the gods of food and drink, usually with mead, and making toasts to them, and can take place indoors and outdoors.

As an academic, writer and art historian, I am constantly adding to my knowledge base and thus enriching my own practice, through the latest archaeological and art historical discoveries. I recently spent a week on a 6th century Anglo-Saxon cemetery dig, observing the many skeletons, jewellery finds and pottery being removed from the ground, to glean more about 6th century Anglo-Saxon life. The result of this will be used in a children's book on Anglo-Saxon life and culture for eight to twelve year olds. Research and writing can help to add and fix new knowledge in my own path, and link the past to the present. Some people call reconstructionism "paganism with homework". I prefer to see it as an exciting, fluid path, constantly updating itself, making it as valid today as it was for our ancestors.

Erin Lund Johnson

The Creideamh Sí is the name Irish monk Seán O'Duinn gave to the pre-Christian, traditional religion of Ireland in his books *Where Three Streams Meet: Celtic Spirituality* and *The Rites of Brigid: Goddess and Saint*. He translates this to English as the fairy faith, and explains, "…the Creideamh Sí was largely a fertility religion concerned with life and growth and prosperity," and, "…it was all-important to preserve good relations with the goddess and the Tuatha Dé Danann in general, in order to secure the fertility of the land…" Through these good relations, "balance and harmony between the different parts of creation was what was sought for in the ancient religious philosophy." In addition to the Aos Sí, and the land goddess of Sovereignty who granted peace and plenty for the people while the tribal king she married ruled justly, the ancestors and their realm were revered by the clan as "the source of its existence and prosperity."

I consider reverence of the Aos Sí, land goddess, and ancestors to be the wellspring of the Creideamh Sí, and my practicing and continuing it one small current in the vast river it has produced, but a current come down to me from my ancestors, to flow down to my descendants. While my forms of reverence are not identical to those of the past, as a traditional pagan, they are grounded in this ancestral tradition, and carry on its spirit in today's world.

Forming and maintaining right relationships of balance and harmony with this triad is central to the Creideamh Sí and my practice of it. Right relationship with the Aos Sí is maintained by making offerings of milk and grain to them at sacred sites during the holidays of Samhain, Imbolc, Bealtaine, and Lughnasadh, the firsts of November, February, May, and August, in exchange for the gifts the land provides, as is prescribed in the Irish tale *In Gabail in tSida*. I maintain right relationship with my land goddess not through the traditional sacral kingship marriage, but by pledging my devotion to her at Bealtaine to live by Truth, Justice, and Honor, that she may continue to bless my home and family with peace and plenty. I honor my ancestors annually at Samhain with the Gaelic *Feis na Marbh*, or Feast of the Dead, sharing a festive meal with them and stories about them with my family, that they may remember and smile on us for another year.

As the wife and mother of my home, I also maintain right relationship with Bríde, goddess of the hearth, to honor her spirit that both cooks our food and brings us together as a family, through morning prayers requesting her blessings upon us, evening prayers beseeching her protection through the night, and weekly offerings from a family dinner in thanks for her gifts.

In these ways my ancestral past inspires and informs my present practice of the Creideamh Sí. To read more about how I practice the Creideamh Sí in my home, please visit my website, Faery Faith and Family Folkways, at http://gaelicfolkway.webs .com/index.htm

Kristan Clark-Gary

Wicca is an actual religion, and was around long before most religions were formed. It has been adapted through the ages and is still widely practiced today. Witchcraft is a practice that has been used by wise women for centuries. Though the two can be traced back before modern religion, medicine and science; they are independent of each other, but intertwined just the same. They have survived persecution, adapted to modern ways, and thrived just the same.

Wicca and the practice of witchcraft date back centuries; and though some practices and beliefs were discarded with the changing of the times, many of them are still widely used and many beliefs have survived. Traditional Wiccans believe one must be initiated, by a high priestess, into a coven. However, many modern eclectic Wiccans initiate themselves with a private ritual or their own coven of few, and practice their craft solitary.

A few other practices of Wiccans from the past that have been discarded or rarely used are sacrifices to the goddess and her god, performing ritual skyclad (or nude), and sex magic (this is where the high priestess and priest engage in sex during ritual to raise the cone of magic within the circle). Many beliefs and practices held true throughout the centuries. Typically, Wiccans believe in a goddess (often represented in triple form) and a horned god (her consort and child); they celebrate the eight Sabbats; use similar tools such as an athame, alter, candles, chalice, besom, etc.; they have a book of shadows; they follow the Wiccan Rede, and the law of three; they follow the lunar and solar cycles; understand the five elements and their importance; natures cycles; and the complexity of spell work and wonder of the magic all around us.

Along with most Wiccans, I worship a goddess (triple in nature) and her consort (the horned god). The goddess(es) go by many names, but I personally feel they are all one and the same. As an eclectic solitary Wiccan, I do not belong to a coven and was not initiated by a priestess. I mostly practice my religion alone, though I have a large community and do take part in group rituals with other Wiccans. I describe witchcraft as a science. Everything is made up of energy… everything! Witchcraft is just a way of channeling that energy for a specific result. A spell is just a way of sending out a certain type of energy to get something back. I always ask the goddess and god to bless all my magickal practices; this is how I mix the two.

Part 3

What We Do

Ritual

Magic

Prayer & Meditation

Healing

Herbalism

Celebrant Work

Ritual

Mélusine Draco

When we talk about 'ritual' within the parameters of magical practice, we are referring to the 'body or code of ceremony contained within an often repeated series of actions' for the purpose of generating magical power or energy. Either singularly or as a group, all Circle energy is powered by ritual, from the simplest form of spell-casting to the full-blown 'bells and smells' of ritual magic.

Whenever we make ready for magical working, we will be utilising some form of ritual preparation before we engage the 'powers that be' on a psychic level – by a series of actions, including invocation/evocation. These can be as brief or elaborate as we wish, but it is more effective to keep things simple rather than run the risk of the ritual running out of steam, and the energy dispersing before we've had the chance to direct it. If we focus on the *practical* use of ceremonial items on the altar and not the spiritual elements of the ritual, then the whole becomes merely an observance rather than an effective magical working.

The object of setting up our ritual area within the Circle is to harness energy and prevent it from spilling out all over the place as it continues to build via the use of pacing, dancing or chanting, depending on the custom of our particular Path or Tradition. We set up the ritual utilising the appropriate magical equipment and correspondences, together with a relevant text to be recited, in whole or part, by the participants. Most of the readily available material is usually adapted from practices that have their roots in that doorstep of a book *The Complete Golden Dawn System of Magic* and here we have an alchemical blend of traditional Freemasonry, Qabalah (Western and Hebrew), Eastern mysticism, Hermetic philosophy, Egyptian cosmology, classical Greek and Roman pantheism, esoteric astrology, planetary correspondences, Tarot, geomancy and scrying. Contemporary paganism, albeit 'tweeked' and amended by pagan teachers like Doreen Valiente, uses any permutation of these techniques in its rituals.

'The ritual' is merely the method by which we create a psycho-drama enabling us to draw down energy needed to power any magical act, but when we study Golden Dawn's systems, or Aleister Crowley's *Equinox*, we are looking at lengthy, complicated 'performances' adapted from Masonic rites originally written for group participation rather than solitary. Because of this, the narrative element of ritual has become over-complicated and, more often than not, magically sterile.

For group dynamics to work, it *is* essential to follow a prescribed formula where everyone knows exactly what's going on, enabling them to follow the progress of the ritual with each participant having a role to play. This gives pace and structure to the working, so that at the right moment, the magical energy can be brought 'down' as a *combined* effort, and re-directed or channelled in accordance with the agreed purpose of the ritual.

The solitary magical practitioner does not need such an elaborate build-up. In this case, lengthy preparations can be self-defeating; magical energy won't hang around waiting for all the standard ritual preparations to be carried out by one person, even if it is contained within the Circle. The experienced solitary worker often uses natural ability to raise the energy, which is often instantaneous – being directed before it has a chance to disperse. That said, it *is* necessary to have some working knowledge of the methods of group ritual in order to develop a fuller understanding of the reasons behind the preparations.

As many modern rituals are Golden Dawn-based, they are often reliant on a number of people being available to play the different parts. A solitary practitioner would find the energy needed to 'drive' these rituals through to completion, would quickly evaporate if the Guardians had to hang around while we whipped ourselves into a frenzy, assuming all the parts and generally playing to the gallery. So, we also have to understand *why* all this psycho-drama is necessary and what part it plays in successful ritualised magic.

Firstly, if we make a study of different groups it becomes apparent that few of the participants have any *natural* magical ability – even Crowley himself admits this in his *Confessions*. The carefully constructed rituals were designed to channel the combined energies of the participants with everyone contributing to the raising of the 'cone of power' within the Circle, to a greater or lesser degree. The prolonged psycho-drama with its carefully rehearsed programme of chants, prayers and invocations, slowly builds up the power so that it can be directed into the magical operation. Secondly, in a large number of modern groups, the psycho-drama is merely justification for the ritual, because the participants never do anything other than recite the chants, prayers and invocations without any genuine magical purpose.

The down-side to all this preparation is that is can lead to 'spiritual-mainlining' – creating what many mistake for divine presence – an endorphin rush, caused by the transmission of chemical messages from the brain, that have the characteristic properties of opiate compounds such as morphine. It has been medically proven that there *is* a naturally occurring opiate in the human nervous system that can be induced by the clever use of music/rhythm/dance and language techniques. These naturally occurring endorphins produce this 'spiritual mainlining' effect, and those who experience the feel-good factor resulting from it are often convinced that deity has indeed touched them.

The various priesthoods, pagan and otherwise, have been exploiting this reaction for centuries to convince followers that they have indeed been subjected to a deeply moving psychic experience. Many solitary worshippers can induce it in themselves with repetitive chanting or dancing as an integral part of spell-casting, and these applications have been used throughout the ages as a form of energy building within a sacred space since it helps shift the conscious mind onto higher planes. We do need, however, to be able to differentiate between the euphoria created by the naturally occurring endorphins being released into the nervous system and genuine psychic experience.

Genuine magical practitioners can *consciously* use an endorphin-related 'high' to kick-start their rise through the levels of consciousness, but they do not fool themselves into mistaking one for the other. The power generated by the human body from ritual intent can be immense, which is why it is used throughout Old Craft and ritual magic as a way of producing power. It is also why there is a great deal of chanting and movement attached to most aspects of ritualised magic – to get everyone marching to the same drum.

For the solitary practitioner, things are much less complicated. The main problem is that people are often inhibited and self-conscious – even when working alone – and can't fully let themselves go. It can take a long time before we feel confident enough to do so (which is normal) but the less restrained we are, the better the results. Working through a 13-part ritual defeats the object of the exercise, and the solitary witch is best advised to draw on simple techniques that can create the same effect in minutes as an hour-long coven rite!

Dance can be extremely hypnotic and powerful; adding a chant makes for a dynamic combination, which is why the techniques have been used for thousands of years and by all cultures and creeds. The restrictions of our own home environment may prevent us from hurling ourselves around like dervishes, but the same effect can be created by pacing backwards and forwards within a confined area. If you don't believe this can be done, think of a large animal caged in an old-fashioned zoo. Even though there was barely room to move, the animal paced left and right with a fluid movement in a perfectly controlled rhythm.

Sound and rhythm play an important part in spell-casting and inducing meditational conditions, and we need to understand how best to implement this for solitary working. Many workbooks give vast screeds of litany, which serve as pagan prayers, but for the solitary witch: keep it simple … a repeated refrain of two lines is much more effective than reciting the whole *Hymn To Pan*. The other important thing is to accept that magically, the most childish 'umpty-tumpty' style of rhyme will produce the best results in setting the *pace* for the chant. Group working produces the best results when the whole coven takes part in 'the Mill', chanting and circling to *The Lincolnshire Poacher*!

To reiterate, we need to grasp the fact that *how* a charm is spoken is more important than the actual words, and it's the way the rhythm resonates that gives it power. The famous *Om-Adme-Padme-Om* Buddhist chant demonstrates repetition can focus the mind and shut out the mundane, without having to resort to purple prose and high drama. Sometimes we can feel extremely foolish using someone else's words (especially if they are not fully understood) and if necessary, we must construct our own verses. Ritual chanting is used as a way of altering consciousness and raising psychic power and one of the most ancient techniques in aligning human consciousness with the subconscious realms of the *Anima Mundi*. Put to magical use, the power raised is channelled into the desired outcome, and projected out onto the astral to work the desired changes in the physical world.

In truth, few people would have the knowledge or experience to conduct a ritual *and* achieve positive results from the outset – we all have to experiment and discover what formula works for us as individuals and within the framework of our own natural abilities. Ritualised magic has nearly always been a solitary pursuit and for the solitary practitioner there isn't any script. She or he sets their own stage by creating an atmosphere that feels conducive for raising and channelling magical energy. Needless to say there must be a period of trial and error before we find the formula that works for us – and there's no one to say that we must stick with it forever because all things are subject to change. And since there is no set script for the solitary ritual, it is impossible to say what will happen! We can only echo the sentiments expressed in Dion Fortune's *The Winged Bull*, that creating our own temple atmosphere ought to cause images to rise in our imagination and that we must accept those images as if they were real and alive in our imagination while the rite goes on. That is the true purpose of ritual – to stir the imagination into exploring different levels of psychic awareness, rather than mere pretty spells of the gimme, gimme variety.

This is a form of spontaneous ritual in which we ourselves have to do what spontaneously occurs to us. It enables our subconscious mind to come to the surface and, as we know, there are some very strange powers lurking there. As Fortune points out, what we will come to realise is that behind this subconscious level is another deeper, hidden Mystery because the lifting of one veil leads to the discovery of yet another. At the same time, we are left knowing that that behind all these veils is an inner core, a hidden Truth that only the very select few will ever find. This is the message behind the magical practitioner's creed of: **Knowledge, Wisdom and Understanding**.

With the knowledge, will eventually come the understanding that even if we do not reach the hidden Truth in this lifetime – there will be other lifetimes. If we are elect, we will have the inner peace of knowing that it is so because the sureness of it being there, and the knowing that it *can* eventually be attained, can be reward enough in itself. The *real* purpose of ritual is to attain a higher level of consciousness that will enable us to explore the astral planes at will.

Mélusine Draco originally trained in the magical arts of traditional British Old Craft with Bob and Mériém Clay-Egerton. She has been a magical and spiritual instructor for over 20 years with Arcanum and the Temple of Khem, and writer of numerous popular books including *The Traditional Witchcraft* series and *The Dictionary of Magic & Mystery*. She lives in Ireland near the Galtee Mountains.

Frances Billinghurst

Amongst the shadows, the lone silhouette of a robed neophyte stood before the altar, with eyes resting on a hand-painted symbol placed between the two lit candles. This symbol emerged from meditations undertaken over a series of months.

A series of specific gestures were made, coinciding with the inhalation and exhalation of the breath. Then a pause as a generous measure of granulated incense was set upon the glowing charcoal, releasing its scent into the air.

Facing east, the place of the morning sun, the neophyte intoned words from an ancient language which is still used today in various religious practices. Such religious relevance, held little importance to the neophyte. The sign of a cross was drawn to connect the cosmic and earth energies, as well as two of the directions, north and south. This resulted in the neophyte standing in the centre of their own Universe as the words of the great Hermes Trismegistus had written: "What is the above is from the below and the below is from the above."

In each corner, pentagrams were drawn; the earthly star that represented the five elements. Each of which was activated by the vibration of specific sacred names, with the first being the unspoken name of the great creating force who gave life to all, the Tetragrammaton. The word itself released the hidden meaning of the balance of duality, both divinely as well as physically.

Each movement had specific meaning and purpose, and was performed with precision and care. Each visualisation was held with clarity for what was being created on the physical was being duplicated on the astral, leaving an imprint for all eternity.

The neophyte returned back to the east again where

archangels were called upon. The cross was repeated, centring the neophyte back into the universe they had created, a microcosm within a macrocosm, allowing the resonating vibrations to echo around the room and through the ether.

To the casual observer the neophyte may have appeared to have walked around the room, waved at four directions, and chanted some irrelevant words for today's technologically based society. To the neophyte, however, something completely different had happened. Through the use of their imagination (visualisation), focus (intent) and passion (belief), they had created a ritual and partaken in a magickal art whereby they would be able to access different realms and spiritual planes.

Everything that was used in the rite had a specific purpose. The colours chosen for the candles, the herbs and resin blended in the incense, not to mention the timing of the rite to coincide with specific planetary alignments, were all keys to assist the neophyte to unlock particular areas within their own psyche, allowing them to gain access to hidden realms and knowledge.

Here the neophyte rested, breathing in the incense scent, eyes focused back on the painted symbol upon the altar. A mantra intoned, loud and clear at first, but as the eyes gradually closed and the painted symbol was projected into the neophyte's own psyche, the voice lowered and the words created a gabbled tone. The doors to the hidden realms had opened allowing the neophyte to enter.

Steven Robert Morrison

From the moment that we first looked up in to the sky and, in a contemplative series of mono-syllabic grunts, wondered if there was something greater than us, we have had religious ritual, ceremony and spectacle.

The first shamans understood that if they needed to keep control over the tribe or the clan and to show that they had the power of the gods, they needed spectacle. Covered in a bearskin and skull, or later in a gold mask and surrounded by chanting virgins, then later in a temple with light and wealth reaching to the sky, it has always been about the show. However, these rituals, in whatever form and whenever held, have nothing to do with faith. They are simply religious functions still held for show.

Modern magickal ritual draws many, if not all, its elements from the religious elements of other faiths, philosophies and practices. There is nothing pure in essence, or original in thought, other that the heart or the intent of the adept. Everything is a substitute. We are not in Luxor or Delphi, the cups we use are not fashioned from the skulls of our enemies, and the law frowns upon sacrifice. We have only the lore, the image and the visualization on which to act.

In Christianity the practitioner consumes substitutes for the "body and blood" of Christ, in the form of "bread and wine". Saltines and orange juices would suffice as well. In any religion it is not about the tools, it is about intent. In the occult the same is true, perhaps even more so. This because witchcraft and the occult encourage visualization, trance and the "seeing" of your personal view of the Universal consciousness.

Is a fine silver athalme used in a show ritual any more powerful than a butter knife at a picnic blessing? Or the pencil used as an athalme by an inmate in prison? Does your Deity require exact recitation by rote, or do they care more for speech with emotion? Your "Divine" should accept whatever tools you have at hand. Because the intent in your heart is all that really matters.

Ritual, true Ritual, is not about not about what you have, where you are, or what you say, it is about taking time, the most precious of all our gifts and returning it to "the Source", whatever your concept of that Divine Source is. Whatever and whoever, your Divine is not impressed with the gold, the physical ritual, gesticulation and the smoke and mirrors of the ritual.

To use another Christian axiom that is often thought to be Biblical: "God does not dwell in temples built of stone, but dwells in the heart of every man." So it is not about what you build or have it is "who" you build. Leave the show to the carnival showmen and religious hucksters. You can get the same emotional rush standing on a sidewalk looking at the sky and just saying, "Thank you". In that split instant, visualizing, yourself to be naked on the top of the pyramid praising the sun. The greatest ritual is simply your act of acknowledgment, with your humility and your gratitude. Because in "true faith", you are always speaking and listening to your Divine, and you need impress no one but yourself.

Jennifer Schwartz

The role that ritual plays in my life has evolved over the past 20 years. As a goth punk teenager, I practiced an unspecific form of witchcraft that seemed to have a role in defining my identity and serving as a spiritual base. Raised by atheists in a relatively spiritual free environment, I hungered for some sense of order and belonging. I performed rituals for self-acceptance and to attract lovers and friends. Trivial, yet no less powerful, objects of teenage obsession. Once, when a ritual was too effective and I got more than I bargained for, I stepped back from ritual practice and expressed my spiritual side through a more intuitive spiritual practice based on my love of nature. Synchronicity and divinatory walks were the most magical happenings in my life for about 10 years. Little did I know that these two phases were closely linked and would lead me to perform a solitary initiation as a Wiccan.

I currently identify as a solitary Wiccan and practice Kundalini Yoga. When I first initiated myself as a Wiccan, I was only dabbling in Kundalini Yoga and attending classes in New York City maybe once a week, but was not practicing Kundalini at home. Wiccan ritual, however, was a part of my daily life. I practiced small rituals to cultivate personal growth and have a deeper connection with Mother Nature and the cosmos. Kundalini Yoga is a very spiritual form of yoga, full of mantras and mudras, that although the greater Kundalini community would not describe as ritual per se, has fulfilled that roll for me for the past year. I perform fewer Wiccan/pagan rituals these days, reserving more elaborate rituals for the Sabbaths, and keep my daily practice centered on Kundalini Yoga. Kundalini helps me cultivate self-love, which therefore attracts friends and lovers, establishes and reaffirms my connection with nature and the cosmos, and gives me that sense of community and order that I've sought since childhood. I guess it is the culmination of all the spiritual practices that I've had throughout my life, plus it works out of my physical body.

Ritual is an organic, evolving, living presence in my life. My involvement in it has changed over time to suit different needs, but is ultimately aimed at the same goal; to feel a connection to something greater than myself. Ritual, be it my Wiccan practice or yoga practice, creates a space and time that allows me to achieve that.

Ritual, in and of itself, is totally unnecessary. You have the cosmos inside of every cell in your body. You ARE the cosmos for goddess sake. Ritual is the scenic route. There is no doubt that ritual cultivates a feeling of excitement and power, but everything you eventually get out of ritual, was inside of you the whole time.

Ian Chandler

Pagans hold rituals to mark the passing of the seasons. These rites are not just celebrations but are purposeful and magical acts, reconnecting us to the cycles of nature, reminding us how dependent we are on the natural world, and inspiring us to conduct our lives with utmost reverence and respect for Mother Earth. In that way, we help ensure that the cycle continues not just for today, but also for years and generations to come.

People also have their seasons, and we can hold Rites of Passage to help them and their communities ease their transition from one stage of life to another, or mark their entry into different occupational groups or communities of interest.

Anthropologists such as Van Gennep identified three essential stages in Rites of Passage performed by traditional societies. In the pre-liminal stage, the person separates from their old status or group. The liminal stage represents the transition between the two states. The post-liminal stage incorporates the person into the new state or group. At each stage, symbols and actions are used to represent the journey being undertaken. In *The Ritual Process*, Victor Turner describes an Ndembu rite: *"Almost every article used, every gesture employed, every song or prayer, every unit of space or time, by convention stands for something other than itself"*.

Today in the West, people still undergo Rites of Passage. Weddings are the most obvious example. When a marriage proposal is accepted, the couple move from the pre-liminal single state to a liminal engaged state. They are both married but not married until the actual wedding, which marks the transition into the post-liminal state of being a married couple. The wedding itself reflects these stages over a shorter timescale. The stag/hen night is the pre-liminal stage where the betrothed say goodbye to their unmarried state. The liminal stage is when the couple dress in their wedding finery and are not allowed to see each other. The lifting of the veil after the wedding symbolises entry into the new wedded state.

However, many life stages are not explicitly celebrated. There is a still an urge by the person experiencing the transition to mark it somehow; but without the process being supported and held by the wider community, the experience is fractured. For example, adolescents want their family and community to recognise that they are no longer children, and so make their own symbolic gesture to mark their separation from the old state (such as, for example, by having a tattoo or piercing), but by failing to honour and complete the rite by welcoming them into the new status of young adults, society leaves them with no clear identity or status.

Just as we try to protect the natural world, as pagans we also need to hold the human world together and support the individuals within it to find their place. Rites of Passage that are clear, purposeful and held with love and respect by the pagan community are one way towards this.

Magic

Harmonia Saille

In past times, magic was used by the rural population and educated alike, but varied from culture to culture, and was sophisticated or unsophisticated depending on the practitioner. In modern times, these practices also vary from culture to culture and from practitioner to practitioner depending on their ability and often their beliefs. Accordingly, nothing much has changed.

Magic is frequently categorized into different types: High, Low, Sympathetic, Contagious, Ceremonial, Transformative and so forth, which themselves may have more lists of diverse forms of magical practice attached to them. There are many crossovers between magical practices, and similarities as well as differences. Here then is but a brief overview of just a few types of magical traditions that are practiced within paganism today.

What is Magic?

Magic has perhaps been most commonly described by Aleister Crowley *as "the science and art of causing change to occur in conformity to the will."* Ronald Hutton says something similar: *"Magic...consists of a control worked by humans over nature and by use of spiritual forces, so that the end result is expected to lie within the will of the person or persons working the spell or ritual."* (*The Pagan Religions of the Ancient British Isles*, reprint 2000.)

The predominant word here is "will". As magical practitioners we can add all the elements of magic to workings such as tools, ingredients, ritual, symbolism, invoking of deities or spirits, to a spell we like, but it is all useless without will.

When we cast a spell or charm, we are purposely promoting change. This is done through altering physical reality (or matter) in a way that harmonizes with the power of your mind. It is in essence mind over matter. So we use spells to help create or change events in our own lives and that of others and achieve this through the power of will. It is connected with synchronicity in that it encourages the interconnection between mind and matter, or psychic/spiritual and actual events.

When we cast the spell we tap into the invisible. Great concentration, visualization, and patience are required to make it effective.

But can anyone practice magic? Hutton goes on to say that in theory anybody should be able to carry magic out, but generally practitioners are specialists and just like in the world of nature, magic can be used for good or bad (more on this in ethics). Therefore, training and direction are needed.

Ritual

Ritual helps our mindset. It is a discipline that helps us reach into the unseen. A ritual works symbolically as each movement represents something. Symbols work on a conscious and subconscious level. In the case of the spell, the symbols work on both. However, ritual also reveals a mythical reality. What happens within the ritual is invisible (the altering of reality), a sort of sacred narrative working in the background, but of which the magical practitioner is conscious and believes in (see *Chaos Magic*). Within the ritual we pass through different stages of the spell in order to create it. All the time we are focused on the goal and have a heightened awareness of what is happening, this also helps in summoning up the invisible but powerful energies that make it work.

Magical Correspondences

Correspondences are tables of items such as deities, nature spirits, angels, elements, colors, herbs, trees, essential oils, crystals, seasons, moon phases, time of day, planets and various symbols – for instance astrological or rune – which we utilize for concentrating and directing magical forces. They are used in both higher and lower forms of magic.

If we put lists of correspondences side by side in categories, and then look for correlation between them for a spell, say on protection, and then draw connecting lines, we would be left with a sketch of a web as each correspondence links to another and another. Consequently, this web is also weaved in magical preparation, and is part of the ritual of building up energy, in which the practitioner finds the scope widens, focus is greater, and the spell is more concentrated and powerful.

We choose correspondences from different categories that will suit our needs and purposes, resonate with us, and are appropriate to the time in which we have to complete the task.

Categories of Magic

Folk magic involves the use of simple charms similar to those used for centuries, more often in the rural community.

If you have never practiced magic before, then pagans often find this is a good place to start. Folk magic has existed since man first walked the earth and even though it is an uncomplicated form of magic, this does not mean no skill is required. Often outsiders believe it is all about props, when in fact much forethought still goes into each magical purpose.

Folk magic will often involve herbs and flowers and all manner of household and garden objects such as pins, bottles, candles, small lengths of ribbon, odd bits of paper, the spoken word, pebbles, nails, pieces of copper and brass, wood, bark and ingredients from the larder. It will be used for simple purposes such as protection, love, healing, money, luck, communication, in fact, everyday problems and needs that crop up that we personally or others may need help with.

Candle magic is perhaps the most popular of the folk magic items to use in spells. These are often dressed in essential oils that correspond to the color of the candle (black for instance for absorbing negative energy), so frankincense or black pepper essential oil may be used in combination with a gemstone such as obsidian or an appropriate herb.

This is not to say a spell should be in any way rushed, care not taken, thought not put into it, and most of all lacking the power of will.

Nature magic involves the seasons, and working with them, becoming in tune with them. For nature magic we need to become nature aware, get out there in all weathers, be sentient to it – touch the trees, connect with them, the leaves and flowers. For the person interested in nature, weeds suddenly become magical plants. It is connecting with these plants and trees that we become conscious that they are alive, have spirit, magical properties and healing powers.

In becoming psychically connected to nature, we work with what we have, and that means in the winter using what is there such as holly and evergreens and the energy and spirits of the season, and in summer working with the plants and flowers as they appear throughout the season, as they do not appear all at once.

Practitioners of nature magic will also connect to the spirit of the plant or tree, or the nature spirit that is attached to it and the phases of the moon. Nature magic is often used in combination with folk magic.

Ceremonial magic is generally classified as high magic and will more frequently involve such principles as hermetic teachings, sacred geometry, alchemy, and the kabbalah.

High magic is for the more experienced magical practitioner. Much study will be undertaken, almost certainly training from another practitioner more experienced than themselves. This is often by means a society such as *The Hermetic Order of the Golden Dawn, The Inner Light,* or coven training. There is no easy way to become versed in the skills of high magic, it takes years.

Ceremonial magic will involve ritual; often consecrated or dedicated tools; knowledge of symbolism from many cultures such as astrological symbols and the tree of life, along with invoking and vanishing pentagrams; the planets; the elements; invocation of divine sources; actions and the spoken word. Visualization is also part of high magic (and indeed most forms of magic), meditation and imagination.

Ceremonies will be long, well thought out, and protection will be in place such as casting a circle.

The practitioner of high magic in general will undertake years of training, keeping up with their studies. They will maintain a journal, perhaps even have studied psychotherapy.

Divinatory magic: When we study forms of divination such as Ogham, runes, dowsing, scrying (such as the mirror or the crystal ball), tarot, and I Ching, they speak directly to us. There is the basic meaning of what we see (i.e. a tarot card or rune symbol), and then there is the secret meaning accessed through the interaction of mind, matter and spirit; for divination methods reveal both inner and outer truths. This magical symbolic language is used to communicate between man and the gods or microcosm and macrocosm, and the conscious and the unconscious.

To increase our intuitive abilities we need to practice using them with confidence regardless of our level of ability. The more we use our sixth sense, the better we will become. We have to learn to recognize our intuition and trust in it.

When we divine we are calling on a hidden intuitiveness to help us to interpret what we see, which we can then use for our own everyday life problems and situations and those of others.

Some forms of divination lend themselves well to magical practice, such as the runes (including bind runes), dowsing, or tarot. These are used in the same way as correspondences.

Chaos Magic: "In Chaos Magic, beliefs are not seen as ends in themselves, but as tools for creating desired effects." (*Liber Kaos* by Peter J. Carroll.) Carroll goes on to say that to fully realize this is to face a freedom in which *"Nothing is True and Everything is*

Permitted", and that although everything is possible, there are no certainties. Since the 1970s Peter James Carroll is the name most associated with Chaos Magic. His writings on the subject are a must for the practitioner.

The theory of belief being an active magical tool seems logical to many magical practitioners, though some would agree it is not necessary. In this, beliefs are seen as true and, as I reported above, beliefs become a mythical reality (see *Ritual* above). In Chaos Magic then, belief is used as a tool to exact change, but it is not the only component of this form of magic. Chaos Magic also borrows from many other forms of magical and spiritual practice such as Taoism (and other forms of Eastern mysticism), Gnosticism, and Shamanism.

In some ways Chaos Magic resembles shamanic magic in that it often uses an ALC – or an altered state of consciousness – to perform magical acts (though it is also used by many other magical practitioners).

Shamanic magic: In shamanic magic, as stated above, an altered state of consciousness is used for magical purposes often for healing. Seidr (various spellings) is perhaps one of the best known forms of shamanic magic, but also Hedge Riding/Magic.

Seidr is a form of ancient Norse magic that according to myth was principally performed by women. Although some men also practiced it, it was thought of as unmanly as the practitioner, having moved into a trance state, became vulnerable to earthly dangers. This was the case with Odin himself. The goddess Freyja was a proficient practitioner of Seidr magic, which was practiced by the Vanir. When Freyja joined the Aesir with her father Njord and her brother Frey, it is said that she passed her knowledge on to Odin.

Seidr and Hedge Riding have a strong association with shamanism, in that the practitioner uses a trance state to perform magical work. The trance enables the practitioner through an altered state of consciousness to gain access to the astral planes.

In this trance state, the practitioner can prophesize, divine the future, influence the weather, shapeshift, and all manner of spell work and magical acts. In their journeying the practitioner meets with spirits and elementals to ask for assistance to carry out magical work.

Seidhr and Hedge Riding are often thought to be dangerous forms of magic; however, if properly taught and guided the novice should be perfectly safe. And guidance in the early stages for the novice is essential.

Whatever form of magic such as those above or others, one thing is clear, training is needed. Even with the lower forms of magic, study and training should be in place before we start practicing. Magical training is in general ongoing and the practitioner never stops learning.

Ethics

This article cannot end without some reference to the ethics of magic. Magic is often described as black, white or even grey. But is it the magic that is good or evil or is it the working of that magic? It is indeed the intent that is black or white and it is commonly agreed that magic is a neutral force, and it is indeed what you do with it that is positive or negative.

Spells, positive and negative, have been around since ancient times and used in many cultures. However, a negative spell does not necessarily translate as "evil" or "black". A binding spell is classed as negative as it is cast to prevent one person from harming another or others. It is up to the individual if they think this is in opposition to their personal ethics. A love spell (in that one person is willed to love another and against what is natural) would be a negative one too, and most people would agree that this type of spell should never be employed. We cannot force another to love us. Moreover, this would be a false love and not a real love and would not in the long run be beneficial to the recipient. In Norse mythology this happened to Frey when he sent his servant Skirnir to woo Gerd, giving his magic sword to him as a reward. Skirnir accomplished his task with the use of magical runes. However, the loss of his sword causes the downfall of Frey at Ragnarok. Translating this into modern times, let us say that a woman uses a spell to attract a certain man, and to cause that man to fall in love with her. The man does fall in love with her but turns out to be abusive; the woman then finds it hard to rid herself of him. The spell backfires and so it causes her downfall. It is often a case of be careful what you wish for.

Many pagan magical practitioners follow the threefold law: *"Eight words the Wiccan Rede fulfill, An it harm none, do what ye will."* (The *Rede of the Wiccae*, Lady Gwen Thompson.)

Not every person believes in the law of karma, and some people do cast negative spells as long as they are not meant intentionally to harm another, possibly for protection or to prevent harm being done. Others cast negative spells regardless depending on their belief system and culture.

Whatever you decide, whether you follow the ethic above or your own personal ethic, it is generally agreed within paganism that you should not cast spells without much forethought over the possible consequences. Even with positive spells the practitioner needs to think about what the possible consequences could be. If in doubt, avoid it. If you think it is negative, listen to yourself, it probably is. There is a fine line between what is right and what is wrong, but experience will help in the long run.

Harmonia Saille is an author and Hedge Witch who holds workshops on spirituality, divination and other subjects both locally and at international spiritual events. She is the author of *Pagan Portals: Hedge Witchcraft* and *Pagan Portals: Hedge Riding* and lives in Ireland.

Elinor Predota

Whether one categorises magic as nature, folk, ceremonial, divinatory, chaos, or shamanic as Harmonia Saille does, as questing, changing or making as some Druids do, or simply as white or black (or occasionally grey), it is generally agreed that desire, intent, and most especially will, are essential ingredients for its performance.

Eight words the Wiccan Rede fulfill: An it harm none, do what you will.
Doreen Valiente

Although I am not a Wiccan, I have always been fascinated by the final statement of the Wiccan Rede. Many people interpret it as saying that it's okay to do whatever you want, as long as you don't hurt anyone. But a single sentence in Marian Green's excellent book, *A Witch Alone*, set me off on a different path many years ago. Green writes: "'An' in Old English means 'In order that' and 'will' is your soul's true will, not the whim of the moment."

So how does the Rede read? For me, it now translates to this: "In order that your actions harm none, do only what your soul truly desires and wills." That sounds rather different, and puts a completely different ethical spin on the practice of magic. To understand the implications here requires less by way of 'whatever you want' and more by way of careful theological consideration, deep self-knowledge, and attention to the inter-connectedness of all beings in the Web of Life.

My own journey of understanding regarding will, magic, theology, self-knowledge and interconnection has taken me from an unwillingness to practice spellcraft at all to happily using spells as a natural expression of who I am. My thoughts in choosing to perform or not perform magic have shifted from, "Who am I to impose my will on the world?" to, "I have as much and as little right to exercise my will in the world as any other being."

The question of spellcraft, of magical ethics and even of

'white' and 'black' magic all comes down to how one views and relates to power – one's own innate power in the world. Magical action and inaction are no different to any other action or inaction. I have no way to know what the effects of any of it will be. There are effects that are predictable and ones that are unpredictable, ones that I desire and ones that I don't. Ethical choice depends upon being willing to take responsibility for the effects of both my actions and inactions, whether magical or mundane, regardless of whether they are the ones I intend or not.

Orla Clancy

Magic is so fluid. You can adapt it to suit your life. Just forget the basic rule: "An it harm none, do what ye will."

I deliberately spell the word without a 'k'. Our ancient ancestors who first used it did not read or write, but passed on their lore through stories and actual memory, so they weren't finicky about how the word looked.

But, as I said, magic itself is fluid. I'm more Pagan than Wiccan, but I still use small spells when I want to find a convenient parking space, for example, or a table in a restaurant. I have also woven spells around my home to protect it from intruders and burglars and anyone who may seek to harm us – it also keeps my cats safe. Knowing there is an umbrella of power over my home that renders it invisible and impenetrable to undesirables is reassuring.

Some years ago there was going to be a huge house built between my small bungalow and my nearest neighbour's house. Neither my neighbour nor I wanted this, and I decided that there would be no building there, and that this would work out well for everyone involved, so I did a spell to that effect. Our legal attempt to block this building delayed construction by three months. In those three months, the daughter of the family, whose money was earmarked to finance the construction, met a man from the UK and fell in love with him, and decided to put her money into a house there instead. Even though legally there was planning permission to build beside mine for the next five years, she built a life someplace else. She's happy. A good spell.

I am a visual artist. Art contains elements of magic. Lines and pigment are transformed into something else entirely. You can be methodical as you like, but at a certain point you get into a state of Zen, and something ... happens. You work on a piece for a while, and step away from it, and you come back and realise that you've created something special, a new entity almost.

But my favourite everyday magic is in my kitchen. Recipes are widely available, online. The kitchen is where so many worlds meet: science, because cause and effect come into play – and if you don't watch what you're doing, your meal can burn; creativity, because you might have to tweak a dish to make it work; and magic, because you are blending diverse ingredients and adding a tiny flavour of your own to the pot. Certain herbs and spices have special properties.

I am intrigued by Serbian-born scientist Nikola Tesla, who believed that humans could harness the power of nature by harnessing the power of the atmosphere. I love the thought of energy being available to everyone freely. It's simply using the elements – the air, the water, creating electricity which comes to earth as fire. Aether is the fifth element that links them, and perhaps someday we'll have 'aether' towers every 100 km or so, to harness the power from the skies. As part of my own spells, to ground them I think of my body as a conductor of power, like a metal pole conducts lightning into the earth. Tesla was onto something.

Magic is everyday, but extraordinary. It is symbiotic, but like a river in its force and ability to shape our lives. Its ordinariness is its strength – humanity might have so many differences in opinions about so many things, but the elements that make up magic remain a common denominator.

As a people, all we have to do now is learn to use this great gift well.

Ali 'Zelanna' Button

I like to call it Magick, as opposed to magic, to show the difference between what magicians on stage perform and what we do. Not everyone uses this distinction, but for me, it is a trapping for my mind to help me feel 'in the mood', to focus and gain a higher state of consciousness. It makes it feel special. I also like to set the right ambience before I start. I find some background music helps me focus, something with no words or sudden booms to distract me. It drowns out the sounds of life going on around me, and focuses my attention solely on the purpose for the working. I like to light some incense with an association to the working I am about to do, plus it smells great! I also light candles on my altar, and work by just their light alone. This all helps me feel as if something special is occurring. It helps me focus, and starts to build expectation and energy. I assemble the tools and ingredients for the spell within this ambience, though as I have grown within my chosen path these have become less and less. It helps when you are just starting out to have all the trappings, but you soon become aware that all you really need is yourself.

My Magickal workings always begin by cleansing and releasing any excess energy. I use a very personal visualization to do this, and you should always find something that feels right for you. I feel strongly associated with the element of Water and as such I visualize myself stepping under a waterfall and seeing dirt and debris wash away from myself. This dirt and debris is the excess and negative energy that I wish to release. Bringing negativity into your Magick can be extremely unhelpful, and can prevent effective spellcasting. I also ground myself once I have finished. I have always associated 'grounding' with Earth so I like to touch the ground/floor and visualize any excess energy flowing out through my palms. I can't really stress enough how important it is to ground. I spent many years being very lax with this, and as such I suffered tremendously. Trust me when I say a hangover is NOTHING in comparison! From this point, I usually like to sit quietly looking into the candle light, or meditate for a little while before raising any energy for the spell. Like many things, raising energy will feel different to each individual and although you can learn the techniques for doing this, no one can tell you how it will feel for you. I know when I have raised energy because I feel very shaky. It's almost how you feel when adrenaline is coursing through your body. This will be very personal to you, as will the spell itself.

As Above, So Below. As Within, So Without. To Know, To Will, To Dare, To Keep Silent.
An It Harm None Do What Ye Will.

Danette Wilson

I am a person who has always believed in Magic. I am constantly learning, and on my quest have met many wonderful and knowledgeable people. I am deeply connected to the subtle flows of energy in the world around me. I have also seen many transformations in my own life because of it.

I was born on a Wednesday during the witching hour, Celtic on my Dad's side, blending Scottish and Irish heritage, with my Mom's side blending a Grandpa Gypsy tarot reader from Budapest, Hungary, and a Grandma from Bratislava, Slovakia. I didn't realise until later in life that it was no wonder I had been in love with Magic my whole life.

They say the teacher comes at the right time. I believe that. For when writing a story on Witches, Laurie Cabot and the Sully Erma VOODOO video rang loud and clear. Power, strength, together we stand. I'm all about that. As a speaker, and teacher, she made sense. In her videos, and her books too. I wanted to study with her and followed through to 2nd Degree. As my life has progressed I have always wanted to expand learning, and submersing myself in other religions; it became a lot like my love of travel from living with the Masai in Africa, to climbing Tulum in Mexico, to tracing the path of Dracula through the Romanian countryside. My travel started to take an occult turn, blending learning, too, on trips. Life is a journey. I have loved and been blessed with many teachers from learning Hoodoo with Lucky Mojo and Cat Yronwode, or Strega with Lori Bruno, Voodoo with Bloody Mary, Folk Magic with Orion Foxwood, Starr Casas. I wanted to get to know places as well, whether Salem, or New Orleans, in the middle of Stonehenge or Avebury and stand in places out of time, and in time. Walking between the worlds in those places is on a daily basis, it seems. The ethers sing of MAGIC, it's in the air we breathe.

Tempestuousness of the heart and soul. Isn't that what we Witches want? To be free, to be wild, to laugh with crazed laughter at our foibles and fantasy, without a care? That's what cancer taught me. Even though you're losing your hair you tell yourself you are beautiful in the mirror every day, and know in your heart that you are a survivor. You can get through this. You will, you do and you dare to laugh even in crisis, and you are able to move on.

Magic IS spells, it is intent. It is also a vein that runs through us making us want to read all the books, and meet others with the same interests. But whether in a coven or all alone, you are at the core of the life you weave.

Prayer & Meditation

Nimue Brown

There isn't a clear distinction between prayer and meditation in any religious tradition. The nature of both practices means that to do one has at least the potential to involve the other, so the grey areas are inevitable. Prayer leads to a calming of the mind. Meditation can open the mind in a way that brings us to prayer. I think generally modern Pagans focus more on a meditation tradition. We have a better described and more widely shared meditation tradition. By comparison, there isn't much coherence of prayer tradition in Paganism. Generally individuals pray privately and alone, or use a small handful of agreed communal prayers for ritual. Compared to the vast body of prayer texts you can expect to find in most religions, even when we bring in ancient texts, Pagans have far less material to hand. That doesn't mean we aren't praying, just that we aren't all praying in the same ways.

One of the main reasons for this relationship with prayer is that, unlike other religions, Paganism in its many forms does not direct you towards a specific deity, or even a pantheon. Common prayers are tricky without an agreement about where these are directed. We might as individuals feel moved to pray to The God and The Goddess, to specific deities from any of the ancient pantheons, or to our ancestors, manifestations of spirit, or our own higher consciousness. We might even undertake something akin to prayer as a formal expression of gratitude without identifying a specific entity to offer that to.

While prayer suggests petitioning the divine for favours, this is not the sole reason to pray. All the major faith traditions have far richer and more complex prayer traditions than petition alone. In essence, the aim of prayer is to open the seeker to the divine, or the numinous. How you think of the numinous and what you understand it to be, is a whole other issue, separate from the mechanics of prayer. Prayer can be approached as a disciplined activity – like meditation – with very little belief or certainty required. It is simply a way of being open and seeing what comes. Thus one does not need belief in deity to explore prayer in private. It is only shared, public prayer that tends to require consensus.

In meditation, we are also concerned with opening our minds, although not necessarily to some concept of deity. To do this, we begin by creating a degree of inner calm. A mind in turmoil cannot be turned towards any meaningful, spiritual work. There are many simple grounding and focusing exercises designed for just this purpose. In sitting still, paying attention to breathing, deliberately relaxing muscles and so forth, we allow our minds to slow down a little. By concentrating attention on simple things – mantras, images and concepts – we let the usual white noise in the mind die down. In this process, a clearer inner voice emerges and we become more capable of having a single, deliberate flow of thought.

In my experience, it is difficult to pray without first entering a calm, meditative state. I have no inclination to approach the divine blabbering whatever happens to be going around inside my head. That would be neither respectful, nor productive. Even if all I mean to do is petition for help, it still makes better sense to do so from a place of clarity. The calm mind is far more open, far more able to listen and be aware as a consequence of not being distracted by its own noise. I find that whether I aim to pray or to meditate, the calm mind is more receptive and more able to work and experience deeply. Cultivating peace and the ability to become peaceful is essential work in any spiritual path, I feel.

Many people meditate solely for the purpose of relaxing the body and cultivating calm. Meditation does not automatically lead to prayer, but it does reliably help the practitioner develop a more spiritual life. Taking time to think and feel in this way, changes and enriches us. In developing the capacity to be calm and open, meditation creates possibilities for growth. We might use that quiet space to pay more attention to our thoughts, feelings and physical condition so as to become more integrated within ourselves. We may seek to clear the mind so as to be more fully immersed in the moment. Alternatively, from the place of calm we can delve into deep contemplation of just about anything. Time given to deep contemplation in turn enriches understanding and opens the way to inspiration. New connections form in the mind during such work, fresh insights are made, empathy and compassion increase. Spirituality is a condition of mind, not a facet of belief. One can have belief and no spiritual practice at all, and equally one can have spiritual practice without holding belief.

Pathworking meditations, with constructed narratives, take us into the landscape of the soul. This kind of meditation can be used to deliberately change our thinking, as well as being a tool for understanding the psyche. Visualizations can help us to muster intent, creating belief in what we mean to achieve and our ability to act. By seeing the goal achieved in the mind's eye, we can progress towards it. In this way, visualization can overlap significantly with magical undertakings. The skills and discipline of meditation have considerable value for anyone wishing to explore magical paths.

Shamanic journeying can also be understood as a form of meditation in which the shaman travels into realms of spirit to seek insight. Here again the boundaries between meditation and prayer blur. This appeal to spirit can be very much akin to prayer. Rather than casting prayer out into the ether, in the hopes of being heard, journeying brings you closer to the intended recipient. The dedication of seeking can be understood as an aspect of prayer here as well.

The more established religions have collections of prayers a believer might use. These may be repetitive, and are often rather general. They exist not to make specific communications between the human and the divine, but to place a person in a particular state of mind. In many ways, the rosary, or the Friday prayers of Islam act more effectively as meditations than petitions. They are, however, meditations aimed at making the individual aware of, and open to deity. These prayers can also function to soothe and settle the mind, an effect inherent in meditative work. Often this experience of calm is enough to give meaning to the act of prayer even when specific requests are not granted and a consciousness of the divine is not achieved.

Paganism does not draw on existing prayers in the same way. We don't have the long modern tradition of prayer writing that other faiths have, but both ancient and modern prayers do exist. As a group of people we don't show much sign of being dependant on these. However, if words are not your medium of preference, borrowing from existing material can be a useful way of acquiring tools. Even simple circle chants can be utilised to create the right mindset. In this approach, it is largely the soft comfort of repetition that carries the work, and any words you find relevant and pleasing will suffice. Anything we write for ourselves is at least as valuable as anything we might borrow. With the Pagan emphasis on individuality and creativity, there are many reasons to write your own prayers and meditations rather than letting your spiritual experience be shaped by someone else's ideas.

There are times when meditation can take on a life of its own. Deep in a trance state, the planned work can be changed as new, unintended elements enter the mix. On such occasions, meditation feels less like a contrived exercise and more like an immediate and spiritual experience. We are no longer merely naval gazing or giving the imagination a workout. It can feel as though something beyond us has noticed our intentions and responded. Such experiences can be as alarming as they are profound. Here, the techniques of prayer can be a great advantage: The open, respectful soul, willing to listen, acting from love rather than anger or hatred, is the one best equipped to explore such an experience.

I have also experienced occasions, conversely, when what started as prayer took me towards something more like trance work or dreaming. If you are in a state of being open to the unknown, you are by definition also in a state of willingness to experience something unexpected. We can hold total control of self in both prayer and meditation. However, the consequence of such deliberate control is that little new can come to us. There's a degree of risk in being open, but to experience the numinous is to be moved and changed. If a practice is to be more than a mental discipline, more than a habit of cultivating good thoughts, a degree of surrendering control is called for, so that something else can come in. By this I do not mean submitting to deity. Other religions use prayer and meditation precisely as routes towards total submission, but this is not the Pagan way. We seek awareness and relationship, not submission. However, as with human relationships, there are times when you have to open up and let go to allow things to happen.

Much of what we do in all aspects of our lives, along with how we do it and how we understand the consequences, derives from our intent. The person who intends to pray will interpret their results based on that. The person who journeys shamanically will understand their experiences in the context of that approach. The person who meditates may well not perceive divine or spirit influence even if they have an identical experience to the one postulated for the other two scenarios above. This is the nature of the human condition. We are limited and finite beings, and what we see depends to a degree on what we were looking for. This is as well, because to be truly unlimited would be to lose your mind.

Prayer and meditation are nothing more than sets of tools created by people. These tools enable us to attempt certain things. Just as water-wings are not the only solution to floating, so these are not the only ways to find spiritual experience or live a spiritual life. It may be more productive to think of prayer and meditation as two kinds of door, amongst many doors. On the other side of those doors lies mystery. It might be one big mystery out there, and then again, maybe it isn't. We aren't well placed to tell.

If you choose a spiritual life, then you probably have a hunger in your soul for mystery. Not in the sense of solving puzzles or debunking myths, but a hankering after that which is beyond us. A longing for connection with something more than the self does not even call for belief, in the conventional sense. That we feel a need, does not of course prove that the universe holds a magical answer to it. I would argue that the universe itself is quite enough, whether it has gods in it or not. Still, for many of us that desire for something wonderful, unknowable and still somehow possible to encounter, is a significant driving force. The experience of life and death can bring us into contact with that sense of mystery and wonder. Prayer and meditation are both doors, or tools, that allow us all to become more aware of what was here all along, or what might be, and of that which defies any attempt at description. You could achieve the same effects though dance, drumming or anything else that has the capacity to open you up. Religions across the world all have their arts and expressions, physical trials, and paths to beauty. You might get there through pain, or study, or parenting. Anything has the potential to be a door into a different and greater awareness, providing you have the will and dedication to use it.

The advantage of turning to prayer and meditation is the wealth of supporting materials and communities out there. The Western Pagan community might not have generated much material, but we have a whole world of belief and practice to explore and learn from. Walking entirely alone is hard. Having sources to turn to both for things to try and ways of understanding the outcomes, can help shore up your practice and is very affirming. In our current climate, the line between spiritual experience and insanity is all too thin. A person who works with a tradition and a community has more reassurance, more checks upon their flights of fancy, and more grounding. Assuming of course that the tradition and community they belong to is itself sane and grounded. Some cults and groups are not as dependable.

Even if you do not carry either prayer or meditation forward in your work, it is worth taking some time to explore one or both practices. Both will provide you with skills and mental discipline that make utilising more individual doors a lot easier. Neither activity is strictly speaking necessary as part of a Pagan path. However, both achieve tangible results in terms of expanding the mind and as methods for opening yourself up. This is why they have such enduring popularity. Go to either seeking immediate gratification and 'results' in the form of prayers answered, or visualisations made real, and you are in for a disappointment. Go to learn, to unfurl yourself like an opening bud, and these tools will serve you well.

Druid, author, bard and dreamer.

Nimue Brown is OBOD trained, a founding member of Bards of the Lost Forest, Druid Network member and previously a volunteer for The Pagan Federation. She is the author of *Druidry and Meditation, Druidry and the Ancestors* and *Pagan Portals: Spirituality Without Structure* and lives in Gloucestershire, UK.

Jo Robson

Prayer – a word that evokes mixed reactions in me and one which I have not been comfortable with. Looking in just one dictionary there are at least five separate definitions of prayer, none of which sit well with me. The type of prayer that I experienced as a child would have been defined as a devout petition to God. Encouragement to use prayer as a forum for requesting something desired. So in the simple terms of a child I was asking for things, a nice house, our missing cat to return home, a sin to be forgiven. This did not sit right with me but I could not on my own at the time objectively consider the greater possibilities. I left the church and prayer behind.

Or so I thought until one day when riding my motorbike and having a rather near miss, caused by another's reckless driving, I found myself muttering to the Goddess of Motorcyclists! I am not sure if I am her only follower, but the experience did prompt thought and a return to the questions that I had when younger.

So what did my prayer consist of? A devout petition as it turns out, *help me to keep me safe, give me the patience I need to drive safely, the skills to anticipate and avoid and the strength to let go the wrongs and the anger.* So back to my dilemma of younger years, asking for things. This has taken me a while of weaving together conscious and subconscious thought, new ideas and a different perspective, which will no doubt keep developing over time. I believe that the divine, however you define that, is within every 'living' thing on this planet including me. So prayer is in part a call to the divine within myself, but equally important it is a conscious act. In the context of riding my bike with a prayer I am consciously telling myself to calm down, let go, concentrate and engage the skills that I possess that keep me safe.

It has taken a long time to incorporate prayer into my daily routine, but the benefits are wonderful and I would highly recommend it. My routine has developed over time and my next step will be to write my own forms of thanks and devotion. My prayer is a space to contact daily with the divine, previously when busy and unable to get a chance to meditate I have felt very disconnected; my daily prayer helps to keep me connected. It is also a space for me to stop, take a breath, and give thanks – let go of the mundane worries of the day and be thankful for all that I have and am. So for me now, although I am still not taken with the word prayer, I do pray – but with a less traditional definition:

'A spiritual communion with the divine, creating a space where I take stock and express gratitude and appreciation.'

Rebecca M Taylor

The terms prayer and meditation have many different connotations, largely dependant upon one's personal experience thus far with both concepts. In the broader community, prayer is often associated with mainstream religion and prostrating oneself to a specific God, with meditation being relegated to the clichéd idea of the monasteries of Asia/India. Such a limited view of these concepts does them a great disservice; prayer and meditation are both powerful tools, particularly if used in conjunction with one another.

During my childhood I experienced many a Sunday in church as well as a myriad of church Christenings and Weddings. My exposure to prayer in an 'organised' context was great. I was a lover of words from a very young age and absorbed these words of prayer like a sponge, taking them away with me and thinking upon their meaning. My childhood also involved a great deal of time in nature, exploring the Australian Bush, wandering vast ocean beaches and playing in the family garden. I noticed a great deal, I noticed the similarity in feeling of sitting in prayer in church to sitting in wonder in the outdoors. To me, the sacredness of both was obvious and tangible. As I grew older I began to write my own 'prayers' to speak to the divine I could feel outdoors, no one told me I couldn't. I wasn't talking to a God, I was just putting it out there. What I now know as prayer was my way of seeking guidance and support.

My Grandparents introduced me to the concept of meditation in my teens, they attended a weekly Reiki gathering and I was very curious. My interest in Reiki opened me up to so many, varied experiences, not least of which was meditation, both guided and unguided. Our evenings began with a group guided meditation and we were encouraged to sit in quiet, solo, meditation after receiving Reiki. It was within this quiet space that many an insight would come, still does. One can be so caught up in the busyness of day to day life that we forget to stop and listen. Many a time in my own life I have felt swept away with the ups and downs of daily living and when it all threatens to overwhelm me I recall the peace and calm of the meditative state and I work to return there. It is not always easy, but it is always rewarding in some way.

It matters not whether you have tried Prayer and Meditation before or whether you are thinking of trying for the first time. Prayer and Meditation combined provide oneself with the capacity to 'dial up' spirit in the manner to which one is comfortable, communicate(pray) and then open oneself up to the divine(meditation – space to sit within spirit) where insight can come and magic can happen. As with most things, practice makes perfect, give it a go and see where the journey takes you

Robyn Stroll

Every breath, every act, and every thought can all be prayers dedicated to the Gods, and can all as easily become meditative practices. I myself walk the world with a deep-seated spirituality, and so I see in every person an aspect of God and Goddess, and in each action or word a lesson to be had. In return, I seek to venerate that which is around me with mindfulness and respect. When I laugh, it is to share joy with the divine. When I cry, it is to implore their mercy. I meditate deeply on that which I see around me, seeking meaning in people, in nature, in myself.

A prayer need not be simply a call into the dark for help – it can be to praise, to honour, to dedicate an act or event. It can be to pass them a message, or to beg for wisdom. A prayer can take any form, wordless and internal, written prose, or spoken and sung aloud. The only requirement of prayer is that it comes from the heart, to speak to something outside yourself and connect you to the Divine.

In contrast, one need not be spiritually inclined to meditate, although certainly it enriches the spiritual life of the practitioner. Meditation is a powerful tool to seek within, instead of praying to something outside of yourself. Through meditation we learn to calm the mind and observe ourselves and the world. You can meditate to clear your mind, or to sharpen your focus on a single thought.

Prayer and meditation are tools that cross spiritual lines across all global traditions. Every religion has a form of both, sometimes several accepted practices. In the modern Pagan, we find that there are endless ways to going about these practices, and by sharing our methods we can only become more spiritually enriched.

A thing that I have found most interesting is that both prayer and meditation commonly begin with a breath – we breathe in and out to pray, and one of the most simple forms of meditation is to observe our own breathing. How interesting, then, that the Hebrew word 'ruach', meaning 'wind' or 'breath', can also refer to 'the soul' or 'spirit'.

In Buddhism it is said that there are 8 ways to the Centre; that is to say to achieve Enlightenment. Prayer and meditation are two of those ways, bringing us deeper into ourselves and the true understanding of life and what it really means: connection with all things. The differentiation between prayer and mediation is your intention. The limitation on either one is only how far you can push yourself.

A final thought - perhaps the greatest thing that prayer and meditation can both help us to achieve in our everyday lives is compassion for others, truly putting us in touch with our most humane selves as well as our most Divine.

Jenny Watt

I was raised in a home that participated in both the Catholic and Presbyterian religions. I was raised primarily Catholic, a religion that consists greatly of rituals. The prayers and supplications are highly ritualized and, to me, seemed only a one-way conversation with God. We said prayers that asked saints to intercede for us. We said prayers asking for forgiveness. When prayers were said in free form, they consisted of thanking God and asking for more. I know that most of my prayers were rote recitations. I said the correct words, ended with Amen and went on with my life. To me, God was a distant entity who spent all his time listening and granting wishes – or not, in which case, the prayers changed to moaning and cursing an unfair God. At no time were we taught that part of prayer was to listen for responses to our questions and requests, and I wondered why, if God was all knowing, I even had to ask for what I wanted. It seemed like He should already know.

My path to Paganism began with learning to meditate. I read in several Deepak Chopra books about how our greatest desires could be broadcast to the Universe in the silence between our thoughts. It was not our thoughts or words that communicated our greatest desires, but our silence. For me, the silence was hard to achieve. When I'd try to sit in silent meditation, my ADD addled brain jumped from thought to thought so quickly that I would jump up in frustration. On the best days I could maintain a meditative silence for only a few seconds before the thoughts would come racing at me again. I tried walking meditations and yoga practice. I found that I could silence my mind more easily with motion, but I still did not feel like I was achieving true meditation, not like they described in the books I'd read.

Then, one day, I tried a mantra meditation. I started by repeating a sound or a word on each breath in and out. On some days I would say mantras consisting of several words, each said on a breath. Finally, with repetition and familiarity, my brain relaxed and quieted and I felt like I was enjoying true meditation. I not only spoke, but also found silence and in the silence I heard the responses or messages that I needed to hear. It was then I realized that all those prayers I had repeated as a dutiful Catholic child were really nothing more than mantras. They provided a pathway to meditation. The part I had not been taught was the silence and the listening. Now meditation forms a big part of my practice as a Pagan. My meditations have evolved to become a sort of ritual, but the most important part will continue to be the silence and the listening.

Healing

Shirley Laboucane

To my mother's people medicine addresses imbalances in all areas of a person's life; the healing process is holistic, the medicines, prayers and dances nurture the mind, body and spirit. The medicine wheel symbolizes the continuation of all life and through the Creator, Mother Earth and All My Relations a circle is formed and when we each share our gifts and gather in healing circles we can create a harmonious community where healing can manifest. In prayer, dance and ritual we connect to the source of all healing, transformations can occur and healers are born.

We do have the ability to use our hearts and minds to encourage healing in our bodies. Sacred medicines along with spiritual guides help us on this spiritual journey. The heart and mind connection is so important, intuition grows stronger; affirmations are believed, therefore the body releases healing energies to the areas of imbalance. It is these gifts that help us know who we are and our place within the circle of life.

Always pause and become aware of what emotions are within your heart, if there is fear replace it with peace, relax your mind and allow your inner eye to gaze at the energy around your heart. What colour do you see? How does that colour feel? How do you see the energy flowing? Relax your mind and ask yourself ... how do I heal my physical heart and my emotional heart? Then allow thoughts, visions and ideas to float up into your conscious mind.

Most of us will face a crisis at some point in our lives; an illness, loss of a loved one or midlife point where we desire some form of direction and meaning to our lives. We know for sure that many of us are on a healing journey or a journey of discovering who we are. This topic of healing is one that is so personal to each of us, for we all have our own unique perceptions of what healing is and how to achieve it. For myself the medicine wheel is my blueprint for how I am doing mentally, emotionally, spirituality and physically. I actually tune into myself to see clairvoyantly what aspect of me is imbalanced and I'd love to share with you how I do it.

In case you don't know what a medicine wheel looks like I will give a brief explanation. The wheel is a circle divided up into four quarters. Each quarter faces a cardinal direction, the circle represents the natural and personal aspects in complete balance. I visualize the wheel and I allow my mind to rest. I know that the first slice of the wheel represents my spirituality, the second my emotional well-being , the third my physical health and the fourth my mental state. I hold the image of the wheel in my mind, I allow colours , visions , feelings to slide into my mind as I gaze at my personal representation of the medicine wheel. Gradually I see blue come into the second quarter, which is my emotional health, and I allow my mind to rest on that blue. I experience with my heart how the blue feels. Next, I place my face in the blue and I allow any words or feelings to float up into my conscious mind. I will take note of what is shown to me and I will do this in all four quarters of the wheel. Afterward I will go over what I have been shown and move forward into a direction that helps me to heal.

The medicine wheel is awareness of physical self; it is a shamanic experience that I embark on when I journey into the wheel.

My relationship with the Creator is my top priority; this is tended to by prayer and ritual but it has to be more than words spoken and songs sang; it must be lived and felt from within myself … then there can be peace. When I have peace spirituality then I can have peace and healing elsewhere in my life and body.

Walking in faith means that I trust that a higher power has a plan and a purpose for my life; when my heart and my mind trust in the source of healing then my body responds to healing ceremonies.

Mother Earth gives birth too, nurtures and sustains all life, she provides us with our food, medicines and shelters. If we allow ourselves to be open and receptive to the Spirit that dwells in all things we find wisdom and love and also the way forward to health.

My relationship with Mother Earth is akin to living in one's parent's home and treating it with respect. I know that she is in charge here I'm aware that she graciously shares her bounty with me and I know that it is a gift that I am allowed to gaze upon her beauty. This makes every sunrise precious, every healing herb a gift; I give thanks to the Creator for my existence and to Mother Earth for my home. Offerings are made not to do a deal with her, but come from a place of gratitude and respect. Following the wisdom of the medicine wheel one realizes the sacredness of plants, crystals and all our relations of earth. When healing and insight is needed there are certain steps that I must make, this practice is done to make sure things are done in a respectful manner. Drumming and dancing settles me and helps me to become aligned with the energies of the Great Spirit and of earth, this is followed by a purification ritual; then my ritual.

Smudging releases thoughtforms held within my energy field, smudging clears my space and calls forth ancestors and angels to assist me.

An herb is lit such as sage. As I burn this plant I give thanks that it has offered itself up in order to help me. I bring the smoke around my head to clear my mind, I bring the smoke around my ears so that I can hear from spirit, I bring the smoke around my eyes so that I may see the truth and see psychically what the root of the problem is, I bring the smoke around my mouth so that I will not be afraid to speak the truth and then I bring the smoke to my heart so that my heart will be encouraged to show me the way forward.

Mother Earth is our greatest teacher and healer. The Creator has blessed her abundantly and she blesses all her children well.

If we listen, observe and respect her she will in turn help us to heal. She maintains our lives ... our food, our water the air we breathe all come from earth. Some people look at me oddly because I carry crystals with me and wear a pendent of healing oils, but many people do not realize the interconnectedness of all life and how powerful those connections are for healing.

My bond to the Creator comes through nature. At every opportunity I escape from my busy life and commune with nature and this is especially true when I am ill. Because I work with nature and divination I have spent a lot of time connecting with Mother Earth and the divine. What I have discovered is woods, fields, and rivers all have their own energy – an atmosphere that is unique – and visiting these places can influence how I feel and how I look at situations in my life. I am drawn to walk in the woods when I need to focus on specific areas of my life. There is something about the energy of the forest that urges me to direct my thoughts and actions in very precise and methodical manner.

When I'm feeling expansive and need to explore all my options I am drawn to an open field. I offer my tobacco and then I listen for the Creator's voice ... then when life seems to be chaotic I am drawn to a pond where I can sit and appreciate the stillness of water ... nature has this way of balancing me and restoring my equilibrium.

Being born an empath I get a real sense of how humans can make earth sick. I'm talking about another kind of pollution here. I'm speaking about how people's actions, such as fighting and drugs, can damage earth's pure energy. If you happen to live in an area that has this kind of activity, you could be exposed to negative energies that can harm your health. Trust your instincts about how the energy feels where you live. If you know that there has been a past of this type of activity or if you sense that there is something off about your home than the land probably needs to be cleansed. When we give back to Mother Earth by cleaning up after ourselves or after our fellow humans she blesses us … healing the land is also part of healing ourselves. If we live on land that has been sickened in some manner it is only a matter of time until we ourselves become sickened; this can be environmentally or energetically.

In the teachings of the medicine wheel, self is sacred. It is important that we value who we are and our place within the Circle of Life. Therefore, I make a pledge to myself that I will value my life and all that the Creator and Mother Earth give me. I will develop a good mind and I will examine myself daily to know my strengths and weakness and tend to my inner fire. Being attuned and in tune with nature is important, but it is also important to have a mind that is well connected to your heart … your most powerful intuitive center. I feel that when we meditate; when we develop our intuition; then we can trust our instincts. We can have a better handle on what is going on with us health wise. Tending to our inner fire (spirit and mind) we can better monitor what our bodies are doing and what our bodies need.

For example, I had had some issues with blood pressure, but before a doctor could tell me I was already being drawn to ideas of diet for heart health, a vision of wild blueberries came to me. Later I found out that these berries help in circulation.

One of the legends of my people is the story of why the Creator created people.

Long ago the animals, birds and fish called out to the Creator, "We give you thanks for all we have, everything is so plentiful but we have no purpose in our lives." The Creator gave this great thought and so he created man and woman. The Creator told the creatures of the earth that they would have to take care of humans for they were weaker and not as wise as the animals, fish and birds. But eventually humankind grew greedy and killed an animal. The Creator was angry and wanted to destroy all humans, but the creatures of the earth begged the Creator to save the humans. The Creator told the creatures of the earth, "You have shown wisdom and compassion for the humans, therefore, I will not destroy them all but they will no longer be able to talk to you or hear you. If a human lives in a kind way and follows my path, they may ask me for one of my spirit animals to guide and keep them on my path. This spirit animal will only come to humans who have a good heart."

That is why in my personal path I rely on my earth teachers or totems to assist me in healing and shadow work; when I journey into the medicine wheel I depend upon them to keep me grounded and in the present moment.

A candle is lit from a single spark and makes rooms open within my heart, a flame blessed signals the beginning of ritual and through prayer and offerings my pain is released to the four directions. The burning of herbs releases my pain and soothes my soul again.

Shadow work is an important step in any healing process. I imagine healing would be difficult without facing our fears and taking an honest inventory of our lives and our habits. Shadow work refers to a process of understanding yourself and illuminating the aspects of ourselves that have been wounded. It involves a journey inward and that journey would be perilous without my totem guides with me. Swan and deer have been my life-long spirit helpers they ground me and keep me present when I journey into the medicine wheel.

When I stand in the darkness of my shadow the deer and swan are there to support me and help me face the unconscious habits and beliefs that are influencing my life, sometimes for the detriment of my well-being.

There are many creative ways to peer into the shadows. I also use divination. Divination can reveal things about ourselves, others and situations that we might not have been able to see. It is a powerful tool in the healing process and one that often gets overlooked. Divination can reveal problems lurking in our subconscious minds and offer clues on how to uncover and deal with the darker aspects of ourselves.

Medicine is more than taking a pill, it is the purification of smoke, the beauty of a crystal to transform fear into love and it is the wisdom that can only come from your heart. Through the medicine wheel and ALL MY RELATIONS I am restored, replenished and re-balanced.

Shirley Laboucane is a descendant of aboriginal healers from western Canada. Her early life was filled with Sundance ceremonies and learning about the Medicine Wheel. For the past several years she has held many workshops and performed native ceremonies for the public. She continues to work full-time, giving psychic readings to clients, and is always eager to share the wisdom passed down to her from her ancestors. She is the author of *Healing Divination* and *Walking the Path: The Cree to the Celtic*.

Kate Brunner

Healer was never an archetype I felt comfortable calling my own, and yet the Ladies of Avalon insisted on calling me to a path infused with the power of profound soul healing. As a member of the Sisterhood of Avalon, my spiritual practice consists of a core Cycle of Healing that can also be visualized as the archetype of the Quartered Circle; cousin to the Medicine Wheel, but anchored in the energies of our Avalonian Mysteries. The westernmost position on the circle marks our Station of Descent and the most common entrance into our Cycle of Healing. Here, in the autumn of the day, week or year, I begin to delve into the work that will lead me to discern the Shadow aspect or soul wound I am called to heal. At the nadir of our Cycle and the southern position of the circle stands the Station of Confrontation. Within the embrace of the winter, I stand and face the root of my soul wound. I must have faith that, despite the darkness, true understanding of my Shadow's dis-ease will illuminate the path to healing. The easternmost position is occupied by the State of Emergence and leads back up to the Light Half of the Cycle. It is here that, taking with me the lessons of the Dark, that I begin knitting closed and truly healing the wounds within. At the circle's apex, the Station of Resolution celebrates my accomplishments, the successes of my healing work this Cycle. Ever present and anchored within the center of the Avalonian Cycle of Healing, the Station of Integration makes itself available to me at any time, always allowing me to pause and see the whole of my healing work across all Cycles. These are the five continuously cycling Stations of the Avalon's Medicine Wheel.

Meditative shamanic practices, along with a great deal of study and ritual, help me work my way through the Stations of the Avalonian Cycle of Healing over and over again. My very first turn through the annual Cycle lanced the deep, festering wound in my marriage, producing a much needed balm for my husband and myself. My second healed and made whole my sexual self. My third taught me profound lessons about the healing art of self-nurturance. Halfway through my fourth, I am experiencing how Avalon can not only heal old wounds, but also staunch the flow of my heart's blood from fresh soul injuries cause by the abrupt loss of friendship.

The more I work with our Avalonian Cycle of Healing, the more whole I become. The more of myself I heal, the more I am able to midwife the healing of others. Avalon, the Isle of Healing, itself, brings me closer and closer to the gifted Healer that truly lies within. For more on the Sisterhood of Avalon and our Cycle of Healing, please see our website http://www.sisterhood-ofavalon.org.

Shaun Johnson

Acting as a channel or conduit for healing energies is actually a simple process, though some like to make it elaborate and mysterious. Conceptualizing it, however, is less straightforward and more contentious, especially in a rational, secular, materialistic society. Any conceptualization is likely to be a subjective one but, whatever the approach, the main test of any healing technique is whether it makes any difference to the health of the patient or not.

Healing shouldn't be seen as an end in itself but more as a siddhi, a phenomena or by-product of spiritual development work. Otherwise, it becomes a distraction, a spectacle. Nor should healing be seen as acting exclusively on the physical, material plane. The purpose of healing is the alleviation of suffering on all levels and should be approached with that attitude in mind.

The ability to attune oneself to the patient shouldn't be underestimated. The closer the attunement, the more significant the outcome. A healer needs to be able to blend their energies and aura with that of the patient until almost another self is created, a self that is beyond self, that is neither the patient nor the healer. In strictly esoteric terms, it is a sexual process, a form of sexual magick.

All healing should be given without any expectation of result. An attitude of observation, of experiment, is necessary, and it is important to monitor any results. When the healing energies are being channelled, however, the desire for improvement should never be the focus. This is particularly important when it's someone you desperately want to help as, under such circumstances, healing is often unsuccessful. This may be for a number of reasons – that the intrusion of the self gets in the way of the healer acting as a channel; or that desperately wanting to heal someone introduces an element of doubt into the proceedings that prevents the healer placing their trust completely in the hands of the ancestors, or spirits, or orisha, or energies.

There is a need to treat all patients, known or unknown, liked or disliked, physically present or not, with the same degree of compassion and with what the Buddhists call metta, loving-kindness without attachment.

Michael Bertiaux has described healing as a process of initiation, and it certainly is a transformative process, both for the patient and for the healer. The patient is initiated by the healer, who is opened up to the healing energies on all levels, meaning their experience of suffering both now and in the future will change, and in channelling and having contact with the initiatic energies the healer is opened up further spiritually. From this experience develops humility, empathy and compassion to a degree that allows considerable progress along the Path, developing further siddhi along the way, but always focused on the ultimate goal of becoming one with the Light.

Samantha Allison-Belle

Everything is energy and healing is a set of practices to focus and channel energy to improve health and well-being of self, individuals and the planet.

The first healing method I personally learned was spiritual healing via the NFSH, who do four very thorough learning courses. I realized how to use the process of energy channeling, how to protect my energy field and to balance chakras and clear and boost a person's energy to help them.

Healing Trust courses extend to meditation, muscle, how to heal oneself, bedside manner i.e. dealing with death and the dying, trauma, and also visualization techniques.

Later I took Reiki to master's level – which has an effect of making you face Karma and use earth energy (Ki or Chi).

After learning reflexology, Indian head massage, shiatsu and OHB Kinesiology, and dowsing, I spent a few years developing healing arts and shamanic workshops: Spirit animal, drumming, vision quest, dance, singing your soul, EFT, yoga and meditation put together as half-day workshops.

So a mandala session colouring followed by a meditation and yoga followed by art or drumming.

I am available for private healing sessions and have seen amazing results, but still the basic energy clearance and energizing technique I was first taught holds true and strongest, bringing in light and energy to boost and balance a person's energy field. This works in person, but also as distance healing. For more information contact *The Healing Trust* or *Optimum Health Balance*.

Amy Aldridge

Healing must be a journey for everyone. Each person has to find out what works for them and that can be something that can be innate or must be learned through trial and error. For me the discovery of healing came in the form of music. I think it was something I began discovering back in high school, but didn't recognize until later that it was the beginning of a pattern, a pattern of healing that works.

My discovery began with situations in high school and college that were particularly anxiety-ridden. I realized that listening to music, singing, playing instruments all helped to alleviate that anxiety and began to transform me. Even now, I sing to help alleviate sadness and muster through physical and emotional pain. If I feel overwhelmed with life or am having issues with anger, there is nothing that balances me like going to band rehearsal and playing my clarinet. While in college, I discovered listening to meditation music helped alleviate stresses I wasn't aware were building up. I've recently returned to that mode of healing once again.

Music can set the mood of a situation, tell a story, play with your emotions, heighten your awareness, and it can heal. I've brought my discovery of music now into the spiritual side of things as well as I start exploring things like Tibetan singing bowls, tuning forks, drumming, singing, chanting, binary beat technology and many other things.

One can witness singing and dancing incorporated into rituals no matter what their spirituality. It can help one open themselves to the energy around them, pull energy in from elsewhere, open their minds to that energy, and it can be used to help project that energy to others. The healing properties of music can work on a personal level or in a large group. From mothers singing to their sick child who gets better to playing music to a coma patient who suddenly awakens after a long period of time, the evidence from around the world that music heals is phenomenal.

Herbalism

Rachel Patterson

Mother Nature provides us with a huge host of medicinal and magical plants, pretty much every plant in the wild or in your garden has magical properties and medicinal uses too (not all and please, please double check before ingesting any plants as some of them might be poisonous!).

The use of herbs in medicines and magic goes back thousands of years, from the wise woman picking herbs to cure ailments in cattle to the traditional Chinese medicines for health. Tribal society saw plants as sources of knowledge and wisdom; they were respected.

Some of the oldest written records of herbs being used as medicine were found on clay tablets made by the Sumerians in ancient Mesopotamia, dating back well over five thousand years. Papyrus has also been found in Egypt, documenting healers, physicians and dealing with health issues, these date back to 1550 BC.

Chinese herbal medicine has been around for thousands of years too, and the Indians have sacred writings called the Vedas, which date back to the 2nd Century BC. The Ayruveda is the Indian system of herbal medicine. The Greeks and Romans were influenced by these early civilizations and the Romans were responsible for bringing with them a lot of the common herbs we recognize today.

In the Middle Ages herbalism flourished. Many people carried on the tradition of herbal medicine as knowledge of diseases and understanding of health increased in Europe. In America it was the Native Americans that had these skills and in Australia the Aborigines carried the herbal knowledge. Right across the globe people have always learnt about and worked with herbs.

Even animals have the sense to eat certain plants when they

are feeling unwell, such as a dog eating grass to relieve gastric distress.

The first anaesthetics used were herbs and a lot of our most recognized over-the-counter medicines that we use today were derived from plants or in actual fact still contain plant matter. At one time herbs were aligned with what ailment they cured by their signature, it is referred to as the 'doctrine of signatures'. The shape, colour and appearance of the plant was associated with parts of the body that it looked like and, therefore, assumed that it would cure an illness there.

Some large pharmaceutical companies are now seeing the benefits of using herbs in their medicines and are also using them in their beauty products. Science it seems has finally caught up with the knowledge of the wise woman (or man)!

Let's go over some basics of herbalism first:

Only buy or harvest what you need

If you are gathering your herbs in the wild or from your garden, only take what you need, leave enough on the plant for it to survive. Herbs do not keep forever so don't have huge stocks, even dried herbs don't last indefinitely.

Storage

If you are drying your own herbs, or if you have purchased them dried, keep them in a cool place out of sunlight. Dark glass jars are the best form of storage vessel. If you dry your own herbs, make sure you do so correctly so that they don't rot and make sure they are properly labelled with the plant name and date you collected it.

From the wild

If you do forage in the wild, please, please make sure you can correctly identify the plant that you are harvesting or the results could be disastrous. Please also make sure that the plant you are intending to harvest from is not protected or endangered. Do make sure you only take a little of the plant and leave enough for it to survive properly. Make sure the plant is not near any fields that have been sprayed with pesticide or near car fumes.

Ingesting

I can't stress this enough, if you are intending to ingest the herb or plant you have collected please make sure you have identified it correctly and that it is not harmful in any way.

Safety

Please do not give herbal mixtures to pregnant women, babies or young children unless you are 100% sure it is safe for them to use. Herbs are considered to be safe because they are natural. However, while they are safer than many chemical medicines, this is only true if they are used properly. Inappropriate use of some herbs could be dangerous; this includes combining them with prescription medicines or using them to treat a serious illness without consulting a doctor. Some may not be used in pregnancy, some herbs cannot be used in combination with aspirin, and some herbs irritate the stomach. Some herbs should not be used for children (under 11 years of age).

Illness

If the illness you are intending to treat with herbal remedies is major, please get a professional diagnosis and let your practitioner know what remedies you intend to take. Some herbal remedies can react badly to modern medicines.

Cleanliness

When preparing herbal remedies please keep everything spotless; your work surfaces, jars you keep the herbs in, your hands, any utensils you use. If you are intending to make and use herbal remedies it is advisable to have at least a basic understanding of the human body and how it works. This will enable you to distinguish symptoms common to an illness and to know when to refer to a conventional practitioner. If you are intending to set up in business and sell remedies to others, check with your local medical governing body; some countries have strict guidelines, some don't, some will require you to complete formal training.

Magical Herbs

Every herb, plant, tree and flower has magical properties. They will also be aligned to one of the elements too, a planet and often correspond to a particular deity as well.

You can use herbs as part of your spell work:

> *Candle spells* – crush dried herbs and spices, dress the candle with a little oil and then roll the candle in the herbs. Or as you light the candle sprinkle some of the herbs over the top.
>
> *Poppets* – use herbs and spices to stuff inside poppets.
>
> *Medicine bags* – add herbs and spices to your medicine bag, or crush finely and use to 'feed' them.
>
> *Incense* – herbs, plants and spices can all be used in incense.
>
> *Offerings* – used crushed herbs as offerings to deity.
>
> *Washes* – add herb mixes to floor washes.

Herbs can also be used in witches bottles and magic powders; the list of uses for magical herbs is endless really.

Before you use herbs in any spell work you will need to enchant them, to charge them with your intent and increase the effectiveness of the herb. You should charge the herbs just before you are about to use them to make sure the energy is fresh and at its strongest. If you are using more than one herb in a spell you can charge all the herbs together or do them individually, the choice is yours.

So how do you enchant it? Hold the herb in your hand, or put it in a clean bowl and hold the bowl in both your hands. Calm and centre yourself and then reach out with your senses to pick up the vibrations of the herb then place your power hand either just over the herb or touching it. Visualise your intent and then send this energy into the herb. You can also say a chant at this point too if you wish.

Some common herbs and their magical uses:

Lemon Balm – love, success, healing

Basil – love, exorcism, wealth, flying, protection

Bay – protection, psychic powers, healing, purification, strength

Birch – protection, exorcism, purification

Camellia – riches

Carnation – protection, strength, healing

Cinnamon – spirituality, success, healing, power, psychic powers, lust, protection, love

Dandelion – divination, wishes, calling spirits

Fennel – protection, healing, purification

Ivy – protection, healing

Lavender – love, protection, sleep, chastity, longevity, purification, happiness, peace

Marjoram – protection, love, happiness, health, money

Mint – money, lust, healing, travel, exorcism, protection

Nettle – exorcism, protection, healing, lust

Parsley – lust, protection, purification

Poppy – fertility, love, sleep, money, luck, invisibility

Rose – love, psychic powers, healing, love divination, luck, protection

Rosemary – protection, love, lust, mental powers, exorcism, purification, healing, sleep

Sage – immortality, wishes, longevity, wisdom, protection

Medicinal Herbs

Herbal tea – this is one of the easiest ways to make an herbal remedy. You use the leaves and/or the flowers of a plant for tea. Use a glass or ceramic pot or cup to infuse the herb. Use one or two teaspoons of the herb, pour on hot water and brew for at least 5 minutes then strain. You can drink it warm or chill it and drink it with ice. It can also be used as a mouth wash, gargle or hair rinse. (Only keep for a maximum of 24 hours).

Decoction – this is a good way to use plant bark, berries and roots. Chop fresh or dried herb and simmer in water for about 20 minutes. Strain and then drink. This can also be used as a mouthwash or gargle. (Only keep for a maximum of 48 hours). Use 1 heaped teaspoon of chopped herb material to 1 ½ cups water.

Tincture – these are made by macerating (which means soaking) chopped herbs from any part of the plant in an alcohol solution. Sometimes vinegar or glycerol is used instead of alcohol. The ratio of herb to water and alcohol will determine the strength of the tincture but the most common ratio is 1 part herb to 3 parts water and alcohol. The proportion of alcohol varies from 25 per cent to 90 per cent. Tinctures do have a long shelf life but usually take at least a week to prepare. Place the chopped herb material in a clean, preferably sterilised, jar and stir in the required amount of alcohol. For each 4oz of dried herb material add ½ pint of alcohol solution. Stir, then close with a lid, leave for 10 days, make sure to shake the jar every day. After 10 days strain and put into a clean bottle. Vodka is the preferred alcohol to use, but I have successfully used whisky too. Fresh plant material needs a 40 per cent alcohol solution. Dried plant material can be made with 25 per cent alcohol. If it is below 25 per cent the tincture may decay.

To freeze herbs, wash and blanch then drop into ice water and place in bags or ice cube trays and freeze. This works well with moisture-dense herbs such as basil, chives and parsley.

To make an herb vinegar, cover herbs in white vinegar and steep for 4-6 weeks in bottles.

For herb butter, add 4 tablespoons of dried herbs and a squeeze of lemon juice to ½ lb of softened butter.

For herb mustard, mix tbs dry mustard, the same of salt and a tsp of sugar, mix to a paste with vinegar, split into 4 and mix with 1tbs of herbs.

Herbs also work well in pot pourri – start with a base of rose petals and lavender then add whatever dried herbs you like, add whole cloves or cinnamon. Add benzoin to fix then store in air tight jar for 4-5 weeks, then it's ready.

You can also make lavender sugar – add dried lavender heads to a jar of sugar. It's wonderful to use in cookie or cake recipes, you can also use the stems of lavender on the fire to make your home smell.

Hot infused oil is only used externally. You need to put your fresh herbs in a jar and cover with oil – olive, almond or sunflower. Put the jar in a saucepan of water up to its neck and bring the water to a simmer for 3 hours. Then strain into a brown glass bottle.

Cold infused oils are made in a similar way, but instead of heating in a saucepan of water you put the jar on a sunny windowsill instead.

An ointment covers and protects the skin; a good base for an ointment is petroleum jelly. The jelly is melted in a double boiler and herbs are added, simmered until they are crisp and strained into jars.

A cream is made from oil, beeswax and water and this penetrates the skin. Melt 1oz beeswax in a double boiler; add 1 cup olive oil and mix. Add 2oz of your chosen herb. (If it's too thick add a small amount of water and mix). Simmer for 20 minutes, stirring. Add a drop of benzoin to preserve. Then strain into sterilized jars.

Some common herbs and their medicinal properties:

Mint – antiseptic, antispasmodic, diaphoretic, mild analgesic, mild bitter, mild sedative, relives wind

Lemon balm – antidepressant, antispasmodic, insect repellent, relaxant, relieves wind, topical anti viral

Cinnamon – antimicrobial, aromatic, astringent, mild stimulant, relieves wind

Meadowsweet – antacid, anti inflammatory, anti rheumatic, astringent

Rosemary – anti inflammatory, antioxidant, antispasmodic, circulatory stimulant, digestive tonic, nerve tonic

Sage – antimicrobial, antioxidant, astringent, digestive tonic, oestrogenic, general tonic, reduces sweating

Chickweed – astringent, cooling (topically), demulcent, relieves itchiness

Dandelion – bitter tonic, diuretic, liver cleanser, mild laxative

Cayenne pepper – antiseptic, counter irritant, local analgesic, relieves wind & spasm, stimulant, tonic

Hawthorn – antioxidant, heart tonic, lowers blood pressure, relaxes blood vessels

Harvesting and drying your own herbs

The best time to harvest an herb depends on the type of herb. Most need to be harvested just as the flower buds appear. The summer and autumn are the best times of the year. Early morning is the best time of day to harvest herbs just after the sun has dried the leaves, but before it gets too hot.

The famous herbalist Nicholas Culpeper suggested that herbs all have a link to certain planets, and that choosing the right astrological phase and hour to harvest your herbs would add to their power.

Annual herbs can be harvested heavily. Cut back just above a pair of leaves or a leaf, leaving 4-6 inches of stem. If it's the seeds you require don't cut it back at all, leave it to flower and harvest once the seed heads are turning brown. Perennial herbs should only have one third of the top growth harvested and sometimes just the tips of the leaves. To harvest, the tools I use are a pair of pruners or a sharp pair of scissors, but a sharp knife could be used as well.

To dry bunches of herbs, wash them and dry, then tie the stems in a bundle and hang them upside down in a warm dark place (you can cover them in a brown bag). Leave them for about 2-4 weeks. I use this method for herbs such as rosemary and bay; it works best with herbs that don't have high moisture content. For individual leaves or smaller herbs lay them on a tray and keep in a warm dark place, I use this method for rose petals or sometimes thyme if it has small stems.

If you need herbs to be dried quicker put them in an oven on a baking tray at around 180degreesF for 3 to 4 hours. Or use the microwave putting the clean herbs on a kitchen towel for 1 to 3 minutes, turning them over every 30 seconds. To store dried herbs I prefer to use dark brown glass jars with airtight lids, keeping the light out extends the life of them.

It is a huge, varied and fascinating subject, not only do herbs and plants cure illnesses and ailments they can be used in magical workings, look beautiful in the garden and help us to connect with the magical energy that Mother Nature has provided for us.

Rachel Patterson is High Priestess of the Kitchen Witch Coven and Team Leadership member of the Kitchen Witch School of Natural Witchcraft. She is the author of *Grimoire of a Kitchen Witch*, and three books in the *Pagan Portals* series – *Kitchen Witchcraft*, *Hoodoo* and *Moon Magic*. She lives in Portsmouth, UK.

Calantirniel

Many years ago when I started to study magic, I subsequently learned it is something you are rather than something you do. In this case, study actually meant remembering! I reconnected with the natural world through my relationship with collective energy, and recognizing individual energies as well. One of my favorite tools while doing meditations, rituals or magic is herbs – and really, the plant kingdom. Well, to be fair, this sometimes also includes the fungi kingdom, although my knowledge is not as extensive here. These kingdoms tend toward an immediate response in my experience, where crystals, gems and metals worked more slowly but permanently.

I started with herbs and spices in the kitchen (and flowers in the garden). Before I even read about magical use of the herbs, I noticed subtleties like Cinnamon having the power to attract, while Cumin seemed to have the opposite, repelling quality. One of my first spells for protection and banishment was grinding some Black Pepper in my hand, blowing it with a large breath in the direction I visualized the need, and tracing a pentagram in the air with my index finger while saying aloud an impromptu, deeply heartfelt wish – it worked almost too well!

When I studied more advanced herbal magic material, I was intrigued by so many herbs that I never heard of before – and many did not grow around me. Rather than purchasing a lot of herbs in which I did not create a connection when they were alive, I really strive instead for a bioregional magical practice. But, learning all the uses for what grew around me was overwhelming – I needed help.

I started by discovering what actually grows in my yard and my locality, ranging from researching field guides to attending neighborhood garden clubs at my library. I checked my local university's botanical education department, and my local branch of the Department of Agriculture, especially for noxious weed information. My first yard-find was Bindweed – and I bet you already know how I used it!

Along with *Cunningham's Encyclopedia of Magical Herbs* and Paul Beyerl's *Master Book of Herbalism*, it is amazingly helpful to own at least one medicinal herbal. I recommend Matthew Wood's two-volume set of *The Earthwise Herbal*. He not only imparts the medicinal properties of herbs (nicely divided into the old world and the new world), but he shares the energetic signatures used in homeopathy, acupuncture and even flower essences. On the latter topic, I recommend Clare G. Harvey's *New Encyclopedia of Flower Remedies.*

For free online reading: Maude Grieve's *A Modern Herbal* www.Botanical.com is a classic reference for harvesting, storing, medicinal use as well as the lore about herbs; revealing many clues to their magical use. For those using astrology, Nicolas Culpeper's *The Complete Herbal* designates planetary rulers: www.complete-herbal.com (Latin name cross-reference: www.medherb.com/culpeper_names.html). Another excellent lore-filled herbal is *Plant Lore, Legends and Lyrics* by Richard Folkard, 2nd Edition (1892) http://ia600402.us.archive.org/9 /items/cu31924062766666/cu31924062766666.pdf.

You can find more information by visiting the Herbal Resources at my website http://astroherbalist.com

Katherine Cotoia

The Earth is our home; it sustains us with nutrients, shelter, water, and blesses us with her inherent beauty. From this wondrous place we have the beautiful gift of plants; the part of the plant that sustains it, just as the earth sustains us, is the root.

Root magick aids with creating a solid foundation for spells and herbal magick.

The roots are the life sustaining force behind the plant, making it the most powerful magickal part of the plant. You can work with roots alone, pick one and carry it on you in a small vial made into a pendant. Placing roots like cinquefoil around your home invites financial success. Another idea is to make an arrangement with dried herbs and flowers and placing roots in the arrangement. Try to keep the arrangement magickal by picking herbs, botanicals, and roots with the same metaphysical properties.

A great idea is to cultivate the roots in your own garden. Gather them from the wild, making sure to leave enough for the plant to regenerate, and plant them in your own garden. That way you can ensure that you have enough for your own workings without taking too much from the wild. Whenever you take from Gaia, make sure to leave small tokens of gratitude for the gift she has given you. The fall is the best time of year to harvest your roots.

Make sure you wash your roots before drying scrubbing out all the nooks and crannies. Some roots need to be cut up before being allowed to dry as they are easier to work with this way. Properly research each root before working with it so you are well aware of how to handle it.

A great way to dry your roots is to lay them on a screen or hang them in a cool dark place. Once your roots are completely dry store them in dark glass jars labeled with plant name, where it was found, and the date it was stored. You could also add the magickal and therapeutic properties of the root.

Make sure your roots are completely dried before placing in your jars or you will end up with a moldy, gross mess and I will not even get into the horrors of the smell! Drying can take several weeks; the roots should feel brittle when dry so be patient with them, give them the time they need to dry properly.

If the plant has magickal properties, so does the root. While there are many roots that are well known and used magickally, do not overlook the roots that are growing in your own area just because they may not be listed in an herbal grimoire. It is important to research each herb and root that you intend to work with. Many plants and roots are poisonous and it is important to be well versed on these matters. With that said, I wish you Happy Rooting!

Laura Perry
Harvesting your own herbs for medicinal and magical purposes

adds a powerful element of intention and personal interaction to your workings. For herbs you can easily grow in your garden, such as basil, or those commonly found throughout the landscape, such as dandelions, hand-harvesting fresh herbs poses no difficulty. But those plants that are rare in the wild raise a set of ethical issues you must consider when making decisions about working with herbs. Thankfully, there is a way to gather what you need – and want – from Mother Earth without putting too big a dent in the ecosystems that sustain us all.

Many people who gather their own herbs use the One-Third Rule: never take more than one-third of the plant, or colony of plants, when harvesting in the wild. For many of the common herbs, this allows the plants enough reserve to reproduce and spread in future seasons. But for some of the rarer herbs, even this rule is not sufficient to protect the species.

Take American ginseng (*Panax quinquefolius*), for instance. The root of this plant is used for medicinal and magical purposes. It takes four to six years for the root to mature, and it usually takes that long for the plant to generate one or two berries with viable seed to reproduce itself. Suppose you find a stand of American ginseng in the woods and dig up one-third of them. The next year you go back and, following the One-Third Rule, you dig up one-third of the plants again, with a slightly smaller harvest than the previous year. The following year when you go back to dig up one-third of the plants, you find your harvest is quite small; the plants have yet to produce seed and spread from the initial group. Even carefully applying the One-Third Rule, you could wipe out the ginseng colony in a few short years. This is how American ginseng, goldenseal (*Hydrastis canadensis*), black cohosh (*Cimicifuga racemosa*) and many other powerful herbs have become seriously endangered in the wild.

So what's a well-meaning herb lover to do? First, before you use a rare herb, research to find a more common herb that will do the same job. Chances are, there are several options. If you are motivated enough to seek out herbs in the wild, try shifting your focus and grow those same herbs in your garden, thus increasing the species rather than depleting it. Don't have a garden? A large pot in front of a sunny window will often do the trick. Search online for 'rare herb seeds' to find suppliers. All it takes it a little thought and planning.

If you want these plants to help you, you must show them respect. The ethics you use in acquiring your herbs will transfer to your magic and your medicine. So educate yourself about the herbs you plan to use. That way, you will be working with Nature and not against her.

Heddy Johannsen

Echinacea is a perennial wildflower with immune boosting and blood purifying properties. The plant is known as coneflower and rudbeckia. The Native Americans used Echinacea to treat colds, coughs, sore throats, toothaches, and snakebites long before the Europeans arrived. Echinacea tincture is best to take when you are feeling the early signs of a cold for two weeks. This causes the symptoms to be less severe and shortens the duration of the cold.

How To Make a Tincture

Echinacea helps the body ward off illnesses. The tincture makes a lovely gift for friends and family. The plant contains glycosides, amides, antibiotic, inulin, and polyacetylene properties. Echinacea acts as an antibiotic, anti-allergenic, and lymphatic tonic.

Gather Echinacea root in the dormant season. The plant puts its energy into developing the flowers, stems and leaves in the growing season. The winter season is the ideal time to gather the root because the plant stores its energy then. Echinacea angustifolia possesses the immune boosting properties.

Fill a jar with half a cup of Echinacea flowers and roots of the plant. Be sure that you are gathering the Echinacea root and not the wrong plant.

Ensure the tools, your hands, and the flowers or roots you are using are sterile. Boil the dark colored jars in hot water to remove germs. Wash and dry everything prior to creating the tinctures. A dark-colored glass jar protects the contents inside from spoiling.

The alcohol or vodka, depending on your choice, extracts the medicinal alkaloids and the essence from the herbs. Pour two cups of alcohol or vodka over the flowers, filling the jar. Seal the jar tightly, date and label the jar. Steep the Echinacea for two weeks and shake the jar every two days. Strain the flowers through fine cheesecloth then discard the cheesecloth and flowers. To make a more potent blend, use the root. The root has the highest concentration for the tincture.

Always store the tincture in a dark, cool place, away from sunlight. Start making the tincture on the new moon to the full moon. Hold the tincture between your hands. Close your eyes for a moment, envisioning that you are sending healing energies for yourself or someone else into the bottle. Fill it with love and blessings for the highest good of all. Remember to thank your deity for the guidance that was provided. Use one teaspoon of the tincture three times daily.

Other ways to use Echinacea for health include as a decoction as a wash for infected wounds. Wash the affected area often. Use a 10ml tincture to aid sore throats. Use as a powder to help treat skin conditions such as eczema and boils. Take three capsules daily up to three times a day at the onset of infections, such as colds, flu or kidney infections.

Celebrant Work

Cat Treadwell

We all know that every religion has its Priests. We also know that Paganism is different. Each Pagan is his or her own Priest, needing no intermediary to officiate between themselves and the Divine (in whatever form that may take), nor interpret a non-existent dogma to a congregation. So why would a specific clergy-person be required? What is the point, therefore, of a Pagan Celebrant?

I've always felt that the term 'Celebrant' is itself awkward and not entirely correct. The dictionary definition of a 'Celebrant' is actually 'one who participates in a public celebratory ritual' – so basically anyone at a wedding, funeral, naming, New Year's party... This is not helpful. It also refers to the person officiating in the rite of the Eucharist (showing clear bias in meaning to one particular belief system). The term is clumsy and vague, causing more confusion than is necessary.

I much prefer the title of 'Priest' – but this also creates some difficulties. As above, many Pagans understand that they/we are *all* Priests. However, when dealing with non-Pagan society (i.e. folk of any other religion or none), a Priest is understood to be the person in the special clothes leading that public celebratory ritual. That, at least, is more accurate.

I was once asked by a young person, while on a school visit, why I wore the robes. Didn't I have normal clothes? Of course – I pointed them out, stashed safely in a bag for afterwards. But if you have a person up front, talking about Druidry, who would you rather listen to: the person in jeans and T-shirt, or the person with cloak and staff? Understanding was achieved, in a way that everyone could easily grasp. OK – the robes are your Work Clothes, your Uniform, denoting your role.

I have been called upon to officiate at many public celebratory rites, in my capacity as a public Pagan. Specifically, my chosen path is that of Druid – but this is only occasionally relevant.

What people seem to be looking for in The Person Leading the Rite (whatever their title) is someone to do precisely *that*. An experienced, preferably trained individual who is capable of holding together a group of varied individuals, leading them to a specific purpose. To act as Priest, in fact, as this term would usually be understood by the wider society.

But it's not only the public parts of ministry that Pagans are now being called upon to undertake. Hospital and prison ministries are increasingly asking for Pagans to be on-call as needed. Multifaith groups appreciate Pagan attendees, so that their voices can be heard.

And despite having no specific 'flock', a known Pagan Priest can be called upon to perform the far more traditional, yet private functions of such a role. Being present at a time of crisis; helping with personal difficulties when nobody else can. Sometimes, it's just about *listening*.

The difficulties arise when someone suggests that Pagans *can't* be Priests in the usual way. None of us have been to seminaries, for example, nor been ordained by a recognised Church. Because there are no seminaries or recognised Churches (yet). We're back to terminology again.

Paganism, by its very difference, is cutting new paths through very traditional territory – and causing a fair bit of confusion along the way. Not content with forcing the redefinition of 'Religion' (as The Druid Network did when it achieved Charity status), Pagans are playing with the very meaning *of* religion. Words such as *spirituality, priest, clergy, congregation, rite*... each of these has certain connotations but is now being actively taken and modified to fit the requirements of this fast-evolving belief system.

There are many paths within Paganism. There are both many books and yet no specific doctrine, many Gods and Goddesses, and yet perhaps only two... and that's without considering the animists, atheists and (yes!) Christian Pagans. There is very little, in fact, that is common to all Pagans, except for our reverence of and for Nature, and our active lives within it.

One of the things that I came up against when I first began to act as a public Pagan Priest was the issue of perception, both from within and outside the Pagan community. What surprised me initially was the fact that yes, all Pagans are Priests – but some are simply more public about it than others. It was gently suggested that there would probably always be 'leaders' and 'followers', but I think it may be truer to say that there are those who wish to stand up in the funny outfits and speak for their faith... and those who'd prefer a quieter life.

Of course, we've no problem with Pagan Elders: those who've trod these paths before us, when times were much harder and acceptance far more difficult to achieve. The fact that they did this means that we are as free to continue as we are, and we cannot honour them enough for that. But there is still a way to go. We really cannot afford to be complacent.

Paganism may be 'ancient' in its lineage, but it is a relatively new spirituality. It is slowly becoming more legitimate within wider society, but there are many who will always see the Druid or Witch as the 'weirdo' to be avoided. Sometimes, to be fair, this can be true. Some Pagans see their spirituality as a path to power over others, fame or notoriety in the manner of Aleister Crowley. Very few have his charisma or ability, however, and these egos playing games generally find themselves quickly debunked and forgotten. That is, perhaps, the main difficulty of not having an 'ordained ministry' – there is no authority figure to call 'stop' before others are potentially injured or conned.

Every Pagan worth their salt has to be able to justify their beliefs on demand. We've all heard that simple question: 'So, what's a Pagan, then?' or 'What exactly do you *do?*' The extent of our answer depends on our own deep (or shallow) understanding of what it *is* that we actually do. Those questions still make me question myself, my own beliefs and practices. And that's before we even get into the muddy ground of explaining ourselves in a way that is actually understood. Reciting the definition of 'what is a Pentagram' as learned from a book doesn't really tell anyone anything about why you're wearing it.

I've often been asked, however, why I call myself a 'Priest' at all (if it's not a power trip). The simple answer? With apologies to the movie 'Hot Fuzz', it's *"Because I am one."* In village communities, if a baker makes bread and it is good, he is accepted and his skills utilised so that he can support himself and his family. If his bread is terrible, the business will close and the former baker has to find another trade. The difference between a good and a bad *insert name of skill here* is whether you are supported by those around.

Each of us, if we identify as Pagans to others, represents *every other Pagan in the world*. Yes, really. When we are questioned by a curious non-Pagan, our answer will colour how they view Pagans as a wider group. When Pagans are mentioned on the news, that person will think of you. You'll get asked questions prior to Solstice and Samhain.

Is that part of what makes each Pagan a Priest? Does it colour how you represent yourself as a Pagan? Perhaps. It's certainly why some choose to remain 'in the closet'. As I said, there are those who choose to be 'public' and those who do not. The robes can be worn in public, but even when they're put away, you're still a practising Pagan – no matter what colour your feathers may be.

This does *not* make anyone's Paganism more or less valid. People may be more active in their spiritual practice than others, but their depth of belief is an entirely personal thing, which should not be judged. Nobody is the Perfect Pagan – we were all beginners once, and we are always learning as we move forward in our lives. Superiority is as foolish as egotism; sharing experience to gain understanding is a far more interesting way to connect our stories as like-minded people.

Making the decision to act as a Priest was not one that I took lightly (I confess that I practically had to be shoved into it). But unavoidable circumstances pointed me in this direction, so I made the leap... and, like that successful baker, found myself supported. Every year, I am called upon more and more often to act *as* a Pagan Priest – from small telephone calls to rites at Stonehenge. I now have quite a few 'job titles', and am perceived to have enough experience to speak with authority on this topic (as I am right now).

But that's not what it's about.

The lovely Nimue Brown has suggested that the most apt metaphor is that of a conductor, leading an orchestra: Everyone is a capable musician, but you can't all play together without the guy at the front waving the stick about.' The Priest/Celebrant is the guide, the one who shapes the ritual from concept to performance, helping those who need support, balancing those who are slightly too loud or discordant. They don't take over – their experience guides the creation, in which *everyone* has their part, making it the best that it can be.

It may seem a great idea, to have a tiny taste of 'fame' from such publicity, to be known as a 'Professional Pagan'. But it can also be the most difficult place to be, on that podium in full regalia. It makes you a great target for slings and arrows, mockery in the media, and all of the usual treatment that we give to those brave enough to stand out.

Remember: those who do this are standing *for* the rest of the community. As I said, each of us speaks for every other Pagan when we're describing what we do. Imagine that, multiplied to include everyone who is watching. I always have that awareness in my mind when speaking publicly: do I accurately represent each and every one of those Pagans out there? If I saw myself on the television, would I roll my eyes and turn away, or nod and smile? The responsibility is terrifying, and for someone who isn't a natural show-off, never, ever fun. At heart, I can only ever be myself. But I promised to do my best for my community, and so I do.

This role involves so many other things, you see, as well as the madness of media and the pomp of ceremony. Sometimes it's just me and one other person, as I hold them in my arms while they weep. I raise a glass to a coffin in a crematorium, or light a candle in my garden to guide the way. I put my Self aside to act as Mother, Goddess, Confessor, Minister... Priest. Pagan 'ministry', being a Priest *as* a Pagan *for* other Pagans (of whatever path) has always been about service, not power. I believe that the original advice is that if you have the choice between being an occultist or a blacksmith, it's easier to be a blacksmith. I could joke that nobody in their right mind would *choose* to be a Priest, to stand up and take that flack, to suffer alongside others. There's a reason it's called a vocation. But people do – because there is still that need for them.

John Belham-Payne, of the Centre for Pagan Studies, related a story about Doreen Valiente that I rather love. She often attended rites as Gardnerian High Priestess to his High Priest, presumably acting the part appropriately, with all its associated glory... only to be found afterwards in the kitchen, helping with the washing-up. Pagan Priests, like any other *good* Priests (or bakers, or black-smiths), are real people, with their feet firmly planted on the ground in order to help their heads not become stuck in the clouds. We hold so much responsibility, represent so many, that we must maintain our own balance or be crushed. I like to think this is why so many of those wonderful Pagan Elders have a wicked sense of humour – because we cannot place ourselves above others. We are 'just' Priests, like any other Pagan. We are simply more public about it. We do what needs to be done.

Because these few folk are standing up and having their names recorded in media rolodexes, to be called on for statements at a moment's notice, the rest of the community can go about its business. There *are* those of us who are present, guiding when called upon, willing to help with the blood, the pain, the difficult sides of life, as well as the joy and celebration as we muddle forward together. Our community can grow and evolve, knowing that it is supported – both individually and in all its wonderful, magical, oxymoronic diversity of shared belief.

I've found that Pagans are more active than passive by nature of their connection to the wider world, their awareness of their own responsibility as individuals, community and species. Each of us works in our own way to live our own Paganism, to be true to ourselves, our ancestors, our deities and each other. We explore our own paths, investigate others, laugh and cry together on this journey of life. Ultimately, that is all.

So next time you see the person in the robes raising their hands in Circle to invoke the Powers that Be... consider what goes on outside the rite. Look who stands with them to support them. See the wider picture. Consider where you stand within it. As Pagans, we honour our Priests – as we honour each other. We forge our paths into new worlds together.

Cat Treadwell is a Druid Priest based in Belper, Derbyshire, England. She is a professional celebrant and multifaith worker, Trustee of The Druid Network and Awenydd of the Anglesey Druid Order. She is the author of *A Druid's Tale* and *Facing the Darkness*.

Fiona Tinker

My role as Celebrant is a practical way of honouring my Gods and being of service. Sometimes the Gods like to have a little fun, sometimes they are profound. They are there always.

Join me in naming a baby, on a beautiful Summer Solstice day in Kent. The sun is blazing, but the baby's father has dug a fire pit, with the intention that the fire will be lit as part of the naming ceremony. The baby has Scottish / Irish ancestry and it is to the Gods of Scotland and Ireland that the ceremony is dedicated. Sweat rolling down our backs, sun tap-dancing on the top of our heads, we begin. I get to a point where I ask Manannan Mac Lir to bless the baby with his element of water – and the heavens open. The torrent that was unleashed turned the fire pit into a paddling pool within ten minutes and blessed everyone with the best outdoor shower they'd ever imagined. I think it's safe to say Manannan was listening.

Religious Pagan marriage is legal in Scotland and I am one of the Approved Celebrants who conduct these marriages on behalf of the Scottish Pagan Federation. It is the Celebrant who has the approval to marry couples, which means that weddings can take place anywhere within Scotland. Join me now as I marry a lovely couple on a small-holding in the north of the country. It is a working farm and the chickens are running around in and out of the circle, curious and hoping we drop something interesting for them to eat. The goats are lined up against the fence, with their heads over the top, chewing thoughtfully as they observe the latest peculiar human proceedings. I pause in the Ceremony, asking for a short silence whilst we remember the ancestors and wish blessings on the couple and their marriage. Then I ask if anyone would like to speak their blessing. "Heeeeeeeeeee-Haaaaaaaawwwww," roared the farm's donkey, in reply. A marriage begun in such laughter just can't go wrong!

Funerals are hard. Honouring my Gods through celebrancy work means accepting that I will be called on to conduct passing rites, it is a balance. I cannot pick and choose only the nice bits. Celebrating and blessing a life gone is not easy, particularly if the deceased is young or someone close to you.

Join me in a Glasgow cemetery; a cold, sunny day, wind whistling. This is the last part of these funeral rites, a private interment of ashes into a family grave. I sing out the soul of a man who wandered so much in search of work that all he wanted was his ashes to remain in one place. I sing him home. It is the last thing I can do for him, to honour him. Tears streaming, I sing. And a blackbird comes to join me, sitting on the headstone. He too, sings this beloved soul out. And I know that he is home.

Rufus Maychild

In a couple of weeks I'll be making a presentation about Paganism to our local W3A. I was invited through my being Pagan Chaplain at the nearby prison. I plan to put over a solid 'Paganism is Best' line, but what if my proselytism gets a recruit? Where will I send them? There are local moots, run by wonderful people, not unwelcoming, but they're almost wholly 'social' (gossiping really). In a year there might be a handful of 'open rituals'. Almost all the actual Pagan religious practice goes on either individually, or in a few private groups that are 'invitation only'.

There is simply nowhere at all (nearby) that someone can just go and share regularly – every week say – in Pagan spirituality (what others call 'services' or 'worship') in a public manner. For those not 'in the scene' it's very difficult to locate any sort of Pagan priest/ess or celebrant for life's all-too-frequent passages. Most ordinary folk don't even imagine that there's any alternative to the horrid 'insert-name-here' ceremonies of the established religions.

One of the surprising things about Pagan Prison Ministry is that it's much easier to be(come) a Pagan in prison than outside. In prison, Paganism is a 'public' religion, on the same basis as any other (though there are sometimes 'local difficulties'). We are advertised in the Chaplaincy information leaflets. We meet every week, for an hour of 'corporate worship'. We Call our Sacred Circle into Being, we Speak to the God/dess/e/s, we Share the Cup, and basically do as we wish.

It's actually so much harder for the rest of the community. Personal religious observances can easily happen every day. But we also need to share Spirit collectively. If this happens more than about seven days apart it all becomes too unusual an experience. Not so good either if one has to burn vast amounts of Earth-damaging petrol just to get to the place of meeting, with a handful of folk drawn from far and wide. It shouldn't be such a struggle to find us. Goddess does allow our Circles to be both Open and Unbroken.

Years ago, I was welcomed into ordination as Priest in the Fellowship of Isis. I use the title of 'reverend' where appropriate for my public ministry (and on my passport etc). The strange thing is that I only really get to take on this role inside the barbed wire, concrete and multiple-locked doors. I wasn't expecting that. They say that when the God/dess/e/s Call us, we cannot long deny, but they don't provide a job description in advance.

My dream is that, soon, we will no longer need to write in explanation of Pagan celebrants and priest/ess/hood. We'll just be normal, everywhere, as we anciently were. Likewise our meetings and celebrations. I call on you to make so this, our renewal.

Sarah Buhrman

The Pagan Priesthood is a fascinating subject for me. The commonly known "problem" is that we are all priests and priest-esses, so how do we even come to have any sort of hierarchy of priesthood. However, the issue that I deal with more frequently is the challenge of being a Public Pagan Priest in a place where there are no celebrities.

I live in a rural town surrounded by rural towns. There are, surprisingly, around 50 Pagans in the area. I know many of them, and they are almost universally solitary Pagans. Often this is by circumstance, as many of them are not very "out" and may not know about each other. But just as influential is that the society of this area is very strongly about forging one's own path.

Even in the larger cities in this state, Pagans don't really group together. There are no major covens, no long-standing traditions, no established hierarchy outside of the small groups that work hard just to continue to exist. We like to socialize, and we love community, but once someone says "I'm in charge," we drift away to find a group that is less pushy. Yes, we think of it like that. We bemoan the idea of not having large, well-planned celebrations and groups with established teachers, but when one stands up to fill that void, we look at them with a critical eye as if to ask, "What makes you so special?"

I say "we" because I do the same thing. It has taken me a long time to figure out why my state has such different experiences than those I talk to online. My life-partner moved here from another state, not too far away. He was the one who really drew this to my attention. He says the Pagans here are just different. Not bad, just different.

I'm not really sure how a Pagan Priest here would ever gain the support of the local community. Our community is so loose, we don't usually band together in support of local people from within that community. We don't create Pagan celebrities. And it isn't about Paganism, either; we just don't often create celebrities in any form.

I have been very "out" for as long as I have been Pagan. Even as a beginner, I learned quickly and formed a solid belief that I could support, even as it transformed and grew. I am the Public Pagan Priest in this area. I introduce people to what Paganism is over work-breaks, smoke-breaks, coffee breaks, and more. I give myself the target and I wear it well, from what others have told me.

I am well known in certain circles around the world with an international podcast. I am known to many of the "celebrity" Pagans, those who are Public Pagan Priests on a national or inter-national level. And ironically, most of the Pagans in my small town, in my area, have no idea who I am.

Anne Coleman

So what is it exactly that a pagan Celebrant helps people to celebrate? Life! That is the short answer – in all its many variations. This can be the life of a person or family, in Rites of Passage such as the Naming of a child, a young adult's Coming of Age, the Handfasting of two people, someone's Funeral; or it can be the life of a group including perhaps a Formation Ceremony, Initiation of its members and often an Annual Remembrance of its Patron God(dess) or its Ancestors. Then there are the public or private celebrations of the Seasons and the Year, which connect the Pagan community with the Land and the agricultural cycle from which many city-dwellers have become estranged and distanced. Each of these types of celebration requires a different approach.

Personal celebrations, in my opinion, should be joint creations of the Priest and the main participants, to ensure that a memorable occasion is enjoyed by all. Typically I would organise the order in which things were done – beginning, middle and end, the choreography and the words that were important to include – but leave much of the wording of the rest to the participants. So a Naming, for instance, in the Druid tradition might include welcoming the newborn child, a blessing with water, salt and honey, presenting the child to the people, the Gods and Ancestors and proclaiming her/his name aloud. Then other optional things might be added by the parents – gifts from each quarter and element; well-wishes from each person present; poetry or song; prayers from the grandparents' faith, if different; the passing of a horn of mead or ale around the company and so on. Handfastings, similarly, are built around the most important part – the making of the vows. A good priest should help the couple to formulate these vows and to be quite sure what it is they are pledging each other, but the words should be their own.

Group Celebrations tend to stick to the same format each time, which helps a tradition to be built up within the group, and in this case, the celebrant's main job is to ensure that everyone remembers what they are doing and the order in which they are supposed to be doing it and to prompt them if they forget! Public Ceremonial, often to celebrate the seasons, needs to be more theatrical, to explain what's happening to those unfamiliar with Paganism. A celebrant might have to rehearse and organise a group of people to act out the central myth, while (s)he tells the story and to instruct volunteers in taking round the cakes and ale, as there will almost certainly be too many people for one person to do it all within the allotted time.

As well as these ritual duties, a Priest should also be prepared to give pastoral care and to lend spiritual aid when needed. This could be anything from lighting a candle with someone to acting as soul-midwife when they are dying, to ease their passage.

Further Reading

If you want to further your reading in any of the areas we've covered in Paganism 101 here are some other Moon Books you may be interested in...

Abrams, Dorothy, *Identity and the Quartered Circle*

Andrews, Steve, *Herbs of the Northern Shaman*

Bramshaw, Vikki, *Craft of the Wise*

Brown, Nimue, *Druidry and Meditation*

Brown, Nimue, *Druidry and the Ancestors*

Carter, Mark, *Stalking the Goddess*

Ceanadach, Siusaidh, *A Ceremony for Every Occasion*

Daimler, Morgan, *Where the Hawthorn Grows*

Dancing Rabbit, *The Way of the Horned God*

Day, Kenn, *Dance of Stones*

Dollman, Julie, *Living Shamanism*

Draco, Mélusine, *Pagan Pathways: By Spellbook & Candle*

Draco, Mélusine, *Traditional Witchcraft and the Pagan Revival*

Draco, Mélusine, *Traditional Witchcraft for Fields and Hedgerows*

Draco, Mélusine, *Traditional Witchcraft for Woods and Forests*

Draco, Mélusine, *Traditional Witchcraft for the Seashore*

Draco, Mélusine, *Traditional Witchcraft for Urban Living*

Eastwood, Luke, *The Druid's Primer*

Forest, Danu, *Shaman Pathways: The Druid Shaman*

Hamilton, Claire, *Mother Maiden Crone*

Hamilton, Clare, *Tales of the Celtic Bards*

Hearth Moon Rising, *Invoking Animal Magic*

Heaven, Ross, *Medicine for the Soul*

Herne, Robin, *Old Gods, New Druids*

Herne, Robin, *Bard Song*

Laboucane, Shirley, *Walking the Path*

Martin, Deborah, *Herbs: Medicinal Magical, Marvelous!*

McGaa, Ed, *Calling to the White Tribe*
Meiklejohn-Free, Barbara, *The Shaman Within*
Meiklejohn-Free, Barbara, *The Heart of All Knowing*
Meredith, Jane, *Aphrodite's Magic*
Meredith, Jane, *Journey to the Dark Goddess*
Morgan, Lee, *A Deed Without a Name*
Myers, Brendan, *A Pagan Testament*
Myers, Brendan, *The Earth, the Gods and the Soul: A History of Pagan Philosophy*
Myers, Brendan, *The Other Side of Virtue*
O'Grady, Judith, *Pagan Pathways: God-Speaking*
Patterson, Rachel, *Grimoire of a Kitchen Witch*
Patterson, Rachel, *Pagan Pathways: Kitchen Witchcraft*
Patterson, Rachel, *Pagan Pathways: Moon Magic*
Pfeiffer, Bill, *Wild Earth, Wild Soul*
Raine, Amythyst, *The Gray Witch's Grimoire*
Restall-Orr, Emma, *Kissing the Hag*
Restall-Orr, Emma, *Living with Honour*
Restall-Orr, Emma, *Wakeful World*
Roberts, Llyn, *Shamanic Reiki*
Rutherford, Leo, *The View Through the Medicine Wheel*
Ryves, Yvonne, *Shaman Pathways: Web of Life*
Salisbury, David, *The Deep Heart of Witchcraft*
Saille, Harmonia, *Pagan Pathways: Hedge Witchcraft*
Saille, Harmonia, *Pagan Pathways: Hedge Riding*
Saille, Harmonia, *The Spiritual Runes*
Savage, Mabh, *A Modern Celt*
Sentier, Elen, *Shaman Pathways: The Celtic Chakras*
Sentier, Elen, *Shaman Pathways: Elen of the Ways*
Shields, Nikki, *Starcat's Corner*
Talboys, Graeme K, *Way of the Druids – Rebirth of an Ancient Religion*
Talboys, Graeme K, *The Druid Way Made Easy*
Tinker, Fiona, *Pagan Pathways: Pathworking through Poetry*

Townsend, Mark, *Diary of a Heretic*
Townsend, Mark, *The Path of the Blue Raven*
Treadwell, Cat, *A Druid's Tale*
Treadwell, Cat, *Facing the Darkness*
van der Hoeven, Joanna, *Pagan Pathways: Zen Druidry*

Moon Books invites you to begin or deepen your encounter with Paganism, in all its rich, creative, flourishing forms.